BUT HE'S A HARD WORKER

LIFE IN RITCHEY – A SMALL VILLAGE IN THE MISSOURI OZARKS – 1925-1950

Harvey –

Some of these stories may be similar to your experiences in small towns in Texas.

It was a great time to grow up -- far different from today.

Enjoy!

Ernest T. Smerdon

10 Sept. 2009

BUT HE'S A HARD WORKER

LIFE IN RITCHEY – A SMALL VILLAGE IN THE MISSOURI OZARKS – 1925-1950

Copyright 2008 by Ernest T. Smerdon

ISBN# 978-1-60725-549-9

All rights reserved
including the right of reproduction
in whole or part in any form.

Printed in the United States of America
By Litho Printers and Bindery
Cassville, MO 65625

Contents

Acknowledgements v
Preface ix
Ritchey and Its People 1
The Ritchey School and Pie Suppers 9
Bedbugs 15
The Farm Life 17
The Radio Weather and C. C. Williford 27
The Barn 31
Threshing and Making Hay 37
Jack 'n' Pete and Kate 'n' Beck 47
Nursing Sick Animals 53
The Ritchey Mill and Jollification 57
Summer Canning, Chiggers and Wild Blackberry Jelly 63
Mrs. Marion's Sorghum Molasses 67
Butchering – Liver, Lard and Lye Soap 73
Household Fuel for the Year 77
Floods 81
Fires 87
Wash Day Monday 93
Saturday Night Bath 97
But He's a Hard Worker! 101
The Joy of Rubber Tires 105
Rhythm of the Railroad Gang 107
Baptized in Shoal Creek 111
Ray's Store 115
Raleigh Man and the Medicine Show 119
Party Line – The Original AOL 123
Quilting Bees and Braided Rugs 127
Jobs for the Women 131
Games 133
Telling Ghost Stories 143
The Swimmin' Hole 145
The Traveling Outdoor Picture Show 149
Sunday Afternoon Baseball 153
A Circus Comes To Town 157
The Barnstormers 159
Jack Armstrong – The All American Boy 163
Stealing Watermelons 167
Shivaree 171

The Jolly Workers	175
The '35 Oldsmobile	179
Holidays and Birthday Spankings	185
Experience with Grandparents	195
Epilogue – Ritchey a Half Century Later	199
A Historical Footnote: It Did Happen	203
The Region	205
Appendix I	205
The Settlers	209
Immigration of Smerdon ancestors	212
Appendix II – Biographies of Settlers	217
Judge Mathew H. Ritchey	217
Captain James M. Ritchey	218
Herman J. Rohn	220
Joseph H. Davidson	221
Appendix III – A 1931-32 Ritchey School Survey	223

ACKNOWLEDGEMENTS

Alhough I did the writing, this book has been a family project. My wife, Joanne, also a native of the Ozarks, was born in Neosho, Missouri, the county seat of Newton County. She spent the first ten years of her life there. This was a rural county. Her father was the high school vocational agriculture teacher and her mother had been a concert pianist. Joanne has long had a deep interest in the region. She encouraged this project and provided invaluable editorial assistance and many original ideas. Although this book is about life in Ritchey, Missouri, a small village in the Ozarks, Joanne did not directly experience life on a farm. However, her father worked with the farm boys in the county and her closeness to him made her keenly sensitive to the rural people of the region and their qualities. This book would never have been written without Joanne's cheerful and unflagging help.

An indispensable source of ideas and input came from my two brothers and sister. John, the oldest among us, had clearer recollections of the early 1930s. Having been born in 1925, he never enjoyed many of the benefits of mechanization on the farm, and he spent many boyhood hours, first, following a team of mules, and later horses, assisting Dad. He worked long, hard hours and he played with intensity during the brief time available for that.

John left Ritchey a few days after his eighteenth birthday in 1943, during World War II to enlist in the Navy, and he became a distinguished Navy flyer, something he did for more than twenty years. After retirement from the Navy, he returned to Ritchey and farmed the family farm for a short time prior to leaving to work in the aerospace industry. His four sons went to local schools, and the eldest graduated from the same consolidated high school as we siblings. John, being the oldest among us, saw a dimension to life in Ritchey that the others of us may not have fully realized.

My sister, Helen, was born in 1926. Helen, is the one who could see the life through the eyes of a girl, and she worked both in the house and outside on the farm. The value of young farm girl experiences cannot be overstated. Girls worked as hard as boys, but since it was often around the house, it was, perhaps, less appreciated. Modern kitchen conveniences didn't exist then. Being a strong-willed person and a bit of a tomboy, she had unusual experiences to add to the story.

Helen never left the state and has stayed close to the region and life in the Ozarks. After living in southwest Missouri for 31 years, she and her family moved to Kansas City. Her husband, Harold Barlow, was also a native of the region, and, in fact, as a small boy was a next-door neighbor when his father was superintendent of the Ritchey School. A year has never passed when Helen and her family were not back in the Ritchey area several times. Even today, she and Harold journey there to respectfully place flowers on our parents' graves on Memorial Day, which was called Decoration Day when we were children.

Glenn, the youngest among us, was born in 1935. He stayed in the area until 1957 when he entered the Army as an ROTC commissioned officer. He graduated with a BS in agriculture from the University of Missouri-Columbia. Glenn was the only one among us who might have followed our Dad's footsteps as a farmer. But his Army flying took him to the state of Washington, where he met his wife, Alyce, and ultimately settled there. Glenn's invaluable recollections covered a slightly different time because many modern conveniences were starting to come and farming was becoming much more mechanized. Glenn saw some of the happenings of the late '30's and early '40's through the eyes of a small boy.

I ended up writing the book, but it wouldn't have happened without the help of John, Helen and Glenn. I thank them for their interest and patience, as well as their ability to keep me from going astray at the word processor. Fortunately, in June 1991, we had the opportunity to discuss this project at a large family reunion held at Roaring River State Park in Missouri, only seven miles north of the Arkansas-Missouri state line and less than an hour's drive from where we grew up. The visit to the area rekindled our interest in and love for that unique region. It also tweaked our memories of incidents we thought might be of interest to others. Our children, cousins, nieces and nephews and their spouses were there and all in a very real sense became a part of this project. It was finished by long-distance, since those involved directly and indirectly are now scattered across at least ten states. I deeply thank all for their encouragement and help.

The J. Erle Smerdon Family.

Also, in terms of acknowledging family, I thank my parents. If there are any lifelong lessons that I have learned from my boyhood life in Ritchey, working hard on a small farm, they came from Mother and Dad. They were principled, hard-working people and always insisted on helping others when they could. They taught us by example the value of hard work, honesty and the importance of always doing one's best. Dad was encouraged to be a farmer and stay close to home by his parents, particularly his mother. He dreamed of being an engineer, but that would have taken him away from his family, and Grandma wanted him close. He never lived more than 10 miles from his parents except during his two years at the University of Missouri. In one sense, that was good because our family was always closely knit. But it also was bad because I know he experienced the frustrations of not following his dream. Dad was a good farmer, but he would have been a great engineer. Never once did Dad or Mother encourage us to follow any career path other than what we dreamed of doing. I thank them for that and acknowledge that whatever we children achieved in life, it was due to the principles and ethics we learned and the freedom of choice we were always given. This all was the result of the wisdom and love of our parents.

In the family picture, Helen is in the top row left, John in the middle, and I'm on the right. Mother is bottom row left, dad in the middle and Glenn in bottom row right. The picture was taken just before John entered the Navy in World War II, probably in the spring of 1943.

I also thank Dale Ritter who grew up in Ritchey and was a neighbor of ours. Dale, who now goes by his first name, Howard, was younger than I and about the age of Glenn. He became a government servant and spent his 43-year career in several locations, including Germany and Italy, ending in Texas where he is now retired. He and his son have organized a web site on Ritchey at www.vvm.com/~ritterh. That site provides much very good information about the area.

Also, I thank Larry A. James, whom I had not met until late 2004. He is a retired school teacher in Neosho and is now president of the Newton County Historical Society. He is involved in several historical projects in the region and compiled a book entitled, The Monark Towns and Surrounding Villages, published by the Newton County Historical Society. To locals Monark is understood to mean Missouri and North Arkansas. He also edited and arranged publication of the Biography of Judge M. H. Ritchey, written by G. W. Laurance of Ritchey. Matthew H. Ritchey was among the first settlers in the region and was the founder of Ritchey. Mr. Laurance lived in Ritchey and, and although I was quite young, I remember him well. He was a good friend of my Father.

Finally I thank my children and several friends for their constructive comments. Most importantly, I thank Ed Stiles for reading the book and providing many suggestions that improved its readability.

Some pictures in this book are through the courtesy of Mr. James. The photos of farm scenes are USDA pictures from the National Archives. They are not from Ritchey, but depict rural scenes similar to those I remember. Some of the photos are from my own collection, including several that I took.

My only regret is that my brother, John, did not live to see the finished product. But he saw the early chapters comprising more than half of the book and made valuable suggestions. It would be a better book had he seen all of the chapters and made his constructive comments.

-Ernest Smerdon

PREFACE

I have not lived in my boyhood hometown in southwest Missouri in more than fifty-five years, but I have often thought about the area where I grew up. Since I left, I've moved ten times and have lived on the west coast, the east coast, and at points in between. I also served a stint in Greenland while in the Air Force. Except for a four-year period in Columbia, Missouri to complete my Ph. D. in Engineering after I was discharged, my only trips to Missouri in the last 57 years were to visit family. With my parents now deceased, those trips have become quite infrequent. Although most of my thoughts were about my work and immediate family, I have always had a painting of the area in my office where I could look at it every working day. That picture, reproduced here, shows the Ritchey Mill, Shoal Creek, and the valley of our farm, where I spent long hours as a boy in the fields. In the background is the village of Ritchey with two prominent features: the Baptist Church with its tall white steeple and our large, white house that replaced the house in which I was born on a record cold night in January, 1930. Although that first house didn't have running water, I have thought many times how lucky I was

Painting of the Ritchey Mill by local artist, Don Draper, of Neosho.

to have been born there. I didn't realize it when I was a boy.

My career has been in higher education, specifically engineering education. After I received my Ph.D. from the University of Missouri, I accepted a faculty position at Texas A&M University. After nine years, I went to the University of Florida in a department head position, and then in research administration. After eight years there, I was asked to be Vice Chancellor for Academic Affairs in the University of Texas System. I was in that position for six years, and then moved to the University of Texas at Austin in an endowed faculty position and I taught both in the College of Engineering and the LBJ School of Public Affairs. I also directed the Center for Research in Water Resources. After six years at UT Austin, I was asked to be Dean of Engineering at the University of Arizona, a position I held for ten years. I then went to the National Science Foundation in Washington for three years before returning to Tucson to teach and finally retire. I am now retired but still involved nationally and internationally in engineering education and water resources matters.

Over the years many things were happening in my career and I was too busy to think a great deal about my roots, but I did think of them some. Because of my wife's interest in genealogy, we developed an interest in the history of our family. A second cousin provided a brief account by a great uncle of the trip my great grandparents made with their family from England in 1872. That journey ultimately ended in the Ozarks of southwest Missouri, where they settled.

As I progressed in my career in higher education and worked at several major universities, I had the opportunity to meet and interact with people from all over the world, representing many different cultures. My work as a consultant and adviser in engineering and water resources has taken me to more than thirty countries and into the rural villages in several of them. All the while, as I worked in my profession, I was gaining insight into the peoples of the world and their cultures. I was also developing a deeper appreciation for my own background.

I knew I was an Ozark hillbilly because I had grown up in the foothills of the Missouri Ozark Mountains. I became keenly aware of this in 1947 when, at the age of seventeen, I jumped from a consolidated rural high school, with a graduating class of eighteen, to the University of Missouri in Columbia, which had 12,000 students. I was with 'sophisticated city boys' from St. Louis and Kansas City, places I'd only visited once. Our classes at MU were full of committed World War II veterans. I was in over my head and the only thing that would carry me through was hard work, and I'd learned about that from my parents and my brothers and sister back home. In fact, I learned early on that hard work was the one thing that could help a person overcome almost any adversity. Being a hard worker was a plus that would counter many weaknesses. Mother, a strong Southern Baptist, always tried to see the best in all, and those who did not properly care for their families, and perhaps even visited the tavern, were not her favorites – to say the least. But if they were hard workers, she could always see good in them. When referring to these individuals, she would end her discourse with, "But he's a hard worker." That was a positive. The title of this book comes from that puritan principle.

Being a hard worker was a type of praise. Honesty was another. As a young boy I could not help but hear the people in town lauding my hard work, even sometimes saying directly to me, "You sure are a hard worker." It was a high accolade. Both parents complimented us children for our hard work. They praised us in other ways as well. But Mother or Dad would often say, "You sure worked hard today and did a good job." I could see in their eyes that this praise brought satisfaction to them.

Although I had dated regularly in high school, I had never had a date to a ballroom dance, because we did not do that kind of cheek-to-cheek dancing in Ritchey or at the consolidated high school I attended. On occasion there was square dancing, though. About the most daring thing I had done was smoke a Red Dot nickel cigar and drive a car very fast. We did not have to confront the temptation of liquor or drugs. Yet in subtle ways as a freshman at MU at the age of seventeen, when I talked to city boys, I mistakenly sensed that my background was not quite up to par. A commitment to hard work was the best way to prevent failure. I am grateful for that ethic from my farming parents.

In 1990, after forty-three years, a former classmate contacted me about a reunion of our 1947 high school class. With one or two exceptions, I had not seen any of my seventeen high school classmates since graduation. That intensified my thinking about that rural area where I grew up and the people and experiences we had. My interest was piqued by going back and seeing the successful lives my classmates had led. No doubt, I had matured and gained an appreciation for the culture of the Ozark people. I had developed increasing pride in my heritage. In my teaching, I regularly talked to university students about my background and the experience of growing up in a very small Ozark village with a population of about 212 – a great place to grow up. It was not the individuals that I grew up with, as such, that were of interest, but the experiences we all had there.

This book is about the experiences of growing up in a small Missouri Ozark town, typical of rural areas of the time – from about 1930 to the early 1950's. It describes life, activities, experiences and people in such a setting. I am candid and describe events as I remember them, but nothing I have written is intended to offend anyone because they were all great people.

The book has a short Epilogue commenting on the last fifty years and on the changes that have occurred in these small towns – something that is repeated literally thousands of times as the small farming towns of America wither. I hope that part is not too nostalgic.

It also has a historical footnote at the end, mentioning a sad incident that happened in nearby Pierce City in 1901. I put this in to make the record complete.

The body of this book is a group of somewhat unrelated essays describing personal experiences and incidents that I recall or heard about first hand from others. Each essay is a short story that can stand alone. As a result, there is some redundancy, and I hope it is not excessive. The pictures are to give a pictorial view of what I write about and hopefully add to the story.

One major reference is used in the book. It is an old, leather bound book published by the Goodspeed Publishing Co., Chicago, in 1888. It belonged to my father and is entitled, History of Newton, Lawrence, Barry and McDonald Counties, Missouri. Ritchey is in Newton County. These counties are the four counties in the southwest corner of the state, bordering Arkansas and Oklahoma. References to "an 1888 history" refer to that book. In the preface of that early history the publisher wrote, "The design of the present extensive historical and biographical research is more to gather and preserve in attractive form, while fresh with the evidence of truth, the enormous fund of perishing occurrence, than to abstract from insufficient contemporaneous data remote, doubtful or incorrect conclusions. The true perspective of the landscape of life can only be seen from the distance that lends enchantment to the view."

I hope this book might in a small way add enchantment to the view of life many of us knew while growing up in a small town. In my case, this was in the Missouri Ozarks during and after the major depression of the 1930's.

RITCHEY AND ITS PEOPLE

The village of Ritchey, in the Ozarks of extreme southwest Missouri was laid out by Judge Matthew Ritchey in 1871. Judge Ritchey had moved to the area in 1832 and built a log cabin where the village named after him is located. At that time the nearest post office was a 100 miles away. The location was no doubt selected because it was near the edge of Shoal Creek floodplain, which provided fertile bottom land for farming. Judge Ritchey and his family built a dam and mill on the continuously flowing Shoal Creek. Also, there was a nice spring just north of the village that provided a dependable supply of cool, potable water. Village growth was spurred in the 1860s when the main line of the St. Louis and San Francisco (Frisco) Railroad reached Ritchey. The railroad followed Shoal Creek and its tracks were at the south edge of town. An 1882 surveyor's plat envisioned more development than occurred. Much of the area envisioned for development was never developed, even when the town's population peaked soon after the turn of the century.

Those who settled the region mostly migrated from Europe. They came directly or moved westward from the eastern states, oftentimes from the Appalachian area, which had geographical similarities to the region. Many were from Tennessee, Kentucky, Virginia and the Carolinas. Almost all of the economic activities were directly related to farming. The crops were wheat and other small grains, corn, and hay. Most operations were general farms with cattle, hogs, and chickens as the primary farm animals although just about any farm animal could be found. There was bountiful wild game in the early days and a major food source came from hunting. But by the time I was born in 1930, most of the food was from farms with their vegetable gardens and domestic farm animals. Virtually every home had a large garden and maybe a small orchard. Many families had a few chickens for eggs and meat. A major summer activity was canning fruits and vegetables and storing fall products, such as potatoes and onions, in the cool, dirt floor cellars that most homes had beneath a portion of the house. Home canned products were stored there as well.

The social culture of Ritchey in the 1930s was no doubt like that of thousands of other very small, rural towns in the United States, particularly in the Midwest and Southern farming areas. There were no factories in Ritchey, except for the seasonally operated tomato canning factory and the small water-powered grist mill.

The canning factory was located on railroad property south of the railroad and southwest of the depot. It had a small spring-fed stream flowing under the building. It canned locally grown tomatoes during the summer and early fall tomato season. Many farmers in the nearby Ozark hills would grow an acre or more of tomatoes for this cannery. Except for the manager, boiler operator (cooker), and a few others the employees were all locals, mostly women who washed, peeled and cored the tomatoes

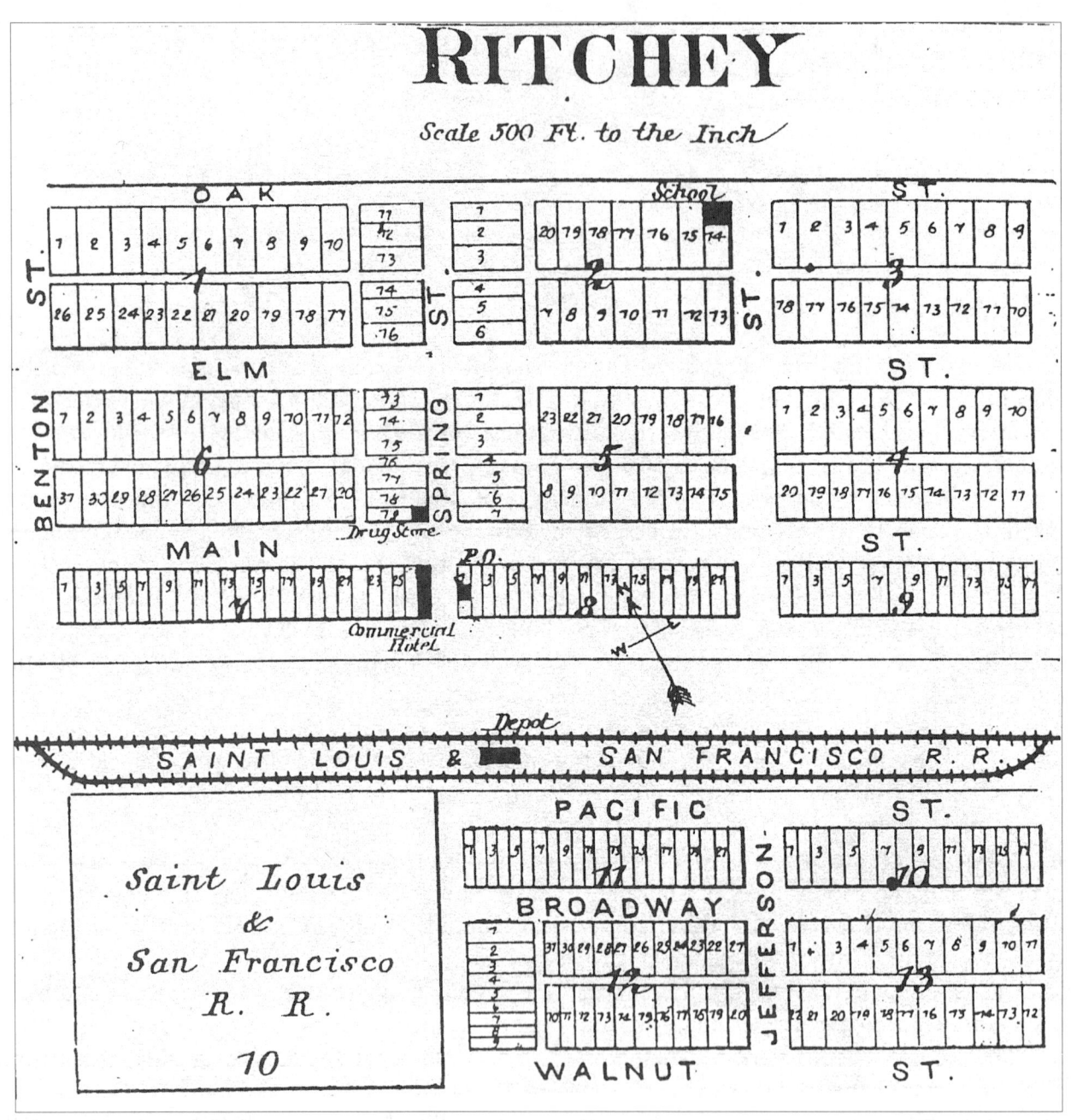

A plat of Ritchey as laid out in 1882 at the direction of Matthew H. Ritchey. The areas east of Jefferson Street and south of the railroad were never developed. Our house was on lots 19, 20 and 21 of block 8. Blocks 3, 4, 9, 10, 11, 12 and 13 were part of our farm since they were never developed. Our barn was located in the middle of Main Street just east of Jefferson Street between undeveloped blocks 4 and 9 of the original survey.

and stuffed them in the tin cans to be capped and cooked. Pay was low and the season was only a few weeks long. But it provided badly needed pocket money for these women.

The mill, located on Shoal Creek and powered by a water turbine, employed only one miller and on a few occasions two. It made prized 'water ground' corn meal and also ground animal feed for the nearby farmers. The farmers grew virtually all of the feed for their cattle and chickens and brought the ear corn and oats to the mill in horse drawn wagons to be ground into feed.

A few residents of Ritchey commuted to nearby towns or to a local sawmill for regular jobs and when the lead and zinc mines in the region were operating, several worked there. The railroad provided employment for a depot agent, and for telegraphers during World War II, as well as for the four members of the 'section gang' that maintained the tracks, right-of-way and fences on their section of the railroad. The railroad provided a house along the tracks for the section gang foreman and he supervised the three other workers.

The gang repaired the tracks, used hand scythes to cut the weeds along the right-of-way, and made sure the fences that kept cattle and other animals off the tracks were in good repair. The railroad was generally responsible for reimbursing farmers for livestock that got on the tracks and were killed by the trains. Rarely, but on more than one occasion, we had a cow or mule hit by a train in the night when the animals escaped from their pastures and got on the tracks. To me, the foreman didn't seem to have to do much physical labor. Since most of my tasks around the farm involved mostly physical labor, I thought that being a section gang foreman would be a great job not involving excessively hard work.

Farming supported most of the families in the region around Ritchey. The town was the support center servicing the nearby farmers and other laborers. But during my early life, the automobile and improved roads made it possible to go to nearby larger towns for this support. During earlier times there had been several retail businesses in Ritchey, but by the mid-1930s there were only a few small ones: York's General Store, Largen's Hardware (with post office in it), and Kistler's General Store (known as Ray's). There also was a gas station, locally called a filling station, an auto repair garage, a blacksmith shop and a tavern (called a beer joint by the locals), and, for a short time, a small restaurant that might seat eight patrons. All of these businesses were one- or two-person family operations. Seldom were more than one or two customers in these establishments at any time. Commonly, when one entered there was no one there except the proprietor.

Very slow business was the norm and, except for Ray Kistler, who was fairly young at the time, most of the proprietors were older. When the owner could no longer work because of health, the businesses almost always closed. Few in the village had pensions or retirement programs, so formal retirement was not the normal course of events. All of those proprietors are now gone and the only business from the '30s in operation by 1990 was the store that once was Kistler's. In the '90s it had a precariously low business volume and irregular business hours.

One nice characteristic of Ritchey was that it didn't take much money to live. I have no idea what the average income might have been when I was a boy, but it was very low. In the 1930's most families did not have cars. In fact, only a few had plumbing in their houses. Water came from shallow wells dug by hand labor. They usually had an old-fashioned hand pump, but sometimes a reel and water bucket were used to draw water. Small three- or four-room frame houses were common.

Electricity was available in the village, but few homes had appliances. So utility bills only covered meager lighting and perhaps a small refrigerator. Home heating and cooking was by wood-burning heating and cooking stoves. The fuel wood was cut locally and was inexpensive. People made many of their clothes at home and store-bought men's work clothes, usually bib overalls and chambray shirts for farmers, were mended over and over to extend their life. Shoes were resoled and repaired at home. My father had a shoe last and he resoled our everyday shoes. Ritchey provided an inexpensive home for older people who had very little income, often from a meager state-provided 'old age pension' of a few dollars a month.

One might think that Ritchey was a dull and lethargic place to live. I never sensed that. All the boys and girls I knew were happy. They were adequately clothed and had enough to eat. Since clothes were usually washed by hand with a washboard in a 30-inch diameter galvanized metal washtub, people would normally wear the same clothes for a few days. Without bathtubs or showers, the weekly bath was in that same metal washtub, with the water heated in a tea kettle on the wood-burning kitchen stove. Mother insisted on our weekly bath without exception. However, some in the rural areas might have bathed less frequently, particularly in the winter in those cold, drafty houses. Still, everyone seemed happy and children and adults alike found a way to entertain themselves. Ritchey was a happy community of friendly, caring people who helped each other.

Ritchey did not have a movie house, so most people seldom saw a movie, locally called a 'picture show.' The exception was during the summer when a traveling outdoor picture show would come to town once a week. Radio was the principal source of outside entertainment in Ritchey homes. A few rural homes that were without electricity had a battery-powered radio hooked to a 6-volt, auto type, lead-acid battery. The battery had to be recharged regularly because, before the days of the transistor, these vacuum tube radios generated a lot of heat and had high power requirements. Other personal amusement was largely self-created.

The men of the town constructed a very nice outdoor croquet court and it was lighted at night, with four bare 100-watt incandescent bulbs that hung on a stretched wire. The court was carefully graded and had a packed sand-and-soil surface, not unlike a clay tennis court, except it was gray. It had two by six bumper boards on the four sides of the court, to which strips of old tire treads had been nailed to give some bounce off the walls. The court was sandwiched between two buildings and there were regulars who played frequently during the summer evenings. Others pitched horseshoes nearby.

There was also the glass-covered, hand painted checker board in Largen's Hardware Store, which was used in the winter when it was too cold for outdoor activities. It was located in the back near the large pot-bellied heating stove that was the sole heat source for the rather large building. Those men with interest in mentally stimulating games would play checkers on winter evenings until Mr. Largen closed the store at about 9:00 p.m. My Father enjoyed checkers and was very good at the game, but farm chores prevented him from spending evenings at Largen's. We had a checker board at home and we sometimes played in the evenings.

Most people did not play cards much. There were many families who, for religious reasons, thought that playing cards, the kind that could be used for poker, was sinful. There were some card games, such as Rook and Old Maid, which were judged okay. But people generally didn't play cards in public. In our family, card games were played in the home when friends visited. We played all kinds of friendly card games at home such as rummy, pitch, hearts and pinochle, using ordinary playing cards. We never played poker. My father enjoyed any game that stimulated the mind and required thought and strategy. Mother seldom, if ever, joined in.

Gossiping was a major source of entertainment for the women of Ritchey. There were absolutely no secrets in the village. Any bit of news would spread like wildfire. The organizations for women were generally associated with one of the churches in town, but there was a women's homemakers club named the Jolly Workers. Such clubs were encouraged by the County Home Demonstration Agent. The agent provided information on improving homemaking skills and raising families. It was at these club meetings that you would hear the women laughing and having a good time. The women would never publicly participate in games like croquet or checkers. But the Jolly Workers undertook many projects to help the community. They performed an important service, which at the same time pro-

Largen's General Store and Post Office.

vided a social outlet for the women away from the confines of home.

The women would also turn work into a social function. For example, when there were big jobs on the farms requiring a large crew of men, such as making hay or threshing the grain crop, these hungry workers had to be fed. The meals prepared for noon-time dinner were feasts, with several meat dishes, potatoes, gravy, many vegetables, several large pies, cakes and the like. The farm wives would help each other on a trade-off basis. The honor code was, "I will help you and you will help me for an approximately equivalent amount of time". Usually no money changed hands, but people remembered when they owed someone a day of labor or vice versa. These were times when the women came together to work and visit. The labor over the hot stoves was hard, but I sense that they enjoyed it, and harvest season was a joyous time.

The children, like the adults, found a way to have fun. No one had many store-bought toys, but, with imagination, a homemade toy could be just as much fun. For example, with a simple 10-cent sponge-rubber ball, eight or ten kids, and adults too, could play 'ante over' for an hour or so. And there were many other games in which there was a lot of running, including 'hide-and-seek,' 'kick-the-can', and 'rolling the hoop.' We also had different kinds of ball games that could be played in any open field or in the infrequently traveled streets. We played marbles on the bare ground and became quite expert at it. Mumbley peg was played on bare ground. It only required a two-bladed pocket knife that could be bought for a quarter.

Although the town had no sidewalks, except for a few hundred feet on both sides of the short street where the stores were, those sidewalks were a source of games. The girls sometimes played hop-scotch on the sidewalk in front of the stores or on the short section of the front walk at school. If a short length of a rope was available, the girls would jump rope for hours. Some would get pretty fancy at it. Jacks was another popular girls game for the sidewalk or an inside wooden floor. This game could get complicated and required dexterity and very good hand-eye coordination.

With toy pistols, homemade or otherwise, boys would play cowboys-and-Indians or cops-and-robbers for hours. This mostly involved running and hiding and yelling, "Bang, you're dead." .

There were special occasions when entertainment among the teenagers took a different form. Halloween was one of them, when the boys would plot all sorts of mischief. On New Years Eve, we all stayed up and laughed and played, and maybe told ghost stories, until midnight when the church bells and the school bell would be rung. We literally rang the old year out and the New Year in. The trick was to be able to get into the buildings at that hour and some might be locked. But we somehow managed. I wonder how many nightmares those chilling ghost stories caused. These and other games that children played are described in the essay entitled, "Games."

Our family was close friends with three other farm families and these families would get together at night maybe once or twice a month, particularly in the winter. Note that in Ritchey the afternoon was called evening and the evening after supper was referred to as night. Also, the noon meal was dinner and the evening meal was supper. Anyway, the men would play cards and the women would visit, perhaps knitting or crocheting while doing so. The children would play games or maybe undertake a project like making popcorn balls or a batch of homemade candy. The candy was usually chocolate fudge, but could be taffy, which was trickier because the taffy pulling had to occur when the mixture was at just the right temperature. No doubt other families had their own circle of friends and had similar experiences. Families talked a lot and played mind expanding games together. And practical jokes were fun and sometimes elaborately planned.

Ritchey was a place where trust prevailed. Most people would not lock their door even if they left for several hours or even a few days. Our house was never locked when I was a child. Neighbors were trusted and you depended on your neighbors. A handshake or a person's word was as good as a written contract in dealing with neighbors. It was a different matter for an outsider. An outsider was anyone you didn't personally know unless a friend knew him or her. A car with an out-of-state license plate would immediately be suspect, particularly if it wasn't from one of the adjacent states. A stranger in town would activate the gossip grapevine and the women wouldn't relax until the purpose of that person's visit was established. We didn't share information with a stranger until we knew what they were about and what they wanted.

Few outsiders came to Ritchey, so people were not accustomed to seeing strangers. An interesting and true story, told to me by Mother who was then widowed, occurred in the late 1960's. A male Peace Corps volunteer from an eastern city was left two miles from the town and told to walk in and establish communication and effective relations with the residents of the town. It was part of his training. He had a bit of a hippy look and sat down on the steps of a vacant house to rest. Before he could get his bearings and establish a plan, the grapevine of the widows and other women in town had pretty much characterized him as a shady character and were preparing to call the sheriff. One of the men in town was asked to investigate and the truth came out. The worst thing the poor guy had done was walk around town and stop to rest on the steps of a vacant house. The security system of the small town was working, and as far as being immediately accepted, this Peace Corps volunteer might as well have been in the depths of a third world country where a different language was spoken.

The village of Ritchey was governed by an elected town board. This board had little to do because the town had no assets. There wasn't any fire protection. If a fire occurred, a fire truck might come from a nearby town, but essentially it would be fought by unorganized volunteers. We also had a Justice of the Peace who occasionally performed marriage ceremonies. One resident was a notary public. There was also a town constable, who, if paid at all, was paid very little. The only time we thought of him was on Halloween when we knew he might interfere with our fun. If anyone needed a law officer, which was rare, the county sheriff would be called.

The elected school board was always active and it was the most important elected body in town. It had a budget, operated facilities and employed teachers and other people. The school, in one sense, was the glue that held the town together. All parents were interested in what went on at school. When towns like Ritchey lost their small schools in the consolidated school movement, the pupils probably got a better education with a wider choice of courses. But the towns lost something. Ritchey School held its last class in 1953.

The post office was a second thing that held a small town together. Dad dreaded the day when the Ritchey Post Office might be shut down. Arthur Largen was the postmaster for many years and he operated the post office from his store. When he died the position was temporary for a short time. Then Ray Kistler became postmaster and operated the post office from his store until about 1973. Upon his death, the Ritchey Post Office was operated on a contract for a short time, but soon closed and another chapter in the life of the town ended. Ritchey is now served by the post office six miles away in Granby, but letters can be addressed to Ritchey so long as the Granby zip code is used.

As more people owned cars and the local, poorly maintained gravel roads were improved and hard surfaced, the importance of the railroad waned. Eventually no trains stopped and the depot was razed. As people traveled to nearby larger towns, they found better shopping and, perhaps, slightly lower prices. Eventually, much of the retail business was lost to Ritchey merchants. The businesses closed one by one. When television came in the mid 1950s, antennas began to appear on the rooftops. The regular social discourse among the residents started to change. One of the cornerstones of Ritchey society, simply visiting and enjoying each other, began an irreversible change. The town would forever be different from the way I knew it as a boy.

Ritchey depot with an inbound train from the east.

THE RITCHEY SCHOOL AND PIE SUPPERS

The school in Ritchey was the 'heart' of the town. School activities involved virtually every family in town and most of those in the rural areas around town. The rural public education system started out with many one-room country schools located so that most students were within a few miles of a school, and could walk, ride a horse to school or be taken in a buggy. These one-room schools had eight grades in them and all of the pupils were taught by a single teacher. That teacher at first had only a high school education and maybe less, but had obtained some type of certification to teach. Most students, particularly boys, would not go beyond the eighth grade. Boys often thought education was not needed for farming. Those that did would have to make arrangements for transportation to a larger town that had a high school. In some cases, the student might find a room in that town if it was too far for daily travel by foot or horseback.

Ritchey was at one time a much larger town and it had its school. The first school was started in 1860 in a brush arbor and later moved to a log house. Appendix III contains information condensed from the original 1932 Ritchey School Survey written in long-hand. It provides a good history of the Ritchey School, which had become a consolidated school in 1929, and in 1932 operated the Ritchey School with 12 grades and two one-room country schools with eight grades. In 1931-32 the total monthly salary for eight teachers in this district was $585, and with 222 pupils, the monthly teacher cost per pupil was $2.64.

By the time my siblings and I became of school age the school was well established and the original two-room wood-frame structure built in 1887 had had a third room added in 1911. But as the consolidation movement continued and more of the students in the country came to Ritchey, the school had to be expanded. Two rooms were added on the east side of the structure (to the right of the three-room school pictured) in 1929 for the high school classes. That left three rooms for the first eight grades. I had not yet started to school when another room was added to the north of the building, providing four rooms for the grade school, two grades in each room. This six-room one-story building was as large as it ever got. The school had a bell tower and the school bell would ring 15 minutes before school started and at 9:00 a.m. when classes would begin. This rope operated bell would be used to call students in after both the morning and afternoon recess and at the end of the noon hour.

The school had a playground on the east side of the building for the first four grades, and a larger one on the west side used for all the other grades. There were no indoor athletic facilities. There was a packed dirt floor outdoor basketball court with two goals mounted on wooden poles in the ground. The sidelines would be scratched in the ground with a stick or a white lime line on the soil for games. It was difficult to dribble on the rough dirt. Also, during and after rains, when it was muddy, we couldn't

Ritchey School, circa 1928. At that time it was a three-room school.

play. The school yard had room for a softball field on the west side, but it didn't have a backstop screen and the right field overlapped the basketball area. A volley ball court could be set up by tying the net to one tree and attaching it to the wall of the school. So at best the athletic facilities were limited and the student athletes bemoaned the lack of facilities. In 1932 the boys' basketball team had a name – it was called the 'Bulldogs.'

The school did not have running water, but there was a shallow well with a hand pump in the east school yard. Instead of a spout at the pump a ten-foot section of one-inch metal pipe was attached to the pump. That pipe, which had quarter inch holes spaced about twenty inches, sloped down slightly from the pump and was capped at the end. It had a piece of gutter hung below to carry the excess flow away to be dumped on the ground near a ditch. For the students to drink water, one student would take the pump handle and pump hard enough so the water would spout up four to six inches at the six holes along the pipe. Six pupils could drink at once. A lone person could only drink at the hole next to the pump and then only when he/she reached out with one hand to the pump handle and pumped it hard.

To satisfy the pupils biological needs the school had two pit privies at the back of the school yard. Each had a wall around it for privacy. The boy's toilet was a two-holer, but behind the wall beside the toilet was a gravel filled pit for the boys to urinate in. I never saw the inside of the girl's toilet, but I presume it might have had four holes.

The room for the first and second grades had low tables and little red chairs. Our first grade teacher was Miss Joslin. She would sometimes have us arrange our red chairs around her and read stories to us. Miss Joslin was a disciplinarian and if you weren't paying attention she would reprimand you. If the offence was repeated, her punishment was to make the offending pupil sit on her lap while she read. I recall that was the most severe punishment I could imagine – and I am afraid that punishment was doled out to me on more than one occasion. All other grade school classrooms had rows of student desks fastened to the floor.

A big event for the school and for the entire town was when a school pageant was held. This would involve the entire student body. The mother's would work on colorful costumes. And there was usually a pageant queen. The pageant would be held on a temporary stage set up in the front of one classroom in the original two-room building. Folding doors could be opened between the rooms so the students at all desks in those two class rooms could see the stage. *Note, the student desks are literally against the shallow stage which was no more than 10 feet deep.* The pageant in the picture was in about 1939 and my siblings, John and Helen, are in it as am I. Glenn would have been about three years old.

Taking photographs inside the school in those days was difficult because the photographic film was slow and lighting was poor. I distinctly remember when this picture was taken. The photographer had a large box camera on a tripod and for lighting he used flash powder placed in a pan on a small pole so it could be held a few feet above his head. He set the powder off with a sparking device like a flint-lock rifle. There was a very bright flash and then a large puff of white smoke that rose to the ceiling. I suppose this was before the days of large flash bulbs and certainly long before the advent of strobe photo flashes. Virtually all pictures then were taken outside where light was better.

Pageant at School.

The Ritchey School was always in a tight budget situation. In 1931-32 the state aid to support the school was only $3,000, and it had 222 pupils. And that had to cover the janitor, coal for heating the school, electricity, operate the school buses, as well as all school supplies including books for the students. These books were used for many years. In 1931-32 the total amount spent on books and other incidental expenses was $2,256.47. So the teachers really had to scrape to meet the needs of the students. The school didn't have a parent-teachers association (PTA) or other regular means of raising funds for the school, except for one – the annual pie supper.

The pie supper was to raise funds and involved the girls and boys in particular. The event would be well advertised. The women and girls would bake a pie and put it in a highly decorated box, usually with crepe paper ribbons and fancy stuff. All women interested were invited to participate. The whole community would bake pies. The crowd would gather in the evening, usually on a Friday or Saturday. All these decorated boxes would be on a table in the front of the room. No one was supposed to know who had baked the pie in each box. Each pie was auctioned off. The man or boy who ended up buying the pie at the auction would, after all the pies had sold, enjoy the pie at one of the student desks with the girl (or woman) who had made it. Husbands usually knew which pie was made by his wife and would usually, but not always, buy it.

Obviously, the teenage boys would want to buy a pie that some pretty maiden had baked, and would try to figure out which pie was hers. So the fun was when the bidding started and more than one boy was trying to get the pie that they thought the pretty girl had baked. What was really amusing was when a married woman brought a pie and the rumors would start that that was the pie baked by this very pretty girl.

These events were to raise money to help some part of the school program in need of support. They were entertaining because a budding romance might begin there. They didn't raise a large amount of money, because no one had much money to spend. But if a boy paid two or three dollars for the pie of someone he wanted to impress, that would be the topic of conversation around town for awhile. A large portion of the community participated. Those events served a worthy purpose for the school and it brought the community together, which except for church activities didn't happen often.

The pie suppers ceased to be held when the high school students started going to Midway. I only remember one or two, but Helen remembers more.

In the spring of the year a photographer would come to the school and take pictures of each class which would go in the small school annual. The pictures were with the teacher and were always taken

Richey School, 3rd and 4th grades, 1938

outside in the front of the school which faced south. Two representative class pictures are provided, one in 1938 of the 3rd and 4th grades and one in 1942 of the 7th and 8th grades.

Note the picture of the 1938 3rd and 4th grades. The photographer told the students to look serious, and those sitting to put their hands together on their laps and those standing to put their hands behind them. Note, all the boys without exception word blue denim bib overalls, and the girls wore cotton print dresses, most of which were likely made by their mothers. There weren't any special schools for students with learning disabilities and if a student had learning problems, he/she would simply fail and not pass on to the next grade. One unfortunate girl in our class had repeated the 3rd grade several times and was much older.

In the war years during World War II, the schools were very patriotic. Everyone was expected to sacrifice and contribute to the war effort. In school we were encouraged to buy savings stamps which could cost a dime to a quarter and paste them in a little war savings booklet. When the booklet was full at $18.75 it could be traded for a war bond that would be worth $25.00 when it expired in 10 years. Virtually every student had some family member or relative in the military service. The 1942 7th and 8th grade class picture was taken in the spring after the beginning of WW II. It illustrates the patriotic emphasis by having the school's 48-star American flag in the picture as well as a sign that says, "We do our part for V" (victory).

The students could buy a copy of the school picture for very little. They were perhaps the only pictures that many students had of themselves as they were growing up. It was not common for families to own cameras in those days.

Richey School, 7th and 8th grades, 1942

BEDBUGS

My father came to Ritchey as a bachelor at the age of 24. He farmed the original Matthew Ritchey farm, which my grandfather had purchased as his second farm. He wanted one farm for each of his two sons, his only children. Matthew Ritchey had founded the village of Ritchey. The farm was at the eastern edge of the village and, in fact, the town was located on the northwest corner of the original farm. So the farm as we knew it was immediately adjacent to the developed lots in the village of Ritchey. In fact, the farm encompassed blocks 3, 4, 9, 10, 11, 12 and 13 in the original surveyor's plat that were never developed.

Dad moved to Ritchey to till that farm in 1923. He first lived in a small shanty, which was immediately across the street and north of the house my parents ultimately moved into when they married. That small, three-room house provided shelter for Dad during his first year in Ritchey. It wasn't a good place to live. To the best of my knowledge, the shack's oak board siding was never painted and had a metallic grey look. The house didn't have a masonry foundation, having been built on a timber foundation. It was a shelter from the rain and wind, and little more.

I recall dad telling of that first year alone in that house. His life consisted of trying to get the farm going and preparing the larger house for his intended bride, Ada Pearl Davidson. She was born on a farm in southwest Missouri near Sarcoxie, but had moved as a young girl to Oklahoma. That house where Dad lived was no more than a place where he slept and cooked his beans and pork, or whatever else he ate. All sorts of insects found a safe haven in those un-insulated wooden walls, which were built on a termite infested wooden foundation.

While I don't recall many of the details of Dad's stories about his life in that house, I remember one quite well. We knew that bedbugs were a menace not to be taken lightly. This wingless, bloodsucking insect infested houses and especially beds. If a house had bedbugs in its walls, as the house across the street did, it was nearly impossible to keep the creatures out of the bed. There was a solution, however, which my father adopted. By placing the legs of his iron bedstead in tin cans that were partially filled with kerosene, the non-flying bedbugs would find a lethal trap if they tried to climb up the bedstead legs to their haven among the bedding. Dad said that while there were bedbugs in the house, they never bothered him. I suppose he became accustomed to the smell of kerosene as he slept. It's a good thing that he wasn't a smoker.

Mother and Dad were engaged before he came to Ritchey. Mother had graduated from high school and was living on her parent's farm outside of Chickasha, Oklahoma and teaching school. They decided to wait a year before getting married so she could save her money from teaching to buy furniture. In 1923 as the Valley View, Oklahoma, school teacher with a high school diploma, she was paid $100 per month, which was a good wage in those days. The $700 or so she saved from her eight month's teaching bought the basic furniture they would need to start their lives together.

Before Mother and Dad were married, a small four-room house across the street to the south had been readied for them. It had a stone masonry foundation. My two brothers, sister and I were born in that house that had a water well, but no indoor plumbing. So the outdoor privy was our refuge for personal biological business. Our house never had bedbugs. So when dad and mother married and moved into the improved quarters, the house across the street was vacant.

After my parents were married, Dad rented out that small house across the street. He obliged them with very low rents. During the 1930's, I seem to recall the rent was $2.50 per month. By then we had an electric pump and the renters came to our house for water and carried it back to their house in an open pail. Dad also provided free water to other neighbors who would come over with two buckets at a time. Since there was no village water utility Dad gladly furnished free water to our neighbors.

Dad once told me he would have preferred not to rent that house and the rent was so low that it offered little income. Still, when a renter would leave, others would appear immediately pleading to rent the place just to have a roof over their heads. I always knew that Dad wanted to raze it and add its substantial garden plot to our own. But there were those who wanted it, and needed it. So we kept renting it off and on until on a fateful day in the fall of 1944 when it caught fire and burned. Thankfully, it was vacant at the time. There was no pride in owning that house, but from time-to-time it was home for some families who called it the Smerdon House.

I never thought of that house across the street as a Smerdon house, but Dad did own it. That fact came home in a rather sick way one fall afternoon when I boarded the school bus to return home from a rather exciting day as a sophomore in high school. When I boarded the bus that afternoon, the driver said that our house had burned. I still remember the flush of adrenaline as I envisioned our wonderful home, then totally remodeled and expanded, and holding all our personal belongings, going up in flames. The loss flashed across my mind in stark detail. It probably was only a short time, but it seemed like hours, before the driver explained that it was not the home we lived in but the small house across the street. Blessedly, it was vacant at the time. That house was never a pretty sight, but it was home to some families over the years and it served Dad during his first year in Ritchey.

I learned an important lesson that day. The bus driver probably was trying to make a joke. But one shouldn't joke at the expense of another person's home or family.

THE FARM LIFE

My two brothers, sister and I were all born in my parents' original Ritchey farmhouse between 1925 and 1935. Dr. Roy C. Lamson was the attending physician. He had to come twelve miles from Neosho and was the son of an early physician who moved to a neighboring town in 1867. Dr. Lamson's mother was Sue Ritchey, daughter of Judge M. H. Ritchey, the founder of our town and the first white man owner of the farm on which we were born.

We lived in that original four-room house until 1940 when it was remodeled and made much larger. It was T-shaped, with an L-shaped back porch tacked on the left side of the T. The house had a kitchen, living/dining room and two bedrooms. None of the rooms had a closet except one bedroom, which had a tiny closet that was only about a foot deep. We didn't have a bathroom or running water at first, but cold running water was subsequently installed in the kitchen in about 1930. There was a dirt floor cellar under the kitchen, which could be entered from the back porch. Many glass Mason fruit jars that mother filled with canned foods each summer were stored there. The fall potato, sweet potato and onion harvest was also stored there, as were lard stands full of lard. We also stored other things in the cellar that we wanted to keep cool, such as fresh apples.

The only pieces of furniture in the bedroom where all four children slept were two iron bedsteads, which were opposite each other in two corners, and a homemade pine box with a hinged lid that was used to store quilts. That quilt box, which was about four feet long, two feet deep and two feet wide, sat between the head of the two beds under a window in the center of the east wall. There was about four feet between the beds and about six feet at the foot of the beds. That latter area held a stand-alone wardrobe and a number of storage boxes. The boxes were at the foot of the beds and adjacent to the wardrobe. We could play in the small space that wasn't occupied by beds or boxes. All four rooms in the house were square and approximately fourteen feet on a side. The total inside area of this house, where six people lived, was about 800 square feet. It was very crowded and, except on the coldest days, we wanted to be outside where we had room.

As a very small boy, I remember that I liked to play under the kitchen table. It was a private place where I could play and daydream and not be under-foot. The barn, which was large and about 200 feet from the house, became a good place to play because you had room to move and you could run.

Other buildings on the farmstead near the house included the smokehouse, the chicken house, the brooder house, the barn and some sheds for hogs. On a farm, with animals to care for, the work is such that all buildings become an integral part of the family's life. A farmer will spend more time in the barn, other outbuildings and fields than he does in his house. Farm chores go on seven days a week. Cows need to be milked, chickens fed, eggs gathered, hogs slopped and otherwise fed. Calves

The Smerdon home and farm buildings in Ritchey.

and horses also must to be fed and watered. And all of this has to be done twice a day, every day.

We always had chickens and Mother incubated eggs in a borrowed kerosene-heated incubator that could be moved into the house. This was done in the late winter or early spring when it was cold. The incubators had to be in a building that had a fairly constant temperature, and the house was the only heated building on the farm. Therefore, in the original house Mother put the incubator in the living/dining room. As the time the chicks would hatch approached, it was fun to peek in the incubator and see the trays of eggs ready to crack and burst open with the life of a baby chick.

When the sows were farrowing, we were always concerned that the litter might have some runts that would be too weak to compete for its mother's milk. Sometimes the litter might include more than a dozen baby pigs, and there was often a runt or two in such large litters. When a runt wasn't able to compete and get enough of its mother's milk, we would bring it in the house and put it in a straw-filled box on the floor under the wood burning kitchen stove, which was a nice warm place. We fed this little pig cow's milk using a bottle with a small nipple. Frequently we failed, but sometimes the tiny pig would gain strength and could be returned to its mother to compete with its brothers and sisters in the double-rowed feeding lineup of nursing pigs. We knew we were giving the pig its only chance for life.

Everyone in the family had chores, and each was expected to complete them without fail. My first chore, like that of my brothers, was to carry in the wood for the cooking stove. There was a wood box in the kitchen by the cooking stove that I was to keep full of the wood, which had been split into small pieces about fifteen inches long and two to three inches across. Since these pieces were not heavy, a child could be assigned that task by the time he or she started school. There was also kindling, often dry corn cobs, to be gathered and brought in to facilitate starting the fire in the early morning, and that, too, was a job for the youngest. These were the first chores for a boy at our house, although I am sure my sister may have been called on to help on occasion.

Helen was expected to help Mother in the house with all kinds of housework, particularly washing and drying dishes, and even the cooking. Since the women and older girls on farms often were expected to help with milking cows, quite young girls were sometimes left in the house to cook. I know that my sister, Helen, could bake the best biscuits I have ever tasted when she was about ten. These were not made from Bisquick or some other commercial biscuit mix. They were made from scratch using the basic ingredients and a rolling pin. Golly, they were good. Mother was the best cook ever, but Helen sure could make tasty biscuits. I was often asked to help with the dishes – usually to dry them.

The women took care of the chickens. We had laying hens year round and roosters for fried chicken in the summer, so there was a lot of work for Mother and Helen. The standard chore with the hens was to feed them, check their water and gather the eggs from the nests. These fresh eggs were often still warm when they were collected. They were very fragile and we had to be careful when we placed

Hen house with nests.

them in our metal pail. Helen had to record the number of eggs gathered. It was not uncommon to have a hen setting on a nest when you gathered the eggs. You just reached under her and took the eggs and left her to do her business.

As a boy grew older, maybe age seven, the next chore assigned was to go get the cows from the day pasture along the creek in the evening. He brought them in to be milked and took them to a different night pasture after milking. Boys did this as soon as they were old enough to open and close the barbed wire gates to the pasture. Since the wire was quite taut, boys in closing the gates developed their muscles at an early age. When cows give birth to a calf, they will go off in high weeds to hide. We recognized each cow by name and when a cow was getting ready to give birth, we carefully watched her. It was a grand experience to be the first to see a new-born calf hidden by its mother in the high weeds.

On occasion we ventured on a cow giving birth or soon after the birth and could watch the mother clean its calf. Biology lessons came early on the farm because we saw the animals being bred and later giving birth. It always amazed me to see a beautiful baby calf hesitantly stagger to its feet less than an hour after being born, and spread its unsteady legs wide for a few minutes to keep its balance before taking its first uncertain steps. A calf had to stand to nurse its mother and soon after birth they wanted to get at that business. So they had an incentive. Those calves became our pets from the day they were born. In a few days after they were taken from their mother in our dairy operation, it would be our job to feed each calf some of its mother's milk, first with a bucket with a rubber nipple at the edge near the bottom. We held the bucket as the very young calf drank its meal. A couple of weeks later it was our job to teach the calf to drink milk from an open bucket. We did this by letting the calf suck our finger and then slowly lowering our finger into the milk while the calf was sucking. By slowly pulling the finger from the sucking calf, it was soon drinking the milk directly from the bucket. They learned to drink quickly.

It may seem harsh to take the calf from its mother, but ours was a dairy operation and the large Holstein cows produced much more milk than a baby calf could drink. It was best for the cow to have that excess taken and doing so kept her production high. You can be sure the calves were fed very well.

For many years, we sold our dairy produce as cream since that did not require the milk to go to market every day. We had a cream separator on the back porch of the house. After the milking was finished, the cream would be separated from the milk. The cream was kept for market and the skim milk fed directly, or mixed with grain, and then fed to the hogs. Those hogs had a tasty diet. Milking was done at the barn, but the cream was separated from the raw milk at the house on the back porch. We washed the milk containers at the back of the house. So the chores of milking extended from the barn to the house and the womenfolk might help with rinsing and scrubbing the milking utensils and with cleaning the separator.

A young boy would learn more biology at the barn than he did at the house or in school. The barn was a place of work, but it was also a place of play. Children around the barn were always playing. It was our zoo. At various times we had mules, horses, cows, hogs, chickens, sheep and, at one time, a few guinea fowl. The latter didn't last long since Dad wasn't overly fond of the domesticated version of that West African bird. We also had a dog or two to help with the stock and a bunch of cats. The dogs were our good friends and the cats were helpful in controlling mice and rats which were always a nuisance around the grain bins. Cats, like the dogs, were pets. But their primary purpose was as

Holstein dairy cattle grazing in the pasture.

working animals: the dog with the cattle and the cats in helping control small rodent pests. Our cats and dog were fed milk and table scraps twice a day. We never had commercial dog food or cat food around. The animals, particularly the cats, worked for their food and were better mouse hunters when they were hungry. These were not house pets. They stayed outside, usually in the barn during winter.

Life at the barn was always most interesting, but also was potentially dangerous. When children were old enough to be released from the fenced-in yard, the play area extended from the house to the barn and even into the seldom-traveled street. Although we were admonished to watch out for cars, there was little auto traffic on the street and, therefore, little danger of being hit. The railroad track was most feared because trains couldn't stop quickly and the sternest of warnings kept us from venturing the 100 yards from the house to the Frisco Railroad main line. But the barn was part of where we lived and young children would aimlessly go there. Parents recognized the danger from the large animals, but as children, we saw adults working with animals daily and often couldn't see the danger. Mother was always concerned that one of us might be hurt by the animals.

My sister, Helen, could easily have lost her life as a result of her aimless wonderings as a small child. I've heard the story many times. On one cool, sunny winter morning when she was about three, Helen wanted to go out and play. Mother bundled her up in her heavy wool coat and, no doubt, told her to be careful and not leave the area where our father was working with a hired hand around the barn. I don't know if Helen made contact with Dad or not, but she somehow ended up in a pen where several sows were kept.

Apparently, Helen grew tired of playing and, having warmed up in the sun, probably became drowsy. The wooden pig feed trough, which was always licked clean by the sows, was a nice place to lie down and rest. Helen apparently fell asleep. One sow found this sleeping child and had her teeth buried in Helen's heavy wool coat and was shaking her like a rag doll. Other sows would have no doubt joined in a feeding frenzy in a matter of seconds. Fortunately, tragedy was averted because the commotion caught the attention of the hand who was working with Dad and he rescued Helen in the nick of time. Other than the abrupt awakening and the frightening seconds that followed, Helen was no worse for the wear. It is frightening to think of the tragic things that did on occasion happen on farms. Our family was very lucky this day.

Despite such near accidents, we all played in the barn regularly. We didn't have a lot of toys, so playing around the house was never as much fun as playing in or around the barn. When we emptied a crib of ear corn, the mice in the crib would move to the bottom and concentrate in the space between the ears of corn that remained. It was always a game when the last vestige of grain was removed, because there would be dozens of mice to be dealt with. The children and the cats were assembled to assist in killing as many mice as possible. We children were not very effective as we tried to stomp on the running and darting mice. But the cats with their quickness could make quite a haul. To most people the fun of that might be hard to imagine, but it was fun and it was part of farm life. Our attitude toward any predator that damaged and otherwise messed up crops or young farm animals was simple; the predators were to be dealt with.

We also had quite a few snakes around the barn and virtually without exception these were harmless, non-poisonous species. We soon learned from Dad that you never killed a snake except in the rare case when it was poisonous. First of all, these snakes would never hurt you and when we did see them, they were always trying their best to get away and hide. Most important, the snakes killed mice and rats, and the latter damaged the grain in bins and left their objectionable excrement in the grain. So snakes, by and large, were our friends and we were taught to protect them on the farm. Sadly, most people killed snakes because they didn't understand them. We occasionally caught and handled some smaller grass snakes and tried to make pets of them. They generally escaped. We had plenty of pets.

We had beautiful barn swallows that lived in the barn during the warm seasons. We loved them and protected them because they were insect eaters and caught these insects in flight. The swallows made sturdy nests of dried mud on the ceiling joists of the barn. In the part of the barn where we milked, the swallows nests were only a couple of feet above our heads, but we never bothered them. It was fun to look up and see baby barn swallows poking their heads over the edge of the nests during the first few days after they had hatched. We watched, but we never disturbed them because they were our friends and helpers.

Pigeons also liked the barn, but we did not let them stay because of their propensity to roost over the grain bins and concentrate their droppings in the grain. A few shots with Dad's 22-caliber rifle at the pigeons and they would leave. Dad taught us to understand that most animals were our friends, and we only would go for those that harmed our farming operation.

The bins of small grain, particularly wheat, were great places for small boys to play. We would climb to the edge of the bin and jump in feet first. It might be as much as a four-foot drop, but your feet would go maybe six inches into the wheat, cushioning the impact. Thirty minutes of fun jumping and playing in the rounded granular wheat was easy to come by. So long as we emptied our shoes and overall pockets before we left, and didn't waste the wheat, we were permitted to play there. It was more fun when young friends who did not have wheat bins were visiting and each of us would try to outdo the daring of our friends.

We milked our cows at first by hand and would do it sitting on a three legged stool about eight inches off the ground. That positioned you nicely for the cow's four teats which were about sixteen inches above the ground. You soon learned that sequential motion of the fingers that fast milkers have, each starting with the forefinger. A three-gallon milk bucket was placed under the cow. Milking was fun the first few times, but since it had to be done without fail twice a day every day of the year, it soon became a chore in every sense of the word. Each of us milked several cows and you couldn't stop when your hands got tired. So, over time, we developed strong grips and muscled arms.

Since we couldn't escape milking, we children found a way to have fun doing it. We did this only when Dad wasn't around, since it was wasteful of milk and, while he enjoyed seeing us have fun in our chores, he would not have approved. The key was in developing accuracy in squirting milk to the side by properly cocking your hand to the side before squeezing the teat. The velocity of the milk jet that we could achieve was surprising and we could hit a six inch target at fifteen feet. We children had several milk fights this way. However, the most fun was when you could surprise your brother or sister. Often, when we would hear a sibling coming to the milking area of the barn we would try to pop them in the face with a milk jet burst just as they entered the barn door. A hit on the nose brought the greatest satisfaction even if you knew that your victim would eventually get even – some way.

This accuracy with the milk jet could be used to feed a cat. The cats learned that if they hung around they might get a squirt of warm, sweet milk. As the jet of milk moved, the cat's quick tracking to keep the milk flow pretty much in its mouth was amazing. The cat enjoyed licking its paws and cleaning itself afterwards.

Young children love to throw. If nothing else is handy, throwing rocks is fun. Baseball and softball were popular games and we always wanted to keep our throwing arms in shape. Around the barn, in the fenced cattle lots, was a good place to practice. We threw rocks at things just for the fun of it. Unless we were trying to get the attention of an animal, we wouldn't throw a rock at it. Generally we would aim at some target such as a fence post, just to see if you could hit it. Rock throwing could turn into a contest this way, and it was healthy fun.

Boy milking a Holstein cow.

Throwing led to another fun activity around the barn. Our corn was harvested by hand and stored as ear corn. However, we had a small, hand powered machine to shell dried ear corn for the chickens. The corn cobs would accumulate around the sheller and were dry and light. In fact, they made good kindling to start a fire and many were used for that. They were also nice objects for young boys and sometimes girls to throw at each other. They were light and would not cause injuries and, unless they were soaked with water, couldn't be thrown too hard. I don't know if other farm children enjoyed cob fights as much as the older three of the Smerdon children did, but we sure had a lot of these playful fights. Helen was a tomboy and joined in with enthusiasm.

I might point out that these cob fights generally occurred when our parents were not around. On occasion, one would find a cob in the wet barn lot, properly soaked with water and other barn-lot liquids. You could get a real zinger with these because, being more dense, you could throw them harder. They made sort of a wet plop when they hit. The satisfaction was high if you hit your target, although as always, you knew that at some time your victim would get even. I guess these wet barn-lot-soaked cobs sort of violated the unwritten rules of cob fighting, but it was still fun to use them.

On one occasion in the 1930's, I remember a small, one-ring circus came to Ritchey by train and the yellow boxcars for the circus animals were put on the railroad siding track. But if you wanted to see a real circus, the big, traveling Ringling Brothers and Barnum & Bailey Circus was the place to go. It occasionally came to Joplin, thirty-five miles away. We went to that larger three-ring circus one time in the about 1940. John and Helen were in their early teens and I was about ten. One act was a man and woman riding two teams of galloping white horses. They were standing with one foot on the back of one horse and the other foot on the back of the second horse. The performer with a white flowing cape held the reins in one hand and waved to the crowd with the other. They circled the three rings just in front of the stands a couple of times during the act. Those circus horses had obviously been trained to run in contact with each other and not at any time separate more than a few inches. We had teams of horses and John felt he could duplicate that circus act.

Our teams of draft horses were Dick 'n Dan and Dolly 'n Daisy. John was determined to duplicate the act, at least to a degree. While Dad was skeptical, it was not his nature to discourage an enterprising teenage boy from trying. We'd all taken falls from horses and another couldn't hurt. It was fun to see John attempt the act on two of our horses that seemed willing to cooperate. But the team would invariably venture apart three feet or so, which exceeded John's ability to spread his legs and stay on top. John did not give up easily and ended up jumping to the ground between the horses several times before he conceded he was not ready to audition for Barnum & Bailey

I think the horses were confused as to what John was trying to do. After all, they had not seen the circus and the notion of a grown boy trying to ride two horses standing up, no less, was a new experience to them. I might add that he had a certain degree of success in riding one horse standing up, but only with the horse walking. I don't think he ever perfected that act for a galloping horse, but he no doubt could have if he had had time and committed himself to it.

While the barn was a place to play, it was also a place to learn about life. We saw sick animals and occasionally we saw animals die. Baby animals aren't delivered by the stork and, as we learned, don't come without the breeding of adult animals. We learned to recognize when a cow or mare was in heat – we never heard of the term 'estrous.' For cows, the term commonly used around Ritchey was 'bulling.' That term was used because a cow in heat tended to mount other cows similar to the actions of a breeding bull. Simply stated, it meant the cow should be put in a pen with a bull if you expected her to have a calf. We frequently saw the farm animals being bred. A female horse could be bred by a male horse or by a male donkey, called a 'jack.' The offspring would be a horse in the first case and a mule in the second. A mule is a hybrid incapable of procreating.

I remember as a boy of eight or so when my father wanted to raise a mule so one of our mares was to be bred by a jack. The mare was very tall and the jack much shorter. I marvel at the contraption the men rigged to assist the jack and make the union possible. No doubt this was a biology lesson that most boys of comparable age didn't get in school.

The baby mules were frisky and very smart. They would do whatever mischief they thought they could get away with and that included kicking you. However, they learned fast and with training and punishment for indiscretions, they would abandon bad habits. One of my jobs was to feed the horses in their stalls in the barn. I would feed them some oats or corn and then climb on them while they ate, all the while talking to them and petting them. I suppose sitting on a tall horse made me feel big.

Later, when I was similarly feeding a young mule, I did the same thing. It didn't dawn on me that the mules hadn't been broken to ride – our horses had. But I guess that these young animals that were growing quite tall knew that I was a friend. After all, I had fed them, petted them and talked to them. Anyway, I was never bucked off in the barn. When it came time to break the mules to ride I told Dad what I had been doing and said I didn't think they needed breaking. He let me experiment by riding the mule outside while he led it. No bucking whatsoever. I had unknowingly broken that mule to ride during the time I fed it in the barn when it was growing up. I loved those mules because they were so smart and playful. At that time we were farming with horses, so we sold the mules when they were fully grown, already broken to ride. To this day I think mules and dogs are the smartest animals we had on the farm.

Most of the time, we didn't have sheep. However, we children had 4-H or FFA projects and often this involved raising and caring for an animal that Dad had given us and that we owned. We kept good records on feed and other costs. Since we had dairy cows, the project was usually a calf. However, one year we decided to have sheep as a 4-H project and Dad bought thirty ewes. Subsequently, to breed our female sheep, he bought a mature male ram at an auction. He was a very fine animal and had the number '7' stamped on his back at the auction. We named him Number Seven. Number Seven was a fine sire for the ewes, but he had a bad habit that, to say the least, was annoying. He would sneak up behind you and butt you, not vicious, but he would knock you down. It may have been his chance to be playful, but since he could hit you hard and knock you over, we never viewed it with favor. You always watched Number Seven out of the corner of your eye.

When I was about fourteen, I remember one occasion when Number Seven happened to be in a small pasture which I was crossing. I had not thought of him until I noticed him pawing in the dirt and preparing to charge. I quickly saw the remains of an old oak fence post with a knot at the end. The post was broken but was solid and about the length of a baseball bat. The knot was at the end making it a good shillelagh. I never thought of myself as a matador, but as Number Seven charged, I used the talents I had. Enjoying baseball, I stood fast until my adversary lowered his head for the last few strides, then at the last minute I stepped aside and swung my weapon with all my might to hit Number Seven's lower face. I popped him on the nose enough to draw blood. He stopped in his tracks, turned and walked to the original spot, turned back toward me, pawed the ground again and started a second charge. With more confidence now, I repeated my side step and swing and again caught him again on the nose with a telling blow.

Again, Number Seven stopped and retreated with his even bloodier nose. However, this time he didn't stop and prepare for a third attempt. He retreated further, apparently having had enough of that game. I do not recall that Number Seven ever played the butting game after that. The farm animals were your friends, but they could hurt you. They had to understand who the master was. Teaching Number Seven his painful lesson wasn't fun, but the alternative could have been worse for us.

To this day, more than sixty years after my episodes on the farm, I look on it as a place that brought joy to my boyhood. Barns and farm life also brought knowledge of biology to many young boys and girls. And we learned useful skills working with our parents. These are skills I use even today.

THE RADIO WEATHER AND C. C. WILLIFORD

Weather was the most frequent topic of conversation in Ritchey. It controlled the lives of farmers, and good weather meant good crops and better income. A farmer seldom finalized his work plans for the next day without checking the weather forecast, generally expressed as 'the weather.' To explain, "What's the weather?" meant "What's the weather forecast?" "How's the weather there?" was usually the first or second topic mentioned in any letter from a farmer or his wife to a person away from Ritchey or in the extremely rare long-distance telephone call. Had timely rains come for the crops or had there been floods or early freezes? A farmer would seldom go to bed without listening to the weather forecast on the 10 o'clock news.

Old fashioned floor model radio.

In the days before television, the radio weather forecast was an important part of every newscast. The weather was the news and it shaped the daily activity of my parents as much as any outside force. The news item of second importance was 'the market' which provided up-to-date prices on agricultural products, particularly the price of live hogs. On weekdays, the Springfield radio station had a special weather forecast at midmorning and at mid-afternoon that came directly from the U. S. Weather Bureau forecast center at the Springfield Airport. That was the regional weather bureau forecast office for all of southwest Missouri. That office was the source of all of the weather forecasts that farmers of the region depended on and those forecasts shaped each workday's activity.

C. C. Williford was the chief weather forecaster at radio station KWTO, and he gave the live forecast twice each day. If Dad was in the field working, which was often the case, he asked Mother to be sure to listen to the weather. At noon, he would check with her to get the forecast– and he'd do the same thing in the evening to check on any changes. If, by chance, he was working in the barn at the time of the forecast, he would go to the house to hear it. Mother would usually call out to the barn that 'the weather' would soon be on, in case Dad had lost track of time. After about 1940, when he put a small radio in the cow barn where we milked, Dad no longer had to go to the house to get 'the weather,' but Mother would still remind him in case he'd lost track of time.

C. C. Williford was an institution in southwest Missouri and no informed person would fail to understand who it was if the reference was only to C. C. In his own way, C. C. Williford had as much prestige among the locals in southwest Missouri as Walter Cronkite had decades later on a much, much larger national scale. After all, the weather was the most important regular news to the farmers of the region. Weather conditions controlled the farmers' lives and well being. And C.C. was a trusted person helping farmers.

The weather broadcasts came from radio station KWTO in Springfield. KWTO stood for "Keep Watching the Ozarks," at least that's what the announcers always said. KWTO was a hillbilly radio station that featured what I now realize was some pretty fair live country music. The elegant words, 'country and western' had not emerged and achieved the broad recognition that they were to enjoy decades later. After all, this was the big band era and that's what young people enjoyed. There was no electronic music in those days and the keyboard was not a separate instrument; it was where the fingers of a piano player hit the ivories.

I had read enough to get an erroneous impression that no one would choose to be born in the Ozarks if he or she could help it. One would certainly think first of more aristocratic places to be born, like California or Florida. I liked C. C. Williford, but KWTO was not then my idea of a sophisticated radio station, nor was its music. I was somewhat self-conscious at being forever blighted by the fact that I was 'a hillbilly,' and listening to KWTO all the time didn't help. I was aware that there must have been radio stations that did not consistently feature the hillbilly music of 'Slim' Pickens Wilson and his group, or the Hayden Family and their repertoire of hymn after hymn after hymn. But our radio was almost always tuned to KWTO, where C. C. Williford provided 'the weather.'

After the advent of television in the early 1950's, the role of the radio became less important. The weather information came from that new small screen black and white TV. Early in the time of TV, the weather forecasters were trained meteorologists like C. C. Williford, not TV personalities. TV weather was good because it provided charts so you could see where the fronts were and one could get a better regional picture of the weather patterns. In due course, the radio weather forecasts direct from the Weather Bureau at the Springfield airport were discontinued. However, the importance of weather was so instilled in the minds of rural farm people that, even in retirement, a farmer or his wife would seldom go to bed until after the TV weather on the 10 o'clock news. Mother and Dad would go to bed just as soon as the weather was over, but not before. It always frustrated Dad if he dozed off watching some boring program on TV waiting for the weather and then slept through it. When he was tired, after a long day in the field, it often happened.

Farm people are gamblers, because they gamble on and are at the mercy of the weather. If the rains were heavy and incessant in the spring, floods would occur and planting would be delayed – or crops were destroyed if they had been planted. The cash flow would drop and needed purchases would have to be delayed. If the rains did not come when the corn was tasseling, a critical time for good production, the yield would be hurt and income would be lower. There was nothing that brought more contentment to farmers than a good slow, soaking rain when the corn or other crops were at the critical fruiting stage. Of course one always wanted a few days of sunshine without rain to make hay, and then have the regular rains to keep all the crops growing. It never worked out perfectly.

There wasn't a better time to relax than during a needed rain. During those cooling rains you could imagine the additional bushels of corn that would result as you dreamily listened to the sound of rain hitting the roof. We had a large, flowered maroon wool carpet in the living room and when the rains started we would come in with our dirty work clothes on. I would nap on that carpet because Mother did not want us to sit in the overstuffed chair or on the divan of the living room suite with our dirty work clothes. The floor was okay, and to this day I can remember the smell of that wool carpet with the not unpleasant faint odor of a feedlot from the dairy-farmer shoe traffic through the years. That big carpet could not easily be taken out to be aired. Ah, but it was a restful sleep, with the rains falling and nurturing the corn and other crops. The farmers napped with a smile on their faces during those needed rains.

When I graduated from high school in 1947, our eighteen-member class unanamously voted to invite C. C. Williford to be our high school commencement speaker. That was the biggest decision that our class had ever made. He would have to drive 65 miles each way, and we planned to raise money to get this great man as our speaker. When our class president, Lena Wheeler, presented the proposal to Mr. Mitchell, the high school superintendent, he told us that he'd already invited a personal friend from Pittsburg State Teachers College in Kansas to be the speaker. What galled us was it had been done without our knowledge. That was our last chance to invite C. C. Williford, an institution in our region and probably the best known person to farmers in the area as well.

The decision had been made and it could not be reversed, according to Mr. Mitchell. This angered our class and we met to consider boycotting our graduation. But we knew we could never explain such a drastic action to our parents and, anyway, graduation was something we had worked long and hard for. We knew it was going to be fun. Still, we had to vent our frustration.

Since all eighteen of the 1947 graduates would be on the stage at the side of the high school gym facing the audience as Mr. Mitchell's speaker delivered his message, someone suggested that we try to embarrass him by pretending to fall asleep during his address. Actually, it was Mr. Mitchell that we wanted to embarrass. What could he do after we had our diplomas? It was agreed by the nine boys in the class that we feign sleep one at a time soon after the address began. Most of the boys had agreed to the idea so we had our plan. We didn't ask the girls to do it because we weren't sure they would cooperate.

Our stunt was immature, but 60 years after the event, I still regret that we didn't have C. C. Williford as our commencement speaker. Although we boys pretended to doze during the address, we were all very wide awake in our 'dozing' effort to send our message of protest.

I can't recall who our professor speaker was, and I have no idea what his message might have been. However, I remember that C.C. wasn't our speaker – this well-known person whom we had never seen, but had heard many times as he gave the weather. C. C. Williford's words affected the lives of all of us and our parents. His delivery was folksy and he always tried to help the farmers of the region. He would have been a good commencement speaker and we would have remembered his message.

THE BARN

Architecturally, to me, our barn was as beautiful as any cathedral or library of the world. It was the landmark of Ritchey, and it was the building to which any new visitor to the town would be referred to indicate without a doubt that they had found the village of Ritchey. Our barn was located immediately adjacent to the edge of town, no more than two city blocks from the post office at the town center. The Baptist and Presbyterian churches, each with its towering white steeple, also stood out. But to my eyes those New England style churches did not have the character of our red barn, with its high arched roof, and two tall ventilators on top.

The barn was painted an earth-toned red and originally had white vertical stripes. The stripes were the galvanized metal strips nailed on to seal the half-inch cracks between the vertical boards that developed as the one-by-twelve oak boards that formed its sides dried and shrunk. These boards, like all the lumber in the barn, came from oak trees grown on the farm. They were sawed at a temporary saw-mill that was set up on the hill pasture when the barn was built and had been nailed on when they were green. The barn wasn't painted for the first five or so years, so the boards were well cured when the paint was applied. That rough-sawn oak soaked up paint like a sponge, and, as a result, the paint never peeled and only faded slowly through the first several decades. The barn doors were also red, with the trim and X-braces painted white, giving the doors a bit of an English Tudor look. The machinery shed doors and doors at both ends of the large hallway that ran the length of the barn each had a pattern of two white X-brace squares on a red background on the bottom half of the door.

The curved roof, shaped like the peace arch in St. Louis, was supported by hand-made laminated curved rafters formed in a jig that was set up on the floor of the barn loft when the barn was being built. Eight, flexible, green oak one-by-three boards were bent and fitted into the curved jig one at a time and nailed together. Since glue was not used to stiffen the rafters, the roof crown sagged slightly as the decades passed, giving the barn roof crown a slightly sway-back look. This roof covered a cavernous hay mow that was about 36 feet wide, 60 feet long and more than 20 feet high at the center. That loft may not seem large today compared to the Astrodome and other gigantic indoor sports stadiums, but it was large enough for any game a child might want to play indoors.

Two large, metal ventilators, which were taller than a man, stood guard at about the one-third points along the crown of the roof. A weather vane stood near each end of the roof crown. The wind pointer on one vane was a horse and on the other, a cow, both always looking upwind. This tall building and its store of sweet-smelling, but highly flammable, hay was protected by lightning rods. A heavy copper cable was connected to the lightning rods and ran along the barn roof. It was grounded at opposite corners. The barn was hit once by lightning when Dad was inside, and I recall his description

The Smerdon barn built in 1926 and yet to be painted.

of the loud crack and flash inside at the instant of the strike. Fortunately, no harm was done by that bolt of lightning.

The barn was whatever you wanted it to be when you were playing. It had all of the stage elements necessary to provide whatever setting was needed for our games. It was our private zoo. Besides the farm animals, there were the working pets of the farm, the dogs and cats that found warm shelter there on the coldest winter nights. Our dogs weren't allowed in the house and that was, with a single exception, true of the cats. It was the hunting ground for the cats, as they would silently and patiently crouch, poised to spring on an unwary mouse or rat. When corn cribs were emptied, the cats could enjoy a hunting frenzy as the mice that had crawled in the spaces between the ears of corn would ultimately be exposed. During those times, catching mice was a game for the cats to see how many they could catch and hold. There were more mice than a cat could eat at one time.

The barn was our aviary and the barn swallow was our favorite among the many birds. They would build their nests on the sides of the floor joists that supported the barn loft. When we were milking the cows or tending the horses, those bird nests, made of dried gray mud, were only a couple of feet above our heads and the swallows learned that we wouldn't harm them. They were totally unafraid of us and would fly into the barn to their nests when we were only a few feet away. Their little homes, which looked as sturdy as a concrete balcony, were safe from all comers.

The swallows would catch insects in flight and each evening in the summer we would marvel at their dexterity in flight. They darted about, sometimes quite low, over the barn lot snatching their evening meal. After their supper was complete, they would sometimes stop and enjoy the view from the electric line that brought power from the house to the barn. Finally, as dusk settled in they would fly to their nests, just over our heads if we happened to be in the barn. They flew in through the same door the cows used. Although hunting some kinds of birds with our BB guns was fair game, we never shot at a barn swallow. Any animal that killed insects or grain-eating rodents was to be protected. And that included the harmless, non-poisonous snakes that we would often see in the grass around the barn and sometimes inside.

The English sparrow was another common bird around the barn. They were gray and dull, not pretty and colorful like the barn swallow with its forked tail and glistening feathers. Sparrows were said to have mites and they would eat chicken feed and occasionally make a mess in it. So we were allowed to shoot at them with our home-made sling shots, BB guns or, when we got older, Dad's 22-caliber rifle. The sparrow was a tiny bird and not an easy target. So mostly we just scared them. Seemingly, there were millions of sparrows around and sometimes we would see literally hundreds of them on the ground in the hog pens feasting on the bits of feed that the hog's sloppy eating habits left lying about.

We could have had as many pigeons as in a city park if we hadn't made efforts to keep them away. These birds also enjoyed the abundant feed in the pens of the chickens, calves and hogs. Pigeons were nice looking birds, with their shiny gray feathers, and they liked to take positions high on the barn roof. What bothered Dad most was where the pigeons chose to roost. It wasn't the feed that they ate. They could fly inside the barn and eat wheat from the bin, and that wouldn't have been so bad if they would have controlled their bowels while they were eating. Roosting pigeons on the edge of grain bins could mess up a lot of grain. We seldom killed pigeons because they were wise. It took only one or two shots to send the clear message that they were unwelcome, and they would leave, often for several weeks at a time. But we could shoot at sparrows daily and they would always come back, usually in a matter of an hour or so.

The stately black crow was the smartest bird among all our avian neighbors. A few were always around because they fed on the corn in the hog feeders, as well as on any other feed they might see. They usually didn't come in the barn. Although we considered the crow to be a pest, we didn't kill many. They were very wary of humans and knew full well that we could be dangerous to them. But, they were not easily fooled. A scarecrow would only work for a few days and the image of crows perched on the outstretched arm of a scare crow was not unrelated to fact.

An unarmed person could easily get within thirty to forty feet of a crow eating corn in the hog pen before it would take wing. But try to sneak up on it with a shotgun and the crow would always take to the air just before you were in range. It was uncanny how those birds would know when you were dangerous. I have tried to trick them by picking up a pole, such as an old hoe handle, hoping it looked like a gun. Those savvy birds would take wing while out of range like they had been fooled only to circle behind you for a closer look before settling back and resuming their meal, now totally oblivious to you and your 'toy gun.' That trick of coming up behind you was a common one as the crow checked you out before venturing too close.

A popular Sunday afternoon hunting sport involved taking advantage of the natural curiosity of the crow. When we were teenagers, it was fun to try to call the crows in with a 'crow call' that made the harsh sound of a crow caw. We would go to a timbered area in the pasture with shotguns and a crow call. The timber provided essential cover as we tried to call the crows in. But the crows were very difficult to fool. They always approached cautiously and if they spotted you, the game was over. I am inclined to believe that they could warn their comrades by cawing if they found a man who was up to no good from their perspective.

I doubt if we ever made a crow believe the crow call sound came from another crow. However, we could make strange sounds with that crow call that were so different from anything in the crow's dialect that their curiosity compelled them to investigate. Don't fret too much for the crows. They seldom fell victim to our shenanigans and usually won the game of wits.

Crows could become pets, and I remember a country neighbor who owned a pet crow. Sometimes a baby crow would fall from a nest high in a tree. These baby birds, still unable to fly, could be fed, nurtured and domesticated. I never found a baby crow, nor did my brothers or sister, and I'm not sure that Dad would have let us keep it even if we had found one. Some around town said, no doubt without basis, that a crow could learn to talk if one split its tongue. Thinking of it now, it sounds a bit gruesome. Nonetheless, in my youth I never doubted whether these smart birds could do anything they wanted to, and if splitting its tongue was what was required, I was sure the crow could do its part.

The barn was also a place to hide. There were dark places, among bales of hay in the loft, behind equipment in the machine shed, and in many other spots. If we wanted to play haunted house, there were ample dusty cobwebs hanging from the rafters forming eerie shadows. If we listened carefully, there were usually sounds of some movement or wind that could take on whatever ominous sign that fit our make-believe situation. The hay loft provided a good place to do things because it was so big and there were a lot of high places to bring in the thrill of height.

There was a ladder fastened to the barn loft that provided access to the hay fork track that ran the length of the barn just under the crown of the roof. This track and hay fork was used to fill the barn loft with hay. Dad used that ladder to access the track so he could repair and lubricate the hay fork mechanism and the various pulleys. It was high and usually there was loose hay under it. We could use that for climbing and jumping down maybe eight feet or more onto the hay. I suspect that activity was not sanctioned by Mother, but it was nevertheless a fun game for us.

Our barn was different from many in that it had a hallway down the middle that was large enough for loaded hay wagons to drive through. At the west end there was a large hole in the floor of the loft about twelve feet by sixteen feet. Hay was hoisted from wagons to the top of the barn through this large opening in the floor and onto the track that would carry it to any location along the length of the barn. There was also an inside vertical ladder that went to the very top of the barn directly over that hole, and if you were really daring you could climb up and be more than 30 feet above the ground. At the time, I couldn't imagine a higher place in the world and gripped the ladder tightly as I made a very careful ascent to the top. The descent was even scarier because you had to feel for each rung in the ladder with your toe as you slowly descended. These rungs were spaced for adults, not for a child's short legs. I didn't make that climb often, but it was a thrill when I did.

I remember Mother telling the story of the time when my older brother, John, climbed that ladder at about the age of three. Dad had gone up to repair the hay fork track and, he was probably deep in thought as he often was when he worked. He didn't notice the baby climbing up behind him. Had Mom been there, she might have screamed and startled young Johnny. But Dad, in his always steady, commanding voice calmly told baby Johnny to climb down and be careful. And that's what the child did. No doubt Johnny had not yet learned to fear heights and his heart probably didn't race as he climbed down, which, I suspect, is more than could be said about Dad as he watched his first baby son descend the vertical ladder below him.

The machine shed always had farm machinery in it and I used to go and sit on those ornate cast iron seats, molded to fit an adult's behind. These seats were typical of the horse-drawn machinery of the period. It was like a child sitting in a car pretending to be the driver. I did a lot of heavy farm work in my mind during those day-dreaming sessions. They seemed to last for hours, but, on reflection, could not have been more than ten minutes or so.

The barn also had a workbench with tools around. I loved that area and spent hours there hammering and building things. The workbench was very heavy and built of two-inch oak boards. I liked to pound nails into that work bench, to Dad's dismay. The oak was so hard that I seldom drove the nail all the way in before it bent. But one end of those two-inch boards was exposed and I soon learned that it was much easier to drive nails into the ends of the boards with the grain rather than across the grain. By the age of ten, I had the ends of those work bench boards fully nailed and the exposed ends were solid metal with nail heads. During those sessions, I tried to nail together any short boards that I could find. To this day I love to work or build things at a workbench and I am sure that's how it all started.

I learned to milk in the barn at a very early age. We had a cow named Mert who was the most gentle one in the herd. So I started with her. I believe she would have stood still and not harmed me if I'd crawled under her, provided she knew I was there. We were taught to always speak to the animals so they knew where we were. Later, when I drove the cows from the pasture, I would sometimes get on Mert and ride her home.

Mert, Whitey and most others were very gentle, but occasionally there were animals that were just plain ornery. Blackie was a good milk producing cow that fit into the latter category. She was always shackled with the kickers, before she was milked. This was a special restraining device that held her hind legs together. Blackie would kick you just for the sport of it. She was lucky to be a good producer, because ill-tempered cows that were only average producers went to market in short order to become hamburger. However, most of our animals were very gentle and that added to the charm of the barn. It was a great place for a child.

THRESHING AND MAKING HAY

Threshing and making hay were hot, dirty jobs. They always occurred in the heat of summer and, since the hay had to be dry before it went to the barn and the grain had to be dry to thresh, there was a lot of dust and itchy chaff and hay particles. These always managed to get under your sweaty shirt. Work in the summer anywhere inside the barn was usually hot because there was no movement of the air. Work in the hayloft was insufferable, like an attic, with no air movement whatsoever.

Yet, there was always a sense of anticipation and satisfaction at threshing or hay-making time. In both cases it was harvest time and signaled success because the crop was being harvested and put in the barn. After all, this was what a farmer dreamed of from the day the crop was planted. We had a general farm with cattle, hogs, and chickens and the grain was their winter food. So we didn't sell grain when it was threshed. It was stored in the barn to feed our livestock. Grain was only sold when there was a surplus exceeding what the animals consumed and that was done to clear the bins for the next crop.

Fruits and vegetables were canned as they were harvested and farm wives felt fulfilled when the

Picture 14: A threshing machine with the operator standing on the machine.

cellar was well stocked with preserved food to see the family through the winter. In the same way, the grain and hay were the winter rations for the livestock, and there was a sense of satisfaction when there was ample feed for the animals during winter. After all, the milk, eggs and other produce from the animals were the main source of income for the family. So threshing and hay making was a time when everyone enjoyed the hard work, even if it was hot, sweaty, dirty, and itchy.

Threshing and hay-making times were also social occasions. Neighbor farmers swapped their own labor as well as use of their horses and wagons and other equipment. The accounting between farmers was very loose, but no one seemed to worry about it. The unwritten code was, "You help me harvest my crop and I will help you harvest yours." There might rarely be some monetary exchange among the neighboring farmers if there was a large imbalance in what each farmer had done for the other, but most often money would not change hands. Each would remember if one or the other owed a day of his labor with his team of horses, and it would eventually be paid in kind. In farming there is a principle of helping your neighbors because you know that you will need his help at some time.

Harvesting related work was as much a cooperative effort among the women as among the men. During harvest men would put in long hours of hard labor, starting when the dew was off and working until darkness approached. The workers had to be fed and a large noontime dinner was expected. Sometimes the members of the crew, who were day laborers and not neighboring farmers with chores to do, were also fed supper. But, usually the farmers involved needed to rush home to take care of their animals and their own chores, such as milking and tending hogs. These men would only have supper

The horses eating before the afternoon's work.

after the work at home was done and that would usually be well after dark.

Since a threshing crew would generally have fifteen or more men and strong boys, preparing the food was no easy task for the women. Also, each farm wife wanted to be sure she provided plenty of tasty food. After all, these crews had the opportunity to eat in many different homes during the harvest season. No self-respecting farm wife would want it said that they did not have enough food when a crew was at her house. The wife got satisfaction from seeing the men and boys devour the meal that she and her helpers had prepared. While verbal compliments were always appreciated, the grandest compliment was seeing the workers take those large second helpings and still have room for a big piece of pie or cake. The cooking crew, like the threshing crew, involved neighbors. The neighboring farm wives and their daughters would arrive in the morning after their own breakfast and morning chores were done. They would help cook, serve and clean up. The women would only eat after the threshing crew had returned to the fields. The helping farm wives generally would not be there for supper because they would need to go home to do their own work, which often included starting the chores on their own farms and doing much of the milking. The housewife's hours were as long as the farmer's since baking for the next day was often done late in the evening or before daylight next morning.

Threshing crews that worked with horses had to be sure that the horses were fed and watered before they could think of food for themselves. The men would be dusty and sweaty from the their work and a large galvanized iron washtub with water, soap and plenty of towels, would be placed under a shade tree by the house so the workers could get most of the dust off before dinner. All washed in the same tub of water. The towels conveniently removed the dirt missed as the worker washed his face and hands in the tub of cold water. Since the farmers didn't usually have a lot of towels, they had to be laundered each night in preparation for the next day. The task of getting the wash water and towels ready for the workers might be handled by some of the teenage girls who were helping. That gave them the opportunity to talk to the crew and to be sure any young boys who might be in the crew were properly attended to. It was always a jocular time as the crew washed up in anticipation of a tasty meal. It also provided a moment or two for a teenage boy to chat with a young maiden who might be helping.

Although the circumstances were a bit different, my parents met for the first time in 1921 when Dad was part of a threshing crew near Pierce City and Mother was visiting from Oklahoma and helping with the women's work. They carried on a long-distant courtship and were married two years later. More than one romance in those days has started under such circumstances.

I remember threshing very well. Even when I was a very small boy and too young to help in a meaningful way, I sensed the air of excitement as threshing time approached. We knew that when the wheat bins were filling we would again have the chance to jump from the high bin wall into the freshly threshed wheat. Our bare feet might sink in to our knees and we could pretend that we were swimming as we thrashed around in the grain, much like you might see children play in a bin of plastic balls today at a McDonalds. Our only guideline was to take off our shoes and be sure we didn't spill any grain out of the bin. We also had to carefully empty the grain from our pockets before we left. Jumping into the wheat was like jumping from several feet high into soft hay or straw and it was something that we all enjoyed immensely.

Dad didn't own a threshing machine for many years, so we had to wait until one of the machines that did custom work was available. These machines were usually owned by one of the wheat farmers on the upland prairie a few miles north of Ritchey. Their main crop was wheat because they couldn't grow corn as well as we could in the Shoal Creek bottom. Corn was our major crop and we did not raise a lot of wheat or other small grains, since we only wanted grain for our chickens and livestock.

The very first threshing machine I saw – and I only vaguely remember this – was powered by a wood-burning steam engine. This must have been when I was about four in 1934. The steam engine had a large diameter pulley that powered the long belt that drove the threshing machine. I remember

Steam engine powering a threshing machine, circa mid-1920's.

the concern for fire that everyone had because a burning spark from the firebox of these steam engines could find its way to the dry straw. Water was kept near at hand to douse any fire that might start.

The threshing machines that I remember best, and the ones on which I was an active part of the threshing crew, were all powered by a large gasoline tractor. While the dreaded fire caused by a spark from a wood burning steam engine was always possible, it was unlikely to be from the tractor. The real fire danger would be from smoking workers who might be careless. Dad never smoked and he was always concerned about smokers accidentally starting a fire. No one was allowed to smoke in our barn.

The threshing operation consisted of five to seven horse-drawn grain bundle wagons with their operators, three to five pitchers working in the field to pitch the grain bundles to a loader on the wagon, two to three grain haulers with their wagons or trucks, the threshing machine operator, and one or two water boys. The size of the crew would depend on the size of the threshing machine, the distance from the threshing operation to the grain fields and the distance that the grain had to be hauled.

My first job on the threshing crew was as a water boy. I was probably eight or nine when I was honored with this assignment. My duty was to make sure that water was available for all of the workers. I used a gallon-size, stone crockery jug with a tapered corn cob stopper to take water to the men. This jug was wrapped with burlap, which could be wetted to help keep the water cool. I would fill the jug with cool water from the well, wet the burlap and make the rounds to all the workers. Everyone would drink directly from the jug. The jug handle was small and only one adult finger would fit through it. So we had a leather strap in that handle and I would use this strap to carry it. Some workers would take the jug by the strap and cradle it in the V of their bent elbow and drink only using one hand. Some exhibited quite a flair as they used this one-arm technique. Since all drank directly from the same jug, some would splash some water out to clean the mouth of the jug.

I would ride to the field on an empty bundle wagon that was returning to be loaded. I checked each bundle pitcher to be sure that everyone got water. I would usually ride back on a loaded bundle wagon to refill the jug and make sure that the jugs kept in the shade at the threshing machine were full of fresh water. Then I would repeat the process of going to the field. Being a water boy was an important assignment, which one appreciated most when he was late getting back to the hot field and the workers complained.

Binder cutting wheat.

Stacking wheat bundles. The young man in the foreground pitching the grain bundle is my Father.

I had several other jobs as I got older, including working in the truck or wagon that carried the threshed grain, sometimes sacking the grain as it was discharged from the threshing machine. However, I knew that I was close to being a man when, at the age of about fourteen, I was assigned to run a bundle wagon, normally a man's job.

The small grain was harvested with a binder that cut the grain and tied it in bundles about eight inches in diameter. The famous original McCormack reaper, patented in 1834, was the start of this automated process. The machine would cut, bundle, and tie the grain bundles with a strong jute 'binder twine.' The grain bundles were shocked in the field to further dry and await the threshing operation. If threshing was to be delayed for too long, the grain would be hauled in from the fields and stacked in high cone-shaped stacks. Then, the early-fall threshing would be directly from the stacks. When I was old enough to be heavily involved, the stacking process was omitted and the grain bundles were hauled directly to the threshing machine during threshing time. But I remember when the bundles were stacked.

The bundle wagons were pulled by a team of horses or mules. The team of horses I used was Dick and Dan. My job was to stack the bundles on the wagon, which was about 8 feet by 16 feet with a stand at both ends to help keep the bundles from falling forward or backward. Since these wagons were loaded to a height of five or more feet above the wagon bed, there was an art to stacking the bundles so none would fall off. There were no sides on the wagon.

In the field, the pitchers would toss the bundles up to the wagon with long-handled pitchforks. I used my pitchfork to place the bundles, interweaving them to make sure the load was secure. Since snakes tended to hide in the coolness under the shocks of grain in the field, pitchers often saw snakes scramble away as they removed the bundles. The snakes were virtually always harmless, and they always tried to escape. Although we never killed the snakes because they fed on our common enemy, harmful field mice and rats, we were often startled by them. A favorite trick of the pitchers would be to slide the pitchfork tines under the escaping snake and flip it up on the wagon to scare the bundle loader. The proper response, if the loader could do so before the snake slithered down into the load of bundles, would be to flip the snake back to the pitcher. The greatest laughs occurred when the pitcher or loader could manage to wrap the snake around the victim's leg or arm. This was funny and usually startled the victim.

I've seen hundreds of snakes come from under grain shocks in the field, but I never saw a single poisonous one. So the game was harmless, except that the snakes must have been frightened out of their wits. Those kinds of jokes and pranks were common on the farm. I remember chiding one pitcher who was afraid of snakes and wanted no part of them. "Those snakes won't hurt you," I said. His reply expressed his philosophy on snakes, "I know, but they'll make you hurt yourself." Needless to say, he was the favorite target of our snake flipping pranks.

It was always interesting to bring a load of bundles to the threshing machine with its noise, vibration and moving belts on both sides. Horses weren't always enthusiastic about pulling the wagon close alongside of the noisy, vibrating machine. Some horses had to be blindfolded and led because of their deep fear of the machine. Fortunately, Dick and Dan were relatively easy to handle and they soon learned that the machine was not going to hurt them.

Unloading the wagons into the machine was steady work. The bundles were pitched onto a moving conveyor so the heads of the grain entered the rapidly spinning threshing cylinder first. For the machine to operate efficiently, the conveyor had to be kept full, but not overloaded. So the unloading work was without break until the load was threshed. Teenage boys could build nice muscles without pumping iron in a gym when they ran a bundle wagon.

It was a good feeling when the threshing was finished and the machine pulled away. Not only were the grain bins restocked, but there was a large stack of straw maybe fifty feet in diameter and twenty-five feet high near the barn. This straw would play an important role in the winter ahead. The stack would settle some and shed water during the rains and snow like a thatched roof, keeping the straw inside dry and warm. We used this straw for animal bedding in the barn and this would help keep the area warm for the stock, including young calves that stayed in the barn for a month or so after they were born. Straw bedding absorbed the urine and solid waste and fresh straw would be put on top to help keep the area clean. During the winter our cows were kept in the lot with the straw stack because the pastures and fields were wet and muddy or covered with snow. The cows always gathered around the straw stack and nibbled at it, forming caves or tunnels that provided warm, cozy shelter for the young animals.

The straw provided natural warmth when the animals' urine and feces became mixed with it. As bacteria consumed the nutrient-rich mixture, they generated heat in the same way that grass clippings decompose and heat a compost pile. The cattle really enjoyed this warm area, as evidenced by where they gathered in very cold weather.

Sometimes when we children were playing around the barn, we would play in the straw caves the cattle had made. It was a warm and secret place. I am sure Mother did not know because she would have been concerned about the straw caves collapsing on us. But they never did. We weren't permitted to play on top of the straw stack. Dad made that quite clear. The reason was that the straw became crusted after the rains and made the stack waterproof. Our feet could puncture this crust and permit rain to enter. Young calves didn't get that message and they liked to climb up on top where they could get a good view. Actually, these calves probably had much to do with the destruction of the stack, which would be gone for all practical purposes by spring.

Much of the straw was ultimately returned to the field. In late winter and early spring, one of the big jobs was cleaning the barn and hauling the manure to the fields. That was an unpleasant but necessary task because the natural fertilizer was good for the crops. Corn needs very fertile fields and we tried to put manure on all the fields where corn would be planted as often as possible. The loading of manure was done with pitchforks and tearing the matted, partially decomposed bedding apart required heavy tugging, no doubt quite good for the stomach and shoulder muscles. We had a horse-drawn mechanical manure spreader that had a conveyor that slowly moved the load to the back as you crossed the field. Rapidly whirling reels with spikes tore the partially decomposed straw so a spreader reel could evenly distribute it on the land in a wide swath. It was our way of fertilizing the fields with recycled straw and animal waste.

We always slept well at threshing time. The days were long and the work was hard. But there was that satisfaction of seeing the bins in the barn fill with grain. It was harvest time. With the good food and rich desserts that always accompanied threshing, we slept well. The problem was getting the dust and itchy particles off your skin. Often we took a bar of floating Ivory soap to the creek and washed there. Slippery non-floating soap would soon be at the bottom of the creek and swept away. On occasion, I have seen Dad wash in the stock tank, since that was warmed by the sun and was a

Mowing hay with a mule drawn mower with a 5-foot cutter bar.

ready pool close at hand. We did not have a bathroom or shower in the early days – and the itchy dust had to be removed. I don't suppose that the cows and horses minded that he bathed in their watering tank. Since the horses didn't have water during the day except at noon, they would drink for minutes without stopping when they got to the tank on those hot days. They didn't bother to question if someone had bathed in their tank the night before.

Hay making was less dramatic than threshing. The crews were smaller and there wasn't any big machinery involved. Also, the operation occurred several times during the summer, not once as in threshing. Our barn had a big hay mow under its arched roof. A large rope, perhaps an inch-and-a-quarter in diameter, was used in the hoist, and the hay which was lifted with the power of a team of horses.

The hay would first be cut, then cured in the field and raked into rows or bunches. The same horse-drawn wagons were used for haying as for threshing. A hay pitcher would pitch the loose bunches up to the wagon where a loader would arrange the load of loose hay in a fashion not unlike loading the bundles, with the loads packed about five feet high. At the barn we'd pull the wagon under the hoist and hay fork. We'd unhitch the team of horses from the wagon and hitch them to the hoisting rope at the opposite end of the barn, where, through a series of pulleys, the hay would be lifted to the top of the barn and pulled along the track. Dad, using a small trip rope, could dump the hay at any point along the length of the barn. Still, the hay had to be moved aside from under the track by hand and that's what Dad did while waiting for the next load to arrive. I believe that was the worst job on the farm because the temperature in the hay mow in the hot summer could reach up to 110 degrees Fahrenheit or more. I have seen Dad come down from the hay loft with every thread of his clothes saturated with sweat.

Raking hay with a side delivery rake pulled by a team of horses.

But, again there was that sense of satisfaction at having the hay in the barn where it couldn't be damaged by rain or anything else. We knew the cows would have good roughage feed during the ensuing winter. The milk and butter we'd enjoy, and which would provide that biweekly milk check on which we depended, would to a significant degree, come from that hay.

Threshing with the old-style threshing machine is no longer done. Today's large, self-propelled combines can harvest all of the grain we grew in a half day or less. The machines combine the work of the reaper and the thresher, as well as all the steps in between, which accounts for its name. One person runs the combine and one or two others haul grain in trucks. Instead of shoveling the grain into the bins by hand as we did, electric-powered grain augers or elevators now do the work with almost no shoveling. The straw is left in the field by the combine, so there is no straw stack for animal bedding or for the calves and boys to play in. There are no longer the social/work aspects of threshing for the men and the women, with the latter working in the kitchen to prepare the meals, and the men gathering and joking at midday and in the evening as these meals were devoured. Much savings in labor has been gained, of course, but something, too, has been lost.

The same is true for making hay. No longer are the barns built with large haylofts. The large red barn with a curved roof and topped by ventilators and wind vanes is a thing of the past. The hay is mowed and crimped for rapid curing with large tractor-drawn machines that mow and crimp in one operation. After being raked into large windrows, it is baled, perhaps with a round baler that makes large bales that can be left in the field until the farmer is ready to use his tractor and hydraulic lift to bring one of the large bales to the cattle. These round bales shed water like the straw stack, so the hay stays good, even when exposed to rain and snow. One farmer can make more hay in a day than the entire hay making crew made when I was a boy. Again, there has been change.

Some might nostalgically say that the change has been bad. While I fondly reflect on the 'fun' of threshing and making hay, I decided in high school that farming was not how I wanted to spend my life. The physical work was very hard and the hours were long. More important, it was repetitious and tedious. Vacations weren't part of the culture since, the stock had to be tended every day of the year. Today's farmers would no more voluntarily return to the old days than a modern housewife would give up her automatic laundry facilities, electric or gas range, dishwasher, running water and refrigerator. Nor is the city homeowner likely to cast aside his power-driven lawnmower in favor of the old push type, powered solely by the pushing of the operator. But at the time we had no other options; threshing and making hay were necessary and satisfying harvest activities that one can remember with fondness.

JACK 'N' PETE AND KATE 'N' BECK

If you ask a modern day farmer how many horsepower he needs on his farm, he might answer with the horsepower of his tractor. Farming a little over 100 acres of cultivated land today would almost certainly not be economical. If it was done, the farmer would likely need a tractor with 40 or more horsepower. The cultivated area of our farm was about 100 acres. When I was a boy and we farmed with four horses or mules, Dad dreamed of buying a tractor. He estimated something around fourteen horsepower would be needed. When he did buy a used tractor around 1945, it was a 20-horsepower model with no hydraulics or power assists for implements. In fact, it had to be cranked by hand because it didn't have an electric self-starter. Nor did it have lights for nighttime operation. Moreover, standard equipment did not include a muffler. So it was very noisy. That was before the days of the Occupational Safety and Health Act, OSHA, which mandates safety devices and noise reduction.

Most of my life on the farm was before the days of tractor power. Then, power came from draft animals, originally mules and later horses. The first draft animals that I can remember were two teams of mules. One team with two males was Jack 'n' Pete and another, both females, was Kate 'n' Beck. Dad and older brother, Johnny, spent long hours in the fields with those mules. Johnny was an early teenager when he worked Kate 'n' Beck. Dad gave him the females because they were a little easier for a boy to handle. In those days there were several mule-drawn farm implements where the mule driver walked behind. These included the one-row cultivators we used to cultivate the corn. Following that cultivator and guiding it with the two wooden handles was very hard work. During those long hours, the worker world talk to the mules to give them directions and maybe just to have someone to listen to our idle conversation during the long days. I was then too small to work in the fields, but I was able to assist. My job on hot days was to take fresh, cool water to the field to Dad and Johnny. Carrying water was an important job for a small boy and you knew that you'd better not forget.

'Giddyup' was the command to the mules to start or go faster. Tired mules often were a bit hard of hearing regarding that command unless they sensed they were headed home at the end of the day. A shout or the sting of a whip would get their attention. 'Whoa,' the order to stop, on the other hand was always heard. In fact, the mules would stop on hearing any word that vaguely sounded like 'whoa.' In the field, when both hands were busy on the two cultivator handles and the leather strap reins were tied together behind your waist, voice commands were used for moving to the right or left. 'Gee' meant 'move right' and 'haw' meant 'move left.' Giddyup, whoa, gee, and haw were the four commands for the mules, but I think they understood a lot more.

I sensed that Dad had a deep respect for Jack 'n' Pete and Kate 'n' Beck. A mule is naturally more intelligent than a horse and, for example, would not overeat if a gate happened to be left ajar to provide

Jack 'n' Pete and Kate 'n' Beck heading home.

easy access to an open granary. A mule would eat until it was full and then stop. A horse, on the other hand, would eat itself sick. Horses and cows would founder from overeating and, in extreme cases, it could be fatal. But a mule was too smart to do that. In many respects, mules were superior farming animals to horses. They were lighter, but very strong, and had great endurance. However, horses had a more glamorous image than mules, and by the 1930s most farmers in the area were using draft horses.

Our mules weren't just draft animals. On occasion, we children would ride them. Riding a mule was quite comfortable even without a saddle, and they were not too bouncy when they would run. Small children always enjoyed the opportunity to ride the mules. Jack, Pete, Kate and Beck were all very gentle and riding them was quite safe in our eyes.

I remember one occasion when that didn't prove to be the case. John, Helen and I were all three riding bareback on Pete from the creek pasture to home. John was in front, being the smallest, I was in the middle, and Helen was at the back. Pete was walking peacefully down a narrow lane with barbed wire fence on both sides when we came to a low area with a narrow muddy ditch across it. Mule logic dictated to Pete that he should jump the ditch, which he did. Unfortunately, none of us anticipated the jump and we all three were thrown. We weren't hurt, except for Helen who fell with one arm over a barbed wire fence. Helen had a nasty cut under her arm that required a visit to the doctor for stitches. Pete meant no harm. There may have been an occasional fall when riding the mules, but it wasn't the fault of these gentle animals.

Sadly, one night the mules escaped from their pasture and they ended up on the railroad track. The engineer of an on-rushing locomotive must have seen them in the strong headlight, but he couldn't stop the train. He frantically blew the engine's steam whistle, which, no doubt only frightened the animals, and they must have started running down the track away from the train. Long speeding freight trains can't stop in less than a mile. So in an effort to clear the track the engineer just hung on the whistle rope making that frightening and continuous sound. Once heard, that sound is never forgotten. Our poor mules hadn't been trained to dive to the ditch, so their natural intelligence was to no avail. One by one the train overtook them and each met its final fate. Jack 'n' Pete and Kate 'n' Beck were no longer available to help with the farming. That was a sad day for our family.

The train track was about a hundred yards from our house so we regularly heard the trains and the warning whistle that they were required to sound at each crossing. There was the whistle code the engineer would use to communicate to the caboose when he would start the train or initiate some other action. But that eerie, continuous, warbling whistle warning that something was on the track was the one that would invariably awaken my parents from the deepest sleep in the middle of the night. You could only pray that the farm animals or whatever else might be on the track would get off because the trains could not stop. Mother always exclaimed, "Stock on the track!" when she heard that sound.

Our next draft animals were horses. Again, we had two teams, one male and one female. Dick 'n' Dan and Dolly 'n' Daisy were the draft animals that I worked during my boyhood days on the farm. I wasn't a good horseman, because I was too impatient. I always wanted to get the work done faster than was possible with the animal power of horses, regardless of how good they were. I must have been confusing to the horses because I would work them very hard scolding them instead of praising them. Then, when I got very tired I'd realize that horses were tired, too, and I would hug them and talk to them and even cry with them. They always had that look in their eye suggesting that they understood. I hope so, because I was not always kind to them in word or action.

On occasion a farmer would take a child to the field when the housewife needed to run an errand where it was inconvenient to take a small child. In a sense, he would be babysitting. But if the work involved working horses and moving across a field, he couldn't leave the child unattended in the field. So the common practice was to have the child ride one of the draft horses, holding on to the round brass balls at the tops of the hames at the horse's collar. I think all young children of the time experienced riding on a walking horse, while clinging tightly to the hames. I know I did.

A working farmer babysitting a young son.

Even if I wanted to be on a tractor that wouldn't get tired and could do more work, I learned a lot from my many hours of working with horses as a boy. You can talk to a horse and not appear to be stupid like you would if you talked to a tractor. A tractor doesn't have eyes that look at you and communicate with you. A tractor can't show appreciation. But still, I wanted to work with a tractor so the work could be done faster. Maybe that's why I became an agricultural engineer.

One of my dreams was fulfilled at the age of fifteen when Dad bought a used Farmall F-20 tractor. By then my older brother, now called John instead of Johnny, was in the Navy. During the summers until I left the farm at age 21 to serve in the Air Force, that tractor was my home in the summer just as much as the farmhouse. Even though we had a tractor, we kept the horses for several years because there were many things that a team of horses could do that a tractor couldn't do as well. For example, at hay-making time the horses could pull the hay wagons as the loose hay, raked into small bunches in the field, was pitched on the wagons and stacked evenly by a loader. The horses didn't have to be driven, and the man or boy loading the wagon only had to give the verbal commands of 'giddyup,' 'whoa,' 'gee' or 'haw.' Also, horses had enough sense to pull the wagons alongside the piles of hay that were in rows on the ground. Unlike a tractor, they weren't blind, and they could see the small piles of hay. The horses knew what we were doing, and they would respond without a driver continuously at the reins. The same was true at threshing time, when the horses would pull the wagons that carried the bundles of grain from the fields to the thresher.

This was a transition period, and it was common for farmers to keep their horses, even after buying their first tractor. But progress eventually changed that. The haying operations changed and hay was baled instead of being put up loose in a large hay mow, where it could be pitched down and fed to the cows and horses in the winter. Small combines, which cut and threshed the grain in the field came on the scene and the old-fashioned threshing operations died. Dad kept the horses and put them in a pasture, sort of in semi-retirement. For entertainment we sometimes rode these horses, particularly Dick and Dan, but mostly Dan. We didn't have saddles, and the male horses didn't have the backbone ridge an inch or more high extending down the middle of their back as the older mares did. Riding these older mares bareback was an experience to be remembered.

For a draft horse, Dan was long legged and very fleet of foot. We enjoyed riding him. We could go to his pasture and easily coax him to us and ride him bareback with no bridle, guiding him by slapping him on one side of his neck or the other. Dan would stand gently to let you get on, but as soon as you were firmly in place, he was ready to go as fast as he could. As he galloped at full speed, about all you could do was tightly hang on to his mane, the only handhold available. As the horses were used less as draft animals and spent more time in the pasture, they became a bit more wild and difficult to control.

I remember riding Dan one time when I went with Helen to the pasture to bring him to the barn. Dan liked to come to the barn because he might get some grain. We didn't have a bridle with us, but we caught Dan in the pasture and both of us managed to get on him, Helen behind me. When we got on the road from the pasture to the barn, I foolishly urged Dan to go faster. Soon he was galloping at top speed. He was having fun running to the barn and ignored our cries to slow down as we were bouncing wildly on his back. Helen was hanging onto me and I was hanging onto Dan's mane. All the time, we were both being pushed forward by Dan's galloping action. At the last corner in front of the barn, Dan made a high speed and abrupt left turn into a gate. Helen sailed off crashing into a stake at the base of a culvert. I was so far forward by then that I could lock my feet together under his neck. Good thing, too, because as he turned I spun around and was left hanging inverted with my feet and legs locked around Dan's neck in front of his front legs.

Fortunately, Dan's good sense and training as a work horse made him stop immediately. He stood perfectly still until I could drop to the ground inches in front of his front hooves. He didn't move a muscle as I did so and seemingly waited to see if we were okay. I wasn't hurt but Helen had a deep bruise on her side from the solid stake that had stopped her fall. Helen, bless her heart, again got the worst of the deal. Fortunately, she was not permanently injured.

My ride on Dan a year or so later was solo, which was a good thing because it was a harrowing experience. Dan probably hadn't been ridden for a year and unbeknownst to me had become just about uncontrollable without a bridle. Dan was pastured in a field down by the creek, immediately adjacent to a small pasture at the Ritchey Mill. That pasture had a young mare in it and I now realize she was of more than a passing interest to Dan. I was going to drive Dan to the barn for some task. I couldn't get him to leave the fence where he was leaning over nuzzling the mare. She didn't seem to mind at all. These horses were only separated by the barbed wire fence.

I caught Dan and hopped on his back with the notion if I couldn't drive him to the barn, I'd ride him there – of course without a bridle. I slapped him and got him started to the gate out of his pasture, which was away from the mare's pasture. Dan ignored my efforts to steer him and made a high speed circle and returned to the mare. Not to be deterred, I slapped him more aggressively and was able to get him to the gate about 200 yards away. However, instead of going towards the barn as I'd planned, Dan again circled back toward the mare's pasture which also abutted the field we were now in.

There was a tree-lined ditch next to the mare's pasture fence, which turned out to be a problem. About four feet separated the small trees and the mare's fence. The trees had low-hanging limbs, about the height of a horse's back, extending over the fence into the mare's pasture. Despite my frantic efforts, Dan made another wide circle and headed straight for that tunnel made by the trees, their low limbs and the barbed wire fence.

You'd have thought Dan was in the Kentucky Derby the way he was running, with me hanging onto his mane for dear life. Like a steeplechase winner Dan bounded that ditch in one great leap and headed full speed down that narrow tunnel between the trees and the fence. I glued myself as low as I could to his back, all the while being pummeled by the low-hanging limbs as we went by. The mare was running with us on the other side of the fence seemingly encouraging Dan in his sprint. I don't know if I looked up or what, but a low limb caught me and, wham – I was swept off over Dan's rump. He stopped immediately and looked around, apparently to see if I was hurt. He just stood there perfectly still seemingly inviting me to get on again. I was as angry as I've ever been and determined not to let him win. Dan stood quietly as I mounted him again and when he felt I was securely in place on his back he took off like a shot.

As we passed the corner of the mare's pasture, Dan again bounded the ditch and again started on still another wide circle back to repeat the tunnel trip, with the mare running in her pasture to meet us at the tunnel. He seemed to be having fun. I wasn't!

One more effort to steer him from his determined course convinced me beyond any doubt that I was not in control. For the first time in my life I voluntarily dismounted from a horse that was running at full speed. Fortunately, the field where I landed, and bounced a couple of times, had no rocks and the soil was relatively soft. The tumble I took was better than being swept off by a two-inch limb in the stomach. The only thing seriously hurt was my pride.

Dan won this one, and I learned a lesson. You don't try to ride a horse bareback without a bridle away from a pasture containing a frisky mare in heat, particularly a horse as determined as Dan was that day. He clearly was enjoying his dreams in the pasture more than the thought of some grain he might get in the barn. I never had an occasion to ride Dan again after that day.

For many years, the horses and mules were an integral part of our farm life. The mules met a tragic end. But the horses spent their final years in lazy retirement. Although farming is much more efficient with tractors and other powered equipment, a tractor will never be your friend and companion like a horse or mule. And a tractor won't challenge you like Dan did that final time. Although, I didn't like what happened then, over 60 years later, on reflection, I admire his spunk. The mules and horses were an unforgettable part of our lives in Ritchey.

NURSING SICK ANIMALS

When I was a boy, the total animal count on our farm at any one time was about 30 cows and calves; 40 or more hogs, including brood sows; four horses or mules; 150 chickens; a half dozen cats and one dog. For a few years, we had about 30 sheep as well. The population would vary as baby animals were born and others would go to market. We had all these animals to feed and care for, in addition to our own family of six.

Just as our family generally depended on home remedies for most ailments, instead of going to the doctor at every sniffle, our sick animals were mostly treated by us. A farm animal had to be quite sick for an expensive veterinarian to be called in from one of the nearby towns. So watching for sick animals was a part of farm life. Since animals couldn't tell us how they felt, we had to watch for symptoms.

We were particularly attentive to animals at birth time and a few days thereafter. As a boy of ten or so, on more than one occasion I was asked to watch the birthing process to see that all was going well. In most cases, things were fine but sometimes action was called for. I remember one time when we had a young heifer that, unfortunately, a bull had gotten with, and she had been bred too young. She was quite small, and if her calf was large there could be problems because her birth canal was not as large as a fully grown cow's. Dad kept our bull in a separate pen so young heifers would not be bred too young even if they were in heat. But occasionally a neighbor's bull would get in our pasture or animals would otherwise accidentally get with a bull. And then the potential damage was already done.

I was instructed to watch this heifer closely because Dad said that we might need to help her give birth and perhaps save her own life. It was a normal birth with the head and front feet coming first and barely visible. But the calf was too large for its mother. The poor heifer, try as she may, could not get the large baby calf's shoulders through the birth canal. She must have been in pain as her eyes rolled with each strain. It was apparent that the heifer couldn't manage alone. I called Dad who entered the picture by securely tying small, but strong, jute ropes around the baby calf's front legs above the ankles. The ropes had to be used because the partially born calf was bloody and slippery with placenta fluid. We couldn't get a grip on the slippery calf's feet with our hands.

We watched for the poor young mother's strain and at that instant we pulled as hard as we could, gaining a foothold for leverage wherever possible. After a few more strains and hard pulls we were successful. We had a healthy young calf, placenta and all, in our laps as its shoulders passed the constriction and out it came. I can only imagine the feeling of the mother. She certainly had a look of relief in her eyes.

What we had done may seem crude, but it wasn't cruel. A cesarean section was not feasible. The young cow survived and the calf was healthy. She apparently had some numbness and slight paralysis in her hips based on her wobbly walk and unsteadiness in her hind quarters. But that, too, soon passed. This young cow continued to grow and did not have trouble with future births. She became a good milk producer. Boys might laugh as they talked about these kinds of experiences with friends at school, but we knew it was serious business. We knew the life of the calf and her mother had been at stake.

With baby pigs we were most concerned about runts. Since sows had litters of anywhere from eight to 12 or more baby pigs, there was always the danger that one or more of them might be underdeveloped, particularly in large litters. A runt often couldn't compete for one of its mother's nipples and would not survive without help. Also, a large sow would sometimes accidentally crush one of its young when it lay down for the piglets to feed. We often would nurse a runt or injured baby pig in the house, keeping it warm and dry and feeding it warmed cow's milk. We'd use a bottle with nipple for the milk. Although we failed often, sometimes we were successful and then we'd be proud because we had saved a baby pig that otherwise would not have survived.

A sow nursing a large litter of healthy baby pigs.

Sometimes, for reasons that I don't understand an animal might not have enough milk for its baby. I remember a baby lamb that we nursed twice daily until it got old enough to eat solid feed. So, in a sense, we had our own animal hospital on the farm.

Giving grown large animals medication was an interesting experience. When calves were young, they would often get the scours – dysentery. We had medicine to add to the feed to treat this problem. Sometimes administering medication was more challenging, especially for large animals. I remember well the problem of trying to give a horse a large pill for some affliction. The pill was nearly two inches in diameter. I had no idea how to get the horse to swallow that monstrous pill. We couldn't put it in its mouth and have it drink a glass of water. Dad would grab the upper lip of the horse and twist it and lift the horse's head high. With the pill attached to a special device about a foot long I would stick the pill deep in the horse's throat. Sometimes the horse could spit it up. But we'd keep trying until the horse swallowed the pill, usually with Dad rubbing its throat.

Our animals were vaccinated for certain diseases, such as cholera for hogs, and we generally had the veterinarian come out for those inoculation tasks. We used a preventative treatment in the chickens' water for a dreaded disease, coccidiosis. Chickens might also be vaccinated, and we performed that task ourselves.

Animals would sometimes injure themselves. Barbed wire fences helped keep animals in the pastures, but the barbs could cut an animal if it tried to jump the fence, and that sometimes happened. Cows would sometimes cut their udder or teats, and those had to be treated with a salve each time we cleaned their udder and milked them. Animals in summer pasture that we didn't see daily were at risk from flies if they suffered a cut. The flies would lay eggs in the wound and these would hatch, creating hundreds of larvae. If they weren't controlled, these maggots could continue to enlarge the wound and perhaps cause infection. Left untreated, this could cause death. Even though the solutions we used to clean maggots from a wound must have stung, the animals would stand perfectly still while they were being treated and when we copiously coated the wound with pine tar. I'm convinced farm animals knew when you were trying to help them.

On two occasions the treatment we used really surprised me. Once was when we treated a badly bloated cow that had gotten into a granary and eaten too much. Her middle body was distended and the skin behind her rib cage was tight as a drum. The gas inside the cow had made her very sick and Dad feared it would be fatal if he didn't do something about it. He said he was going to puncture her stomach to relieve the pressure. He sharpened the longest blade of his pocket knife and disinfected it carefully with alcohol. Then, as I watched, he stabbed the animal behind the ribcage where the skin was very tight. The foul smelling gas almost whistled as it escaped through that small puncture wound. I have never seen a cow smile, but I believe that young cow, who had turned her head back to watch the proceedings, tried to smile. She soon was back to her healthy self and running with the herd again.

The second case involved Dad's attempt to repair a large rupture in a hog. As his helper, I was to hold the surgical instrument – his sharpened and disinfected pocket knife – and have the disinfectant solution available to clean the wound. We had one of Mother's needles and strong silk thread to sew up the incision. We caught the hog and then securely tied him so he couldn't get up. We worked on the ground in a dry area of the barn lot, on reflection not a very good operating area.

The poor animal had part of its intestines protruding through the abdominal membrane and they were being held by the skin. My job was to help stuff the intestines back into the abdominal cavity, which Dad would sew up first. After that, he planned to sew up the outer skin. The pig was securely tied, but we had no way to anesthetize it. So it was free to squeal, wiggle and carry on during the operation. Dad carefully cut the outer skin and, lo and behold, we had intestines coming out of that pig that almost seemed like an erupting geyser. We quickly realized that the notion of getting all of that expanding mass of intestines back in the abdominal cavity was unrealistic. Our goal shifted to trying to get back to where we started, with the intestines inside the hog under the outer skin. We quite literally had our hands full in attempting that task. Actually, we each needed four hands.

As I reflect on our efforts, it's almost humorous. We were washing the intestines with Lysol water and putting them back under the skin, and we both felt like we needed more hands. But we finally succeeded and actually got the incision sewed up with strong silk thread. The miracle is that the wound healed and the animal survived. But it always had a bulge larger than a grapefruit hanging from its underside. I suspect this is a case where the pig would have sued us for malpractice if it could have.

Young male animals that were to be raised for their meat had to be castrated, and that was one operation that we did regularly. But we never looked forward to it. By the way the small pigs squealed, one knew it was painful. But they recovered very quickly. Dad, with his sharpened and disinfected knife, was quick with his work and we were always careful to apply a disinfectant solution to the wound. I didn't cherish the thought of doing it, but I did learn. In fact, when I owned sheep as a 4H Club project, I was expected to perform the operation on my own male lambs. It was part of learning and accepting responsibility.

While some of this may sound inhumane, I don't believe it was. Our business was farming, and each animal had a market value. You wouldn't intentionally spend more on medical treatment for an animal than it was worth. That was an economic reality that guided all farmers. Each animal had a cash value. Our medical care was not perfect, but we did the best we could with our limited resources, and we saved the lives of many animals. We never had an animal die as a result of our efforts.

THE RITCHEY MILL AND JOLLIFICATION

The first settlers chose the area because of Shoal Creek and its fertile creek-bottom soil. Shoal Creek is a beautiful perennial stream that is fed by springs and seepage from the surrounding hills. As the creek passes through the Ritchey valley, it hugs the valley's southern edge tight against a very steep hill, where rock outcrops form small bluffs. The village of Ritchey is on the north edge of this east-west oriented valley. Villagers looking south see the large trees along the banks of the creek and the wooded hill rising abruptly from the creek's southern bank.

Although Shoal Creek is one of the most beautiful streams in the county, there are many streams that flow continuously and offer potential for low-head water power. No doubt Matthew Ritchey, and

An early Ritchey mill, circa 1900.

The Ritchey mill of my boyhood where I took cattle feed to be ground.

the settlers that followed him, saw the creek's potential for providing water power when they located there in 1832. After all, they would need power for grist mills to grind wheat flour and corn meal as well as for saw mills to convert the abundant timber from the wooded hillsides and valleys into lumber.

Matthew Ritchey and his son built Ritchey's first dam on Shoal Creek. The dam, which was made of logs, provided the water power needed to run a mill for grinding grain. Eventually that dam failed and was replaced by one made of stone and some concrete. Both dams were due south of the village center. The mill pond extended east for more than a quarter mile. The dam I remember is still in place, although sections have failed and the mill pond is now filled with sediment. It was a low dam providing no more than about eight feet of head for the water turbine. Low head power turbines require a large flow of water to generate much power. The wide valley formed by the meandering creek was so flat that a higher dam would have inundated the farm land in the valley. So the mill pond, called Mirror Lake in the early days, although more than a quarter mile long, was confined in the river bed. This bed is formed by the south hill and a natural levee along the north bank. This so-called levee formed over time as the coarser sediments settled out adjacent to the stream during floods.

At one time, there was an ice plant near the creek, just east of the two-story grist mill. The ice plant burned in the early 1930's. As a small child I vaguely remember hearing descriptions of that fire, which could be seen from our house across the valley to the north. The image of that fire is so vivid that I feel like I can remember seeing its eerie glow across the valley. But the fire happened when I was very young

By the mid-1930's, the mill had essentially ceased operation as a commercial wheat flour and corn meal enterprise. The low power output from the low dam and inefficient turbine may have been one reason. However, the mill continued to grind livestock feed with its hammer mill. We used the mill to grind the grain for our small dairy herd and sometimes for our chickens. The ground feed was mostly for cows since the chickens didn't eat so much. The medicines and supplements needed to keep chickens healthy were included in commercial chicken feed, such as that made by Ralston Purina in Saint Louis. Chickens were far more sensitive to their rations than cows, and egg production would drop drastically when the hens were sick or other problems occurred.

Our cow feed was based on whatever grain was at hand. Usually we would grind ear corn, cob and all, some oats and a protein supplement. The protein supplement was usually soybean meal or cotton seed meal, which we would buy. Another protein supplement called tankage, made from dried animal residues gathered at slaughter houses could be used, but we fed that mostly to hogs to supplement the protein in their rations. We didn't add much salt to the cow feed before it was ground because we always had a block of salt in the cow lot. This allowed the cows to lick salt according to their needs.

The feed constituents were loaded in a horse-drawn wagon that had a narrow, high-sided grain bed on it. The same wagons were used for hauling grain and hauling hay, but a narrow, tight, box-like bed was used for grain, while a wide, flat bed was used for hauling hay or grain bundles. We would load the ear corn from the corn crib first, using a scoop shovel, then put oats on top, and finally spread the protein supplement on the oats. The materials would be well mixed as they were unloaded at the mill by shoveling from the wagon into the hammer mill feed hopper.

As a boy, I usually went with my father to the mill to grind the feed. We would take burlap gunny sacks with us to bag the feed as it came from the grinder. When we arrived at the mill, we would pull the wagon onto the large, drive-through scales to weigh the grain and wagon together. Then we'd move the wagon to the grinder area. The miller would open the turbine gates to start the water flowing through the turbine, and the machine would start slowly. Finally you would hear that high-pitched hum of the hammer mill turning at about 2,400 rpm. The hammer mill had a rotating cylinder with hinged metal hammers that shattered the grain so it could fall through a steel screen. The size of the holes in the screen controlled the coarseness of the feed. When we heard that correctly pitched hum of the hammer mill we started shoveling the corn-oats-supplement mixture into the feed hopper. If the grinder was fed too fast, the rotational speed of the hammer mill would slow and grind poorly; so we listened to the sing of the grinder to be sure the speed stayed high.

As the water was released through the turbine, you would see the boils of blue-green water downstream below the turbine. This was the signal for any fisherman in the area to move up close below the turbine outlet. Experience had shown that the fish often would bite better just below the turbine outlet when it's operating. Good channel catfish were often caught that way. I think the turbine stirred up crawfish at the bottom near the outlet and may have stunned or disoriented aquatic life as it tumbled through the turbine, signaling chow time for the fish.

My boyhood job was to sack the feed as it came out of the grinder. The hammer mill sat below the main floor of the mill and the ear corn-oats mixture was fed into its feed hopper through a two-foot-square opening in the floor. I was admonished to give that opening a wide berth because it would be the end of my young life if I fell into that high-speed grinder. The feed was blown up to an inverted cone-shaped dust collector called a 'cyclone separator' where it spun around with dust exiting at the top and the feed dropping to an opening at the height of an upright gunny sack. The large, 75- to 100-pound sacks could be filled easily and dragged to the side on the floor, which was slick with powdery feed dust. A boy could drag the sacks, even if he couldn't lift them.

After the wagon was emptied and the grinding finished, the miller would close the turbine gates, stopping water flowing through the turbine. The pitch of the hammer mill singing would get lower and lower becoming a low-pitched hum as the grinder coasted to a halt. Next, Dad would drive the empty wagon back to the scales to get its empty weight so the net weight of the feed could be determined. The charge for grinding was according to weight. The sacks of ground feed were then loaded on the wagons and hauled back to the barn and emptied into a special bin for cow feed. I sat high on the sacks and waved to friends as we passed through the edge of town, knowing I had helped with an important job. I enjoyed the envious looks of the neighbor kids who didn't live on a farm and work

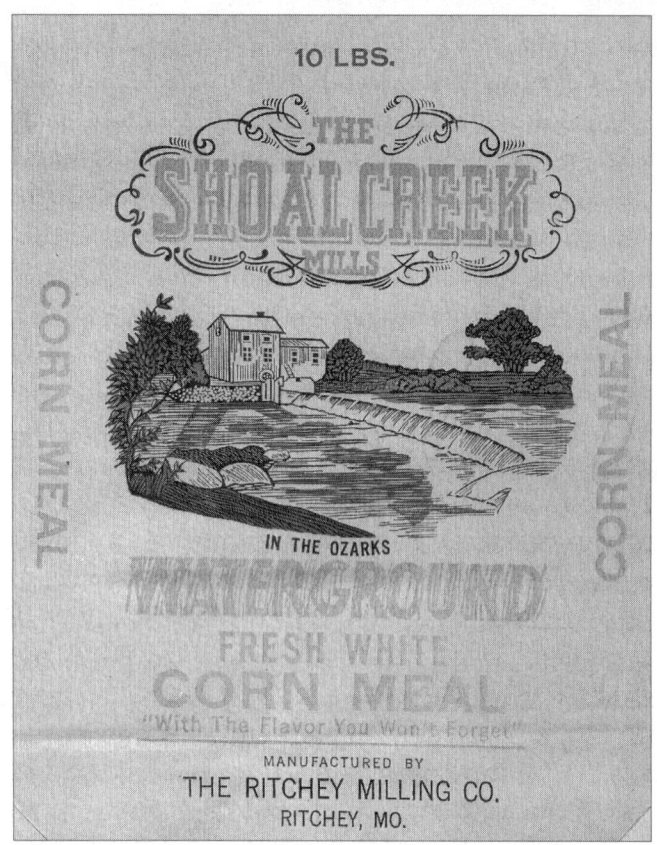

A ten-pound corn meal sack from the Ritchey mill from the early 1940's.

with animals.

At the age of about thirteen, I was old enough to handle the grinding by myself. That was a job that I did many times. It was interesting because the mill was such a fascinating place. In the two-story part of the mill that had once been used to make flour and corn meal, there was a collection of antique milling equipment, all connected by elevators, wooden chutes or other conveyors. The craftsmanship needed to build wooden chutes that wouldn't allow finely ground flour to leak out was extraordinary. A millwork carpenter, known as a 'millwright,' was recognized as a highly skilled craftsman.

In the early days of this mill before my time, the grain was ground with a large millstone. Subsequently, a more modern burr mill was installed. In the burr mill, grain was fed between a rough metal plate and a slowly rotating plate that was covered with metal burrs. The grinding action occurred between the slowly rotating plate and the stationery base.

The mill didn't grind corn meal during the first 12 years of my boyhood, but toward the end of World War II, the grist mill was reopened and made corn meal for human consumption. Mr. William Rodgers, a miller from Tennessee via Oklahoma, came to Ritchey, opened the grist mill and began making high quality corn meal for stores in the region. The corn meal was sacked by helpers in five- and ten-pound size paper bags with a picture of the mill and advertised as 'water ground.' Apparently, that was a selling point, suggesting it was old fashioned, like Aunt Jemima pancake mix.

The old water powered turbine couldn't produce much power when the mill pond was low due to drought or a leaky dam. So a supplementary power unit was added in the 1940's. It was a one-cylinder diesel engine made in 1910. That 'one-lung,' low-speed engine had a straight un-muffled vertical exhaust pipe about six inches in diameter that looked like a miniature smoke stack. When the 'whoom-whoom-whoom' sound of that engine, at about one-second intervals, could be heard across the valley of Shoal Creek, we knew that 'water ground' corn meal was being produced by diesel power. On a perfectly calm day that engine would blow concentric black smoke rings in the sky. At times we could see five or six of these halos rising and expanding as they dissipated above the mill.

Progress does not stand still. When we expanded our dairy herd and purchased a tractor, we needed more cow feed. We built a milking parlor to handle more cows and to qualify for Grade A milk production. First, a traveling, custom feed-grinder mounted on a truck, would come every two weeks to grind feed. Then we installed our own tractor powered hammer mill in the feed supply room of our milking parlor. The ground feed was blown directly into the storage bin without sacking and hauling. Our need for the mill on Shoal Creek had passed. The same was true of other farmers. This was another nail in the coffin of the Shoal Creek mill.

At the same time, the local 'water ground' corn meal was having trouble competing with milling gi-

The Jolly mill, circa early 1900's. This mill existed at the time of the Civil War and at various times both the Confederate and Union troops camped nearby. Rumor has it that there was a whiskey still on the third floor that was not damaged by soldiers on either side.

ants like Pillsbury. So the Ritchey Mill closed, never to be opened again. The regal two-story structure stands today, but that landmark has been slowly disintegrating. The dam has essentially failed and the beautiful millpond, now filled with sediment, is mostly drained. I understand that new owners are renovating the mill as a hobby and possible tourist attraction.

The millpond, where teenage boys once swung from ropes tied high in the tall trees overhanging the creek and jumped with loud yells into the deep water, is now very low. Those pond banks were muddy so the boys would scamper naked as jaybirds, up over hanging tree roots to the dry ground. It was a nude swimming hole and girls knew they dare not venture there unless their intent was to startle the boys who were frolicking in the cool pond. The sounds of boys yelling as they played and swam signaled the message that girls were not welcome.

The Jolly mill was another beautiful structure of considerable historical significance near Ritchey. It was a three-story building located about ten miles southeast of Ritchey on Capps Creek, a tributary of Shoal Creek. The Jolly Mill, like the Ritchey Mill, sat like a jewel in a beautiful setting. Fortunately, it's being preserved, and a park has been established on its grounds. It's sad that the same was not done at Ritchey, until recent efforts began to restore its mill.

However, the Jolly Mill has a history that can never be matched by the Ritchey Mill. Several significant Civil War battles were fought in Newton County and several took place in Newtonia, five miles south of Ritchey and only seven miles west of the Jolly Mill. Skirmishes took place in 1862 on August 8, September 30, and October 2. The Newtonia area had a significant civil war history, being a hot spot that was scouted thoroughly. In early May of 1863, 103 Union troops assessed the resources around the village now referred to as Jolly.

During the Civil War the small town near the mill was called Jollification, not Jolly, as it was known in my boyhood. An 1888 history of the area has a short description of Jollification on Capps's Creek and mentions a sawmill on Shoal Creek, only a short distance from Jollification.

Both Confederate and Union Army troops camped in the vicinity of the Jolly Mill at various times during the war. The men of both armies were no doubt familiar with the early mill, including the moonshine still that is said to have been located on the top floor. The mill would certainly have had water and the grain essential for making moonshine whiskey. According to legend, both armies enjoyed the products of this still at various times. Local history has it that both sides used the area for rest and relaxation, and were careful to be sure that nothing happened to the mill and its precious third floor still. Perhaps that colorful name, Jollification, came from the rowdy results of a few snorts of the mill's 'white lightening.'

SUMMER CANNING, CHIGGERS AND WILD BLACKBERRY JELLY

Several wild blackberry thickets grew on the hill pasture. They were a nuisance because the blackberry bushes were thick and choked out the pasture grass. In the days before herbicides, the only way to get rid of the wild blackberries was to grub them out. Blackberries couldn't compete with the grass in the open sunny areas, but held tenaciously to areas that were usually shady. Blackberries were a pain in the neck and of no value except for the fruit they yielded in the late spring and summer. I hated to pick them from their thicket, which was resplendent with briars, but it was a chore that we children shared with Mother.

The blackberries ripened in June when school was out for the summer. So there was no way to get out of picking them. The dress for blackberry picking was overalls and a heavy, long sleeved shirt. A person only tries to pick blackberries with a short sleeved shirt once. After that, the memory of blackberry briars was indelibly printed in one's mind and the temptation to wear anything but the most protective clothing was routinely avoided. Mother wore a pair of Dad's overalls, one of his blue chambray shirts and a colorful cotton sunbonnet she had made. When stiffly starched, it held its shape and provided complete protection from the sun and the briars.

Besides the briars, there were the chiggers to contend with. Those little blood-sucking mites are impossible to see except, when their transparent bodies are full of blood. That's why they're called redbugs in Texas and some other parts of the country. We usually spotted them only after we started itching and our skin was irritated from the bite, blood sucking and microscopic eggs the chiggers had laid under our skin. Scratching, which could hardly be avoided because the itch was so intense, only made matters worse. I doubt if scratching kept any chigger from completing its life cycle on my body.

Chiggers liked to worm their way into tight areas, such as under the elastic band of our undershorts and under the bands of our socks. Unfortunately, the chiggers weren't totally committed to waistbands and socks and sometimes selected more private body parts for their home. Any place that was warm and relatively moist with sweat seemed to fill the bill as far as chiggers were concerned.

We heard of only one way to keep the chiggers off when picking blackberries – putting powdered yellow sulfur in your socks. But I don't recall us doing that, probably because we never had the sulfur handy. So, chiggers always seemed to get us at wild blackberry picking time.

We always treated chigger bites with rubbing alcohol. I don't know if it killed the chiggers or not, but it sure did sting when applied. It may have just made them drunk. Another way to kill chiggers was to coat them with finger nail polish. The lacquer seal was supposed to suffocate the chigger and eventually remove them when the dried polish was peeled off. The itching usually lasted only two or three days, if we could resist scratching the bites.

We'd usually pick the blackberries in gallon-sized sorghum molasses buckets that had been cleaned. After we picked several gallons, which we would carry back in three-gallon milk buckets, mother would be ready to make the jelly. The ingredients were sugar, pectin and the berries. Mother would cook the berries and, when they were very juicy, she would first press the juice out in an inverted cone

Winter's supply of canned vegetables from the summer vegetable garden.

shaped colander that stood on three legs. She'd use a pointed cone-shaped roller that had a ball-shaped handle to press the juice from the berries. She'd rotate the roller in the colander to crush the berries. Then she'd strain the juice from the seeds using an old cotton tea towel she had made. Straining the berries involved twisting the cloth and was done when the juice was quite hot. It was a hot, messy job. In fact, canning anything was hot and steamy work, and there was no air conditioning.

As I recall, the sugar and pectin were added to the juice and the mixture was cooked some more. After that, the liquid jelly was poured into mason jars that had been sterilized in a large kettle of boiling water along with the lids. The berry liquid would jell quickly. Most of the jelly was put in pint jars, but occasionally quart jars were used. The jars were filled to within about half an inch of the top.

Jam was made without straining out the seeds and pulp. The seeds were very small and some were mashed in the colander, which had very small holes in it. The jam was prepared in a manner similar to jelly. Again, the jars were set in large, rectangular cake pans to catch any drips and were filled to about half an inch of the top.

The final step, after the jellies and jams had jelled, was to melt paraffin to seal the tops. The melting process was a bit tricky because the paraffin could catch on fire. If the paraffin wasn't hot enough, it would form a scum on top. And with wood cook stoves, controlling the heat was not a precise process. The person making jelly had to be careful.

When done properly, the hot paraffin formed a perfect seal with no entrapped air above the jelly or jam, insuring that no mold would grow. If the jars were sealed only with the screw lids, there would be air and some mold would form. Mother always put lids on along with the paraffin seal, but many said that wasn't necessary.

Since paraffin is solid at room temperature, but soft at body temperature, it made a nice substitute for chewing gum, which we seldom had. We children would take a piece of cold paraffin and put it in our mouth. When cold, it would crumble as we chewed. But by working it carefully in your mouth until it warmed, you could work it into a nice, soft chewy substance. Since paraffin doesn't have any flavor, we pretended we had chewing gum. Real chewing gum was a rare treat, since Wrigley's gum cost a penny a stick in those days. That was a lot.

Mother usually saved some berries to make a pie or cobbler for supper. This was very special, and we all looked forward to a large piece of warm, blackberry cobbler, with thick cream on it, for dessert. One jar of the jelly or jam would be kept out and tested to be sure the mixture had jelled properly. It had to cool first, but it seemed that the first taste from that newly made batch that we slathered on a hot buttered biscuit was the sweetest and best in the world.

The jelly and jam from the summer lasted through the year. While it could be kept more than one year on the shelves in the cellar, it would sometimes turn to sugar if kept too long. Occasionally the paraffin seal was not perfect and there would be mold on the jelly that could be scraped away with little waste. On occasion, the jelly with a poor seal would ferment, giving it a wild blackberry wine flavor. Dad particularly enjoyed that. For us, it didn't taste quite right.

Most of the jelly we had was made from wild blackberries, although occasionally mother would make raspberry jelly, crab apple jelly, strawberry jam and peach or apricot preserves. One thing for sure, the freshly baked homemade biscuits for breakfast were always topped with butter and some sweet substance Mother had made. We never thought of the chiggers and itching on those many cold, wintry mornings when we enjoyed that wild blackberry jelly.

Jellies and jams were not the only thing preserved in the canning season. We always had a large vegetable garden where we grew onions, leaf lettuce, spinach, carrots, squash, English peas, beans of several varieties, tomatoes, bell peppers, cucumbers, cabbage, beets, watermelons, cantaloupe (which we called mush melons), sweet corn, sweet potatoes and Irish potatoes. Only the lettuce, watermelons and cantaloupe were not preserved and stored for the winter meals, although watermelon rinds could be pickled. Mother did not do that often, though. The Irish potatoes, sweet potatoes and onions were simply dried and stored in the cool cellar in crates or baskets.

The vegetables were usually cooked in their sterilized glass fruit jars in a pressure cooker. That way, the food could be cooked at a higher temperature than possible in an open container, with water at our altitude boiling at slightly below 212 degrees F. My jobs were helping to pick and clean the vegetables, shell or snap the beans or whatever Mother asked me to do. Canning occurred several times during the summer, whenever there were vegetables to be harvested. The canned food was stored on shelves in the cellar.

Botulinum bacteria could grow in canned food that wasn't heated long enough or to a sufficiently high temperature. These bacteria produce botulin toxin that can cause fatal food poisoning, even in tiny doses. On very rare occasions we'd find a lid of a jar puffed out by pressure inside the jar, a sure sign of botulin toxin. If the metal lids were not perfectly flat, we wouldn't eat the food. Instead we'd bury it to keep it away from any animals.

In the late summer, we would harvest the mature, large heads of cabbage and slice them on a cabbage board that had a special knife built in it. The cabbage was placed in large stone containers in brine made of its own juice, water and salt. The resulting sauerkraut would be preserved for the season. Mother also made a lot of sweet pickles from small cucumbers, but never any dill pickles, which Dad didn't like. I think she used a solution with vinegar in it, but I'm not sure. She also made some beet pickles, using two-inch beets before they had grown to full size and become fibrous.

Although we didn't grow apples or peaches, Dad would buy a few bushels from a local orchard and Mother would can them for desserts. Dad always liked a bowl of sweet canned fruit or some other sweet dessert after supper. Sometimes apples were dried to preserve them and they could be made into a dried apple pie, which was much like a raisin pie, but Mother seldom did that.

A grade school classmate who lived on a farm south of town always brought his lunch to school. It was invariably the same thing, a fried dried-apple pie. That was his lunch. Not knowing much about nutrition, I thought how lucky he was to have such a tasty meal. On reflection, I am sure he would have enjoyed some variety.

MRS. MARION'S SORGHUM MOLASSES

Mother and Dad worked very hard to have enough food preserved and stored so we could eat well in the winter. They did a very good job at that, but the children were all expected to pitch in and help.

Mrs. Marion, who lived across the street, was one of the hardest workers I have ever seen. I don't ever remember seeing her relax, except one time. That was in the winter when, for some reason, I was across the street with Mother at Mrs. Marion's and she invited Mother to have a cup of coffee. I was served fresh Jersey milk, although that's not what I most remember. Mrs. Marion had three small, light-brown Jersey cows, different from our larger black and white spotted Holstein dairy cows. Jersey cream was very rich. Mother's coffee was served in a nice, white cup and saucer. I recognized it because it was one of the cup-and-saucer-patterns that came as a prize in large, round boxes of Quaker Oats – sort of like toys in Crackerjack boxes. Mrs. Marion served her own coffee in similar 'china.' Both women used generous amounts of sugar and thick cream in their coffee.

Blowing saucered coffee.

Mrs. Marion drank her coffee in a way that I hadn't seen before. After she had stirred the sugar and cream in her cup, she carefully poured steaming hot coffee from her cup into her saucer to a point that it was quite full and set the cup aside on the table. Then she carefully lifted the full saucer with both hands to her lips and gently blew across the liquid surface. After a few blows, she put the saucer to her lips and sipped. She didn't spill a drop. Mother's coffee was as yet untouched, apparently still too hot to drink as evidenced by the steam rising from it. Mrs. Marion drank her strong, boiled coffee slowly and obviously savored every drop. But she didn't drink a drop from the cup. She had 'saucered and blowed' her coffee. That ritual, which I have never seen since, was not unlike savoring and slowly sipping a good brandy, but not until the snifter has been cradled in one's palms and warmed to amplify the aroma and its fragrance inhaled. Joanne says her grandmother in Tennes-

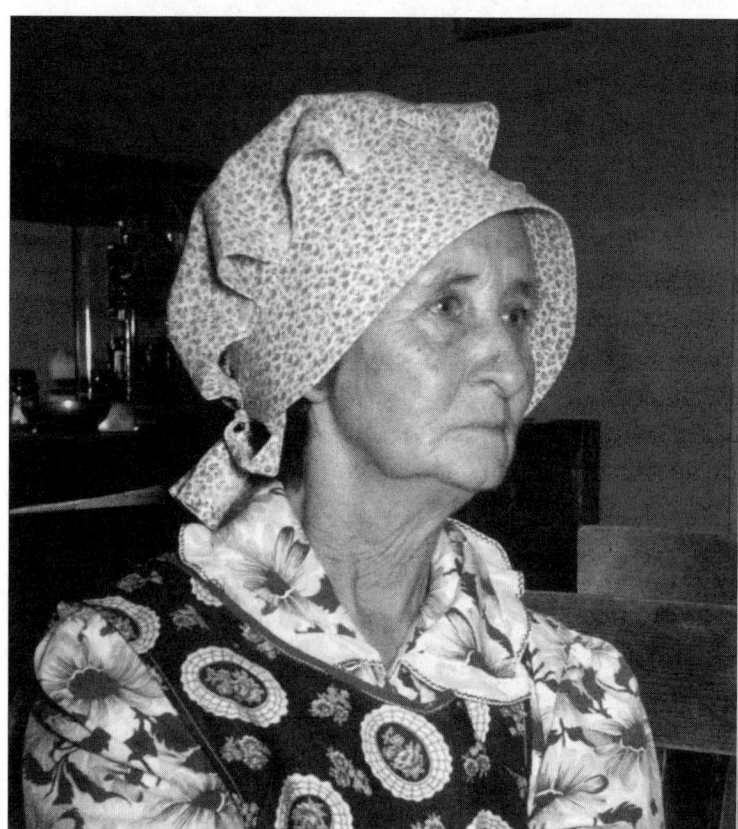

Mrs. Marion in her stiffly starched sunbonnet, cotton print dress and apron.

see drank her coffee that way.

Mrs. Marion was always addressed as Mrs. Marion. Most women went by their first name. I don't even know her first name. Her husband's name was Alec, and he was seldom, if ever, referred to as Mr. Marion. In fact, like several in town, he had a nickname. His was Pedro, pronounced 'pee-dro' by Mrs. Marion. That is how she referred to him.

Mrs. Marion was a very hard worker and that earned her a lot of respect. I thought of her as a lady, not necessarily a lady of culture, for sure, but a lady nonetheless. To my knowledge, Alec did not have a regular job. No one would consider being Constable of the Village of Ritchey as regular work. That job couldn't have paid more than a few dollars a month, if it paid at all – and it didn't take much time. Although he may have been on call, there were no phones in town, save the one in the post office and one or two others, including in later years, the one in our house. The Marion's didn't have a phone. So, to my knowledge, Alec's constable duties were pretty much restricted to Halloween, when he would patrol the town on foot in hopes of keeping the teenage boys from turning over outdoor privies and creating other mischief. Privies were the toilet facilities, usually located on the alley in back of the house, for virtually everyone in Ritchey.

To be fair, Alec did pitch bundles at threshing time and often helped farmers at haying time, but I confess I thought of him as a loafer. He did regularly go to the small pasture that he and Mrs. Marion rented from Mr. Largen, the postmaster, to bring the three Jersey cows home. They had a small barn on the alley behind their house where Mrs. Marion would milk the cows. I never saw Alec help Mrs. Marion do any milking. Since we would milk our fifteen or so cows ourselves, Dad and the children all shared in the milking as did Mother when the men were heavily involved in the field work. But Alec was not seen on the classic three-legged milk stool, the standard seat used while doing that chore. That is probably why I thought of him as a loafer. Perhaps he thought milking was women's work. In fairness, he did deliver milk to the neighbor customers in returnable, glass quart bottles that had snap-in, waxed cardboard paper, milk caps. These were about twice the diameter of a quarter. Of course, the bottles were washed, filled and capped by Mrs. Marion. The dime-a-quart that the milk sold for in those days was a small but dependable income for the Marions. She probably churned butter and sold it as well.

Mrs. Marion always seemed to be working. She had a large vegetable garden, and she spent the summer putting away hundreds of Mason jars full of canned goods. In the spring and early summer, you could count on seeing Mrs. Marion, always in her apron and stiffly starched and ironed sunbonnet, weeding or doing other gardening chores daily. As the sweet corn would grow taller, there would come a time when only the top of her sunbonnet was visible to attest to her daily diligence in the garden. Eventually, the sweet corn towered above her short frame, and she would sort of vanish as she silently worked in the garden.

Having a few cows for milk and butter for your own use and possibly for earning money by selling a few quarts of milk was not uncommon in this country. Most families had a large garden and did canning. I can't say how many people 'saucered and blowed' their coffee, but there may have been others. I understand that those who came from the hills of Tennessee and Kentucky and that general region regularly savored their coffee this way. But, around Ritchey, and maybe in the whole county, Mrs. Marion was the only woman to make sorghum molasses.

There are many varieties of sorghum, locally called cane. Grain sorghum is a short growing variety and its seeds come from the head of the grain. My relatives in Oklahoma called it maize. There is also a sorghum that is grown as a forage crop and often made into silage for cattle. And, of course, there is the well-known sugar cane grown in the southern United States for sugar or syrup. The sorghum cane that's used to make molasses is probably more like the latter – at least the juice is quite sweet.

Mrs. Marion's oldest son, Roy, was a progressive farmer who had a tractor before we did. He would grow some sorghum-molasses cane for his mother. In the fall, as the trees in the Ozarks were turning into a kaleidoscope of warm, fall colors, the sorghum cane would be harvested. The cane, which was harvested with a corn binder or a corn sled, was brought by wagon to a stack near Mrs. Marion's cane roller press. Since her house was less than a couple hundred yards from the front of the Ritchey School yard, we children watched during recess as the stack of sorghum-molasses cane grew during the few days of the harvest. The most exciting day, however, was when the cane was run through the press, powered by Roy's tractor, squeezing the lime-colored, sweet cane juice from the stalks. It was tempting to sneak a taste of the freshly squeezed juice from the storage barrels. I can't say that it tasted that good, but the excitement of slyly getting an illicit taste meant that you drank it with fervor. We paid the price if we were too successful in our sneaky tricks and drank too much raw cane juice – loose bowels beyond imagination. The boys at school had another term for it.

The green cane juice has to be cooked to make that distinctively flavored sorghum molasses. This is done in a so-called syrup pan, which is made of heavy gage tin by a tinsmith. Mrs. Marion's syrup pan was about four feet wide and about 20 feet along. It had two-inch high tin partitions perpendicular to the long dimension that were spaced at about six-inch intervals. Alternate partitions extended to opposite walls along the long sides of the pan, but an opening was left at the end of alternate partitions. The pan was positioned about two and a half feet above the ground on low brick sidewalls to create a long, narrow stove. There was a cast iron door at one end for fire logs and a short chimney, perhaps ten feet tall, at the other. The flames and heat from the burning logs traversed the length of the syrup pan, providing a long, flat cooking surface on which the raw cane juice was slowly introduced at one corner near the fire door. The tortuous path of the juice was a back-and-forth route across the pan, as the liquid slowly made its way through the maze of partitions, all the while cooking and being transformed from a watery, greenish liquid to a golden-brown, viscous and distinctively aromatic sorghum-molasses. The molasses exited into five-gallon containers near the short chimney.

There is an art to cooking sorghum-molasses and, as far as I was concerned, Mrs. Marion was the master artist. The wood fire had to be carefully monitored and she would give Alec specific instructions as to how he should stoke and feed new logs to the fire to keep it just right. Mrs. Marion's instructions to Alec were not ambivalent and she could bark them like a marine drill sergeant. Mrs. Marion was 'in charge' when she cooked molasses. Also, the rate at which the sorghum cane juice was fed into the syrup pan had to be just right to control the continuous cooking process. A valve at the

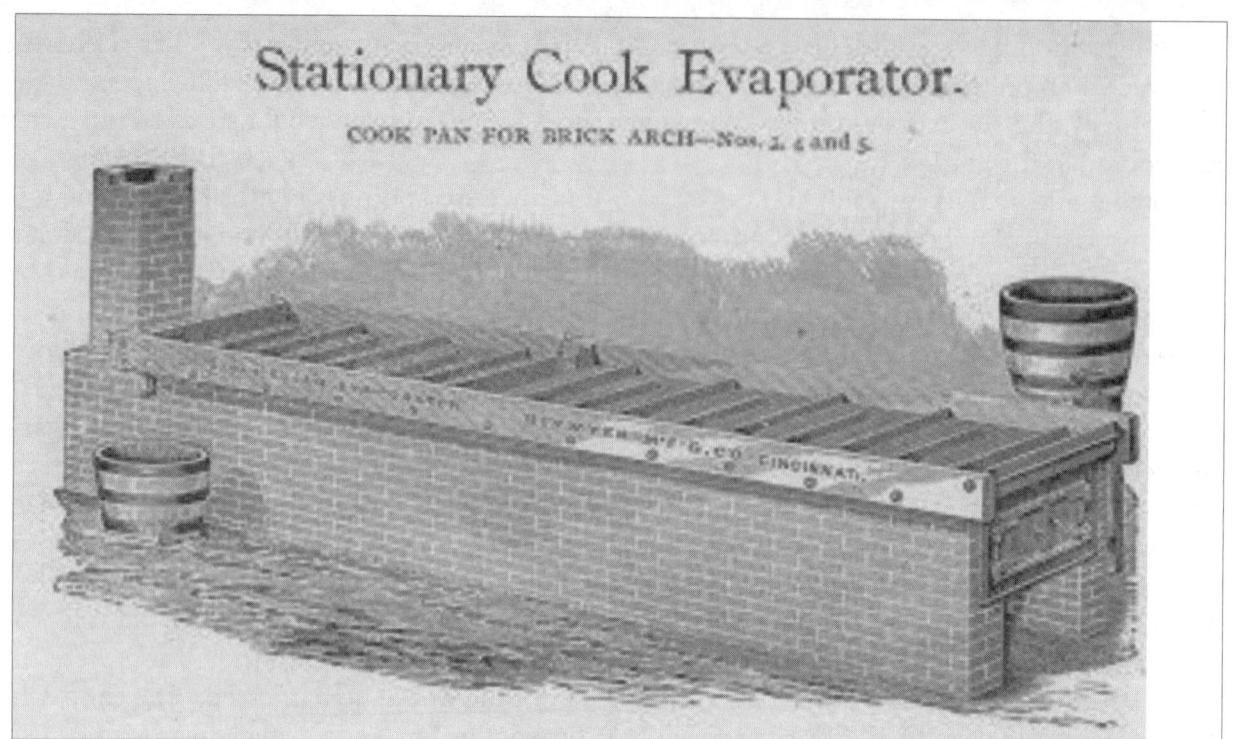

Sorghum molasses cook evaporator similar to Mrs. Marion's.

bottom of the barrel that held the raw cane juice was precisely adjusted to make the flow rate just right. But the main instrument of control was her wooden paddle, shaped like a garden hoe, and attached to a long wooden handle. The paddle was about six inches wide and about three inches high. It would just fit between the vertical partitions that were soldered to the bottom of the syrup pan and was used to accurately moderate the liquid's movement across the pan.

As the molasses cooked and slowly changed color, consistency and aroma, Mrs. Marion would move the cooking juice along its back-and-forth journey for the length of the pan. At the end, the dark brown, highly aromatic and very hot liquid would discharge into a five-gallon reusable tin lard stand. This was the standard bulk storage container for lard, but it was also used and reused for many other purposes. When the molasses cooled it was transferred to gallon reusable syrup cans. These cans had a lid and a bail, not too different from a gallon paint can, except the lid was more easily removed and replaced. We always bought the molasses in the gallon cans from Mrs. Marion, probably at less than a dollar a gallon. Note that Mrs. Marion always referred to molasses as plural and you wouldn't eat 'it'. To her, you cooked 'them' molasses and you ate 'them.'

Enjoying freshly baked, homemade biscuits with butter and molasses was a treat that once experienced can never be forgotten. Cold molasses is very viscous – how else could the bromide, 'slow as molasses in January' come about? It can be wound around a fork or table knife that's been dipped into the molasses bucket or pitcher. Therefore, you never poured molasses – you wound it on your knife or fork, or at least used the fork to sort of drag it out of the pitcher.

The butter was usually at room temperature and relatively soft. That led to my favorite way of eating biscuits and molasses. I would place a large chunk of soft butter in the middle of a saucer of molasses I'd scraped off my knife or fork, and then stir the butter into the molasses with my knife. As I stirred the mixture, the ribbons of yellow butter would blend with the dark brown molasses, making a lighter-brown delicacy for the steaming hot biscuits, which were fresh out of the oven.

A half-dozen biscuits and molasses would give a person the energy needed for almost any task on the farm. No matter how poor you were, hot biscuits and molasses were a delicacy that Mrs. Marion made possible. We always looked forward to the fall when fresh sorghum-molasses would be made. I can smell 'them' molasses cooking now and I see those steaming biscuits fresh from the oven of Mother's wood cooking stove.

Mrs. Marion was truly a remarkable woman. She couldn't read and neither could Alec. Therefore, when she received a letter, which wasn't very often, she would bring the letter over for Mother to read to her. When she came over, she invariably wore her stiffly starched flower-print sunbonnet and an apron. We could see her come onto the porch through the glass in the door. She never knocked until she had cupped her hands on each side of her eyes and put them against the glass on the front door to block out the glare so she could see if anyone was home. I suppose she thought there wasn't any need to knock if no one was there. We never thought of that as being rude. Mrs. Marion was a lady. It was just Mrs. Marion, and she was a wonderful, hard-working neighbor who would help in any way she could.

BUTCHERING – LIVER, LARD AND LYE SOAP

In the late fall of each year, after the leaves had turned and dropped, and the corn had been shucked, it was time to give serious thought to butchering. This always occurred when the days wouldn't be too cold to work outside with bare, wet hands and yet cool enough to keep the meat for a few days until Dad could prepare his special sugar-cure mixture for the bacon, hams and shoulders of the butchered hogs. It was a time that we happily anticipated because we ate more meat than usual, including liver, which was always eaten fresh because it wouldn't keep long, even when refrigerated. Mother cooked fresh pork tenderloins, as well, and they were always a favorite.

This was before the days of home freezers or even commercial frozen-food lockers in town. Since any meat that was not cured with Dad's special sugar-cure recipe had to be eaten quickly, we had feasts ourselves and shared fresh meat with our neighbors. Dad's curing mixture included brown sugar, salt, red and black pepper, maybe saltpeter, and perhaps some other secret ingredients, and it was rubbed into the meat on all sides. Then the meat was hung in the smoke house to dry and cure. The neighbors and friends kept a mental balance sheet on what each had received at butchering time, and they always tried to pay back in kind. So we liked to see the neighbors butcher, at a different time of course, because they would share fresh meat with us, often liver, and this extended the fresh meat season.

We butchered hogs, and that's what I remember vividly as part of my boyhood days. We generally butchered two hogs each fall. It gave us a lot of meat which was okay because pork could be cured with Dad's mixture and would not spoil even without refrigeration. Beef couldn't be cured in the same way, but it could be canned or dried. When Grandpa and Grandma butchered a beef, they would usually share a quarter of it with us. They lived only about 12 miles east. One thing for certain – whether it was a hog or a steer that was butchered, the liver was consumed first because it had to be eaten quickly, lest it spoil.

Our butchering hogs were always very fat, maybe weighing 220 pounds on the hoof. The butchering had to go smoothly, so everything was well planned. Usually the preparation on butchering day started before dawn when we built a fire to heat barrels of boiling-hot water that was used to scald the hogs after they were killed. This loosened the hair and facilitated scraping the coarse and stiff hair from the hog's skin. We used sharp knives to do this and the knives were all sharpened days before. We would do the milking early so the chores could be finished and breakfast completed in time for an early start. Butchering was often done on Saturday so we children could be home from school to help.

The hogs to be slaughtered were isolated in a separate pen close to the butchering area. A rope block-and-tackle, which also was used to stretch barbed wire fence on the farm, was secured to a support pole near the area and used to lift the slaughtered hogs so we could douse them in the barrels of scalding hot water to loosen the hair, facilitating its removal. The water had to be the correct temperature so as not to 'set the hair,' making it hard to scrape off. If Dad could quickly dip his finger in the water three times and not get burned the temperature was just right.

A shovelful of wood ashes was put in the water to act as a cleansing agent and to help loosen the hair. The wood ashes had just enough natural lye in them to serve that purpose. Dad was always the one to kill the hog and severe the jugular vein to drain the blood so the meat would not be bloody. The hog was then

Butchering day.

dragged to the hoist, lifted and doused in the barrels of scalding hot water. After we removed the hair by scraping with butcher knives, the hoists were used to string the carcasses up for the disemboweling, cleaning and cutting the animal into quarters. The innards were put in a washtub and the liver, heart and other edible parts removed and cleaned. We didn't clean the gut for later stuffing with sausage as some did. Instead, these remains were mostly fed to the other hogs that would go to market.

Clean boards were placed nearby on saw horses to make a work area. After cleaning and washing the hanging carcasses, the four quarters of the hog would be cut apart and transferred to this temporary work table. Subsequently, the quarters were cut into hams, shoulders and bacon slabs. As the meat was trimmed, all of the fat went into a container, usually a washtub. The fat would later be cut in small pieces and rendered into lard. We put the lean scraps with a little fat in them in another container to be ground into sausage. We usually gave away such things as the pig's feet, the head and some other parts because there were many people who enjoyed these and considered them delicacies. I sensed that Mother didn't particularly relish the thought of cooking them, and we had plenty of meat. On butchering day, things had to be well organized beforehand so everything would go off without a hitch.

Butchering was exciting, but there was one part which I dreaded. I suspect that Dad dreaded it even more. That was when everything was ready including that big butcher knife that he would use to stick the hog. Dad would get his Remington 22-caliber pump rifle out of the bedroom closet where he kept both the rifle and the 12-gauge shotgun. The dreaded event was shooting the hogs. When all was ready, Dad would take deadly aim and kill each hog with one shot between and slightly above the eyes, putting the bullet directly into the brain. There wasn't even a squeal as Dad made the process quick and painless for the hogs. There were few smiles or jocular talk during the minutes from the loading of the gun until the killing process was over and the work of butchering started in earnest. This part of butchering was serious work. Killing a hog for butchering was not like going hunting and shooting a rabbit or a wild duck. We had lived close to these animals and fed them and watched them grow up. Butchering was a time of mixed emotions.

The cutting and trimming was mostly done by Dad or others experienced in butchering. There was little waste. The fat on the sides of the hogs under the skin was made into lard. The scraps of lean meat were cut away from the fat and later ground into sausage. The front legs from the knee up were called "shoulders" and the hind legs from the knee up were "hams." Today, both of these would be called hams, but we distinguished the shoulders from the hams. They were kept intact, with the skin on them, to be treated with the curing compound and hung in the smoke house along with the slabs of bacon. They could be smoked there, but generally we didn't go through that step since dad liked the hams, shoulders and bacons cured with his special sugar-curing compound. To him, the smoke flavor didn't add that much. These were not the modern tenderized, chemically treated hams you find in the stores today. They were home-cured hams that had a slightly strong, rich and lasting flavor.

The sausage was ground at the house. We had a sausage grinder that was powered by a washing machine motor. The wringer could be removed from Mother's Maytag washing machine and the sausage grinder placed on it. It was a simple process of grinding all of the lean scraps into sausage. The sausage could be canned or it could be eaten fresh. It wasn't cured. While Mother canned some, most of it was eaten fresh or given to the neighbors and relatives. We could keep quite a lot in the refrigerator. One thing for sure, the breakfasts with that fresh sausage, biscuits and gravy were very special during and immediately after butchering time.

The slabs of fat from the sides of the hogs were for lard and had to be cut into small cubes of about three-quarters of an inch on a side. This was a job that was done on a special lard-cutting board, which was a soft pine board about 24-by-30 inches and over an inch thick. The children helped in cutting the fat for the lard. We learned early to be very careful with those sharp knives. We all had a few cut fingers as we learned the process.

The lard was rendered by cooking the fat cubes and scrap pieces in a large round-bottomed cast iron kettle. The process was not unlike cooking the fat out of fat bacon slices. The rendering was done outside with an open fire under the cast iron kettle to cook the white pieces of fat until they were shriveled, brown and crisp. We strained the hot fat through a cotton muslin cloth into a tin five-gallon lard stand. We borrowed a hand-cranked lard press from a neighbor, and it was used to squeeze the fat from the solid material left after cooking was complete. All of this hot grease went into the lard stand, where it would eventually cool and become snow white. We kept the lard in the cellar where it was cool. We used lard for all our cooking. I have no idea how much cholesterol was added to our arteries as a result of cooking with that lard. But, the food was always very tasty.

Cutting and trimming meat. The fat goes in the washtub to be rendered into lard, and the lean pieces into the bowl to be ground for sausage.

The pressed cake, called cracklings, left from the lard press had a very crisp, fat bacon taste, although we did not eat it. It was used as the animal-fat ingredient that Mother needed to make soap. The following is one recipe for lye soap from Mother's family, and she no doubt used a variation of it, since her fat source was the cracklings cake:

Lye Soap

Equipment: Use a cast iron container and a wooden spoon. Instructions: One can of lye, 2.5 pints of cold soft water, 6 lbs. clean fat.

Instructions: Slowly add lye to cold water, stirring to dissolve. Melt fat. Have fat temperature at 85 degrees and lye solution at 75 degrees. Pour lye solution into melted fat in a thin, steady stream with slow even stirring. (Rapid pouring or stirring causes separation.) Continue to stir until wooden spoon can stand on its own. When all the lye is incorporated into the fat, pour into a cardboard or wooden box lined with old oil cloth or an old sheet. Let stand 24 hours. Cut into bars and remove. Keep dry at room temperature for 2 weeks, allowing it to cure.

The lye soap was used to launder the farmers' work clothes and had a brownish color. I'm certain it wasn't kind to the hands. Many a housewife must have had red hands from washing clothes with that strong soap. No doubt that added to the aura of the mild soaps such as Ivory and Lux that were advertised on the radio as being gentle on the hands.

Butchering provided meat for the winter, spring and on into the summer. Usually the cured hams would be a little strong and salty after a year and some soaking was needed to help remove the curing compound before the meat was cooked. This older meat seemed very strong to me, but Dad had developed a taste for it. We didn't have fried chickens in the winter, since the homegrown fryers came only in the summer. So the meat from butchering carried us through the winter, and, on occasion, included a ham bone in a pot of beans. That made a mighty good meal when spiced with a little homemade tomato-and-pickle relish that mother made from garden products.

HOUSEHOLD FUEL FOR THE YEAR

Until the 1940's, we had two stoves, one with a large firebox for heating the house, and another with a small firebox and a large cooking surface for preparing our meals. Although we had electric lights, we didn't have electric heaters or hot plates. Nor did we have an electric toaster – toast was made in the oven. But we did have an electric waffle iron that was often used on Sunday morning when we could have a leisurely breakfast. It cooked one waffle at a time, so we had to eat in one-person shifts. Except for the waffle iron, our electrical appliances consisted of a small refrigerator, a Maytag electric washing machine and a heavy electric iron. Coffee was made in a drip coffeemaker on the cooking stove.

Our household fuel was wood that we gathered on the farm. We never bought wood for heating or cooking. In the early winter, after all of the crops had been harvested, we would cut logs from trees in the hill pasture. We would bring those logs down and stack them between the house and chicken house. Ultimately, they would be sawed into lengths of about 15 inches.

On occasion, dad would sell a few oak trees that were large enough for lumber, to a sawmill. The lumber for the barn all came from the farm, and a temporary sawmill was set up in the hill pasture to make logs from the farm into rough construction lumber. The sawmill used only the main trunks of the trees, leaving the tops and the crooked limbs, usually six or more inches in diameter, for fire wood. When we hadn't sold trees to a sawmill, we would get our firewood by selecting trees that didn't have commercial lumber value or were in areas where the timber needed to be thinned. Dad would deaden a tree selected for firewood by cutting the bark away in a ring around the base of the tree. With the bark severed, the tree would die. He would do this several months, or even a year, in advance of cutting the tree and the wood would dry.

We didn't have chain saws at that time, so all of the sawing was done by hand with a crosscut saw about six feet long and fitted with a handle at each end. This was a two-man job and, in our case, that meant my dad and a boy – John, me or Glenn. Other tools used included an axe or two, several wedges and a sledgehammer to drive the wedges into the wood. Wedges were used to split logs and also were driven into the saw grove when the tree was leaning so the saw blade wouldn't bind, or we said get pinched. Dad could control the direction that the tree would fall by precutting and chipping out the wood with an axe on one side of the tree, and then finishing the cut from the other side and using wedges to control the direction a tree would fall. Dad was good at felling a tree in the precise direction he wanted it to go.

The same horse- or mule-drawn wagons that we used for other farm purposes were used for hauling the long logs from the hill pasture to the area behind the house where they would be cut to proper

Daughter bringing wood for the cooking stove.

lengths for firewood. The hay frame or grain box was removed from the wagons and wooden stakes put in the metal loops on posts that held the wagon bed in place. The long logs would extend way behind the wagon and even drag the ground as we hauled them to the house. A typical log might be up to 20 feet long and eight inches or more in diameter at the large end. The large end of the log was always loaded in the front of the wagon.

It was an art for two people to load these heavy logs on the wagon. We would drag the log beside the wagon and remove the stakes on the sides of the wagon frame. Then dad and I would lift the heavy end up and temporarily rest it on the front wheel hub. Next we would get a new hold and hoist it up to the top of the front wheel, and finally over onto the support above the front axle of the wagon. Last, we would lift the lighter other end of the log up. We learned to get a good hold and lift with our leg muscles so we wouldn't injure our backs when we lifted these heavy logs.

We would stack all of the limbs that were too small for firewood in a pile near the wood collection site and burn them on a day when there was no wind or danger of the fire spreading. Often we took some of the small pieces to the house to be used as kindling to start fires.

After the long fire logs were stacked in a pile between the house and chicken house, Dad would arrange for our neighbor, Roy Marion, to come with his saw rig to cut the wood into lengths suitable for use in the heating stove and for splitting into sizes for the cook stove. Roy's saw rig was bolted to the front of his tractor and a short belt from the tractor pulley drove the large circular saw. There was no protection from the rapidly spinning, 24-inch saw, so we had to be very careful. No children were allowed near it. Usually Roy, Dad and a boy could do the work. The men could take the heavy end of a log and lift it to a special support to be slid into the rapidly spinning saw. The lighter end of the log was on the ground or held by the boy. Roy would position the log so the stove wood would be the proper length. Then with Dad holding the end they would slide the log into the high-speed saw cutting off one piece of firewood. Dad would hold the piece cut wood and toss it into the wood pile. The process was quickly repeated. It's surprising how fast the work went. The wood was usually left in a pile and not stacked further.

If the pieces of firewood were too large in diameter for the heating stove, they were split with an axe or a wedge. Usually, the oak wood had been dead long enough for the spitting to be done with an axe, but if there were many knots, the wedge might be required. One of the jobs for a boy was to keep enough firewood on the back porch so we wouldn't have to go to the wood pile at night to get fuel for the heating stove. Wood on the back porch was protected from rain and would be kept dry.

The wood for the cooking stove had to fit into the fire chamber of the stove, which was about six inches on a side and 20 inches long. There was a door in front and the cast-iron top sections could be removed and wood could be placed in the fire box from the top. Most of the wood for the cooking stove was split into pieces about three inches across. That meant that all of the wood for the cooking stove had to be split with an axe. We boys learned to do that at about ten to twelve years of age. We were carefully shown how to do it and constantly reminded of how dangerous an axe could be. Many serious foot cuts occurred in chopping wood. We used a chopping block or a large piece of wood on the ground so when the piece we were chopping split, the axe would go into the chopping block and not our shin or foot. None of us were injured with cuts from an axe, but it was not uncommon.

One of the early tasks for very young children was to carry in wood for the cooking stove. That stove was used every day of the year and a lot of wood had to be carried in regularly. We had a woodbox close to the stove in front of the west kitchen window. It was about two-feet square with an open top and two feet deep. That wood box had to be filled regularly and that was one my early chores. I am sure that Helen and John also had that job many times, as well, since the wood was not heavy and small children could do it.

Another job was to be sure that there was dry kindling available for quickly starting fires. We used dry wood chips, dry corn cobs or whatever would ignite quickly. If the stove was cold, and there were no burning embers, Mother might use a little coal oil to start a fire but that was never used if there was a possibility that hot coals might be present, lest there be an explosion.

In the early 1940s Mother got an electric range, so the burden of starting a fire to cook with each morning ended. The wood stove was called a cook stove and the electric one was called a range. Later dad purchased an oil burning heating stove. We had a large elevated heating fuel oil tank in back of the house with a fuel line directly to the stove. So, with that purchase, the days of going to the hill and cutting logs for household fuel ended. I am sure no one hated to see the end of carrying in wood for these old wood burning stoves each day.

FLOODS

Ritchey is located on the north side of the Shoal Creek flood plain. The creek itself is across the flood plain immediately adjacent to the steep hills that form the south side of the valley. The flood plain is quite flat and is about a quarter mile wide at Ritchey.

Shoal Creek would be considered a small river in most parts of the country. It is fed by springs and seepage from the hills all along its course and continues to flow even during the most severe droughts. Any stream that periodically floods has a natural levee along its banks, where the coarsest sediment carried by the floodwaters is quickly deposited as the stream overflows. So the lowest point in the valley is always a distance from the stream bank itself. The low point in the Ritchey valley is about a fourth of the way from the stream to the town.

The bottomland of our farm extended from the road south of Ritchey to the east about a quarter of a mile. Our farm comprised the entire valley for a quarter mile just east of Ritchey. Judge Matthew Ritchey, who founded the town and built its first grist mill, was the original owner of our farm.

The Frisco Railroad followed a straight or gently curving line up the meandering valley sometimes on one side of the valley and sometimes on the other. On occasion, when the meanders took the stream all the way across the valley, the railroad track crossed the creek on a wooden trestle bridge. When the creek flooded, the flood water was usually confined to the valley between the streambed and the elevated roadbed of the tracks. But backwater flooding was common in the low areas on the side of the tracks opposite the stream.

Flooded railroad tracks.

Ritchey's buildings never flooded because a small, intermittent tributary flowed out of the hills to the north, right through the center of town. That stream was spring-fed and, although it did not have much flow during droughts, there was always water in the deeper holes in its bed which provided water for livestock. In fact, this small tributary, locally called 'The Branch,' was no doubt a major reason why the village was built at that precise spot.

The floods of geologic past had caused a small and nearly imperceptible alluvial fan to extend into the Shoal Creek valley, and that placed the town's buildings high enough to be protected from Shoal Creek's floods.

Our house, on the southeast edge of the town, was also high enough that water never got to it. But the barn was a foot or so lower and, on two occasions, the flood waters came up to the edge of the barn foundation. We did get water in the cellar at the house a few times when the floods caused the water table to rise to near the surface. The floods at Ritchey didn't normally pose a danger to humans. Our concern was erosion of valuable top soil in the fields between the tracks and the creek, and loss of animals and crops. Erosion was particularly bad when the floodwater's strong current ripped through recently plowed fields. In a few cases erosion was as deep as the field had been plowed, perhaps six

Automobile fording a flooded road.

inches. Literally thousands of tons of nutrient rich soil were lost and that would adversely affect production for several years.

Spring was the most critical flood season when we had our heaviest rains. Still, Dad told me floods could occur at any time and the creek had been known to overflow its banks in every month of the year. Shoal Creek was not a flash-flood stream. It took several days of rain to soak the ground and cause the upstream tributaries to flood or run full bank-to-bank. When all of that water accumulated in Shoal Creek, it would overflow its banks and water would flow down the valley and across the road leading south from Ritchey. Cars could ford that water until it was over the running boards, generally approaching a foot deep. As the flow got deeper, the road to the south became impassable. Then if we wanted to go south we had to detour to the north or east, driving an extra 20 miles or more.

The roads became impassable to cars long before the water was dangerously deep. In fact, except for severe floods, we could wade the flooded area. But wading was dangerous because the floods would wash out fences and there was the chance of getting tangled in submerged barbed wire. There was always the possibility of barbed wire getting tangled in your clothes and the current would pull you under. Most likely, that would be the end. Fear of the wire made us very cautious about wading in the flood waters.

Once, however, I wasn't as cautious as I should have been and it could have been very serious.

Word came to school that 'the creek was up,' and the school bus was taking Ritchey kids home at mid-afternoon while the road was still passable. We'd just started basketball practice, so I decided to stay and practice. A teammate, Chuck Hailey, said he would take me home in his parents' car since there would be no bus that afternoon after practice.

When we reached the south side of the flooded creek, the water didn't look too bad, but it was much too high for Chuck's car. Our house was only a quarter mile away, but detouring around this crossing by car would have involved a 40-mile drive. So I told Chuck I would wade across, since the water only looked about waist deep.

I went upstream away from the fences to cross. So I was less concerned about submerged barbed wire. At first it wasn't too bad, but when I reached the deepest flooded area, the water was waist deep and the current was much stronger than I'd expected. I moved forward very slowly and carefully, mentally planning what I'd do if I lost my footing and was swept away by the current.

Dad had told me that if I was ever caught in the floodwaters I should try to relax and swim perpendicular to the current, letting it carry me downstream to wherever I might finally reach the shore. Trying to fight the current to get to a specific point on the opposite shore would quickly sap your energy and you could very easily drown.

As I inched forward gripping the mud with my toes (I was carrying my shoes and socks), I was forced downstream. I thought what might happen if I stepped into a scour hole, and then tried not to think about it.

I knew I was in a serious situation, but I tried to stay cool and to handle the circumstance one step at a time without rushing or panicking. After what seemed like hours, but was probably less than a minute or two, I realized the water was dropping below my waist as I inched forward. I was across the deepest part and I breathed a sigh of relief. Walking got easier, and soon I was slogging knee-deep out of the muck.

Suddenly, I realized how cold I was. And then I noticed that through it all, I had kept my shoes, socks and wristwatch dry. These were all valuable items, and the Depression-era need to save expensive possessions had apparently remained strong, even in my subconscious. I was just a few hundred yards from home now, and I scampered across the tracks for the house, with its warm stove and dry clothes.

When I got home, Mother looked startled and demanded to know what I'd been up to. I put on my coolest demeanor and casually told her that I'd crossed the flooded valley on the way home. I assured her that it was no big deal and that I zipped across with no more problem than you'd have crossing the street. She didn't buy it and told me never to do that again. But she wasn't too hard on me. I think she was relieved that I'd made it home safely.

One spring we had a terribly big flood and floodwaters were up when we went to bed. During floods, we would often go down the road south of town and see how high the water came up along the very gently sloping road. You could place a stick on the road at the waterline and if the water was rising, the stick was soon in the water and floating away. Conversely, with a declining flood, the water receded from the stick. On that night, the water was rising when we went to bed.

I was in deep sleep when Dad awakened me at about two a. m. and said to get my clothes on right away. The hog pen was flooded and the pigs were drowning. I had never seen a flood so immense. The flood water was way up to the southeast corner of the barn. All the cattle were on the hill pasture, so they were safe. I dressed quickly, took a flashlight and went to the hog pen, where Dad was already out in the water working to get the pigs to safety. The main problem was that the sows had recently had litters and the baby pigs couldn't cope with the situation. Except for Glenn, who was too young, the whole family was in the water that night using the flashlight to locate and then try to herd swimming pigs through a gate and onto firm, if muddy, ground.

We floated a flat-bottom washtub as a small boat for the baby pigs. Wading in water three feet deep and holding the floating wash tub, we collected the struggling piglets. We finally moved all we could locate to another hog pasture north of the barn and well above the flood waters. After this ordeal of an hour or so, we went back to bed. By dawn the water had receded some and we could survey the damage. Of the fifty or so baby pigs, we probably lost a third of them. We also lost a couple of shoats. They should have survived, but apparently swam the wrong way and got way out in the deeper water.

That flood was very devastating. All the corn that had been planted was lost. And some of the fields where the floodwater had been deepest and the current the fastest had suffered very severe erosion. In one cornfield, the six inches of loose, plowed soil was almost completely gone. While losing a crop was bad, losing that soil was worse and I definitely sensed that in comments from Dad. But he never complained or felt sorry for himself. Floods were just another natural event that we had to deal with.

We had a lot of fencing to rebuild and that could be done before the fields were dry enough to work. Floods brought additional work for all of us. And yet, during the actual flood, after we had protected the animals by taking them to higher ground, there wasn't much to do. We mostly waited for the water to go down, and that might take two or more days.

Dad was a voracious reader and would read anything he could get his hands on. As a boy I never enjoyed reading much because I always seemed to have other, more interesting, things to do. But that particular flood lasted so long that even I took up reading along with Dad. I still remember the two books I read in those couple of days. One was a chronicle by Eddie Rickenbacher about a downed military aircraft crew spending more than 20 days on a small raft in the Pacific Ocean. That book, "Seven Came Back," seemed a fitting story to read during a flood. At that time Ritchey seemed to be floating in an ocean of its own.

Mother was a worrier. Dad did not outwardly worry, but Mother fretted about the losses. Dad would settle in a comfortable chair and read, seemingly oblivious to all the havoc the water was causing. I remember that Mother would interrupt and ask many questions, such as his estimate of the damage and the problems the flood was causing. Dad generally would ignore most of the questions and only look up occasionally to comment. I recall one time when Mother had asked several questions and made comments about the flood damage; Dad finally looked up impatiently and said, "I know Ada, but what the hell do you want me to do about it?" The message was consistent with his philosophy. There was no use worrying about those things he couldn't change.

During those big floods, the railroad suffered major damage. Although much of the roadbed was above the high-water line, there were some low areas where the rushing waters from stream tributaries, or the main current, crossed the tracks and washed the gravel from around the railroad crossties. Sometimes there also was damage around the bridges. This meant that all railroad traffic had to stop until the tracks could be inspected and repaired. Temporary repairs would be made so the trains could pass slowly and the tracks would be permanently repaired later when there was more time. The railroad would hire temporary labor during the time after floods, and it paid well, maybe more than 50 cents an hour. This far exceeded the normal labor rate of 25 cents an hour. One year, my older brother, John, worked for the railroad for a time after a flood. I wanted to, but I wasn't old enough, and I had to help Dad repair the downed fences until the fields were dry enough to work. After all, John was a teenager and he needed some spending money for dates and the like, and it was a good opportunity for him to earn some 'big money.'

Even if we did have occasional floods to deal with, farming in the bottoms was much better than farming in the rocky hills around Ritchey. Our land was more fertile and less droughty than the shallow, rocky hill soil. And our corn crops were better than most of those grown on higher ground with

Great Grandfather Smerdon, who emigrated from England in 1872.

Dad's corn averaging over 50 bushels per acre, just about the highest in the county at that time. Even if we had a few days of travail every so often, we wouldn't have swapped farms on an acre for acre basis with any of our neighbors.

Historical postscript: My great grandfather emigrated from Devonshire, England in 1872 and ultimately arrived in southwest Missouri in 1873 about 10 miles east of Ritchey near Pierce City. My Great Uncle Will describes a flood of July 3, 1875 on Clear Creek, a tributary of Shoal Creek. Uncle Will's account follows:

"THE FLOOD – JULY 3, 1875

A never to be forgotten experience happened this summer. On the night of July 3, 1875, there came up one of those terrible summer deluges with thunder and much lightening, and the upper reaches of Clear Creek and its drainage were flooded. About three o'clock in the morning Father was awakened by the roar of the rushing water in the creek and got up to investigate. The muddy water was about to come into the house. The floor was only eighteen inches off the ground. They awakened the children and said we all must get, as this was within fifty yards of the main channel of the creek. We waded out to higher ground in the darkness as we had no lantern. We could only see where we were going by the flashes of lightning. We waded water for about 250 yards. I remember it was waist deep to me and sometimes up to my armpits. We went to our nearest neighbor's home, a James Looney, who very kindly took us in for a few days until the water ran down and we could clean the house where the water had been four feet high in the house as shown by the mud on the walls.

At daylight next morning, the rail fence that we had followed in wading out was all gone. Everyone said that if we had been one hour later coming out we would most likely all have drowned as we were on the down stream side of the fence. The next day some folks were taken out in boats from their homes in the bottoms. This was the first Fourth of July that I remember. In the year 1875! My mind is as clear on this as though it had happened quite recently. I waded in front of my mother. Mother carried brother John, who was a baby. Father carried Sister Emily, and Brother Tom, who was next eldest to me, held Father's hand as he waded along by his side. He sometimes lost his footing and just floated along. Rail fences were swept away and lodged in drifts in the timbered bottoms."

Baby John, my grandfather, was born on August 29, 1873, so he would have been about 22 months old when this flood occurred. Great Uncle Will (b. Dec. 21, 1867) wrote this in 1941, toward the end of his life. He would have been about seven and a half when the event occurred. Grandpa subsequently owned and farmed that farm. In fact, he spent his entire life on that one farm. However, the buildings were moved out of the creek bottom. Grandpa's house and other buildings were on a hill overlooking Clear Creek and its valley. No longer were homes built in the floodplain, as was this log cabin of Great Grandfather Smerdon. I remember one grain bin constructed of wood with hand made square nails and wooden pegs that had been on this original flooded site in 1875. It was subsequently moved up on the hill and still stands.

FIRES

In Ritchey you wouldn't talk to very many people until you realized that several families had a personal experience with a fire that adversely affected their lives. It could be a house or a barn that had been destroyed by fire. We didn't think of it much, yet we knew that a fire could have a devastating effect on the family. Dad didn't smoke and was very strict regarding smoking in the barn, where there was always dry straw litter and the hay loft, which was often full of dry and highly inflammable loose hay. One spark and it would be gone. No one in our family smoked, so his admonitions were mostly for the hired help. He was also very careful about putting hay in the loft that was too green or wet, which could lead to spontaneous combustion. We had lightning rods on the barn to protect it from lightning. The barn was tall and it was hit by lightning once that I know of, but with no damage. The house was surrounded by tall maple trees, which provided some protection from lightening, but it did not have lightening rods.

I can't say that we boys didn't experiment with smoking dried corn silks or mullein, a weed that grew in the pastures. On reflection, I know of no earthly reason why we smoked these things except to feel grown up. Dried mullein leaves could be crumbled to look like tobacco. We smoked these in the corn cob pipes we made out of carefully selected large corn cobs and pieces of maple twig for the stems. We would cut the cob to the proper length and hollow the center of the cob out with a pocket knife. The bowl of the pipe was quite small in diameter, so we couldn't get much smoking material in it. Then, we would drill a small hole in the side for the stem. We'd then cut a green maple twig about three-eights of an inch in diameter and, with a stiff wire, poke through the soft pithy center to hollow it out. You might have to try three or four stems before you got a good one, but we persisted until we had a homemade pipe.

When neighbor boys and I smoked dried corn silks or mullein east of the barn and out of sight of the house, we stayed away from the straw around the barn because Dad had instilled in my mind the dangers of smoking near the barn. There was no exhilarating effect of the smoke except a feeling of being grown up. The main effect was the sore tongue from the blazing hot smoke that came straight through that hollow stem with no filter or other means of cooling it until it hit your tongue. If it hadn't taken so long for the sore tongue to heal, we might have smoked more of the stuff since smoking was the grown up thing to do according to all of the magazine ads.

I guess it's natural for small children to play with matches. I vaguely remember one time that I had some wooden kitchen matches in my bib overall pocket. I guess I had taken them from the big nickel box of kitchen matches Mother kept in a drawer close to the cooking stove. I couldn't have been more than six years old and I don't know why I had the matches. I had gone to town for something and on the way back I stopped to play with the matches in front of an old barn, which was across the street and west of our house, just east of the alley. This barn was no longer used and partially collapsed. I was out front, not in the barn, but I accidentally set the dead grass on fire. I thought I had stomped it out before I rushed home. Anyway, later I recall someone telling of the grass fire that they extinguished just before it reached the barn, where no doubt it could have ignited that dry, old barn in short order. Although I was very young, I knew in my heart that I had nearly caused a major fire. I never played with matches again and, for that matter, I never told anyone of the incident until this writing.

In those days, there were too many fires. Maybe it was because there were no nearby fire departments. And the codes for electrical wiring and for stoves were non-existent or not enforced. Coal oil heaters and stoves that were not vented were used to heat homes. At night, light was provided by coal oil lamps with glass chimneys. No doubt there were many other fire hazards that were too often ignored.

The original Ritchey mill was built south of Ritchey on Shoal Creek in 1835 by Matthew H. Ritchey. That mill burned and its replacement, the second Ritchey mill, was built on the same location after the Civil War. This second mill made flour, cornmeal and ground cattle feed. For a while, that mill was run by John H. Barrett, who built an ice plant east of it. That plant furnished ice for the entire region, including Joplin and Webb City. The ice plant adjacent to the mill burned on July 24, 1936. I have a fuzzy recollection of seeing those flames leaping into the sky as I watched from a south window in our house, which was about a quarter mile due north. I have pondered, as I write this, whether I actually saw the flames when I was a little more than six, or whether I simply recall the vivid descriptions of the fire by others. I don't really know for sure, but I definitely think I saw the fire.

At one time, Ritchey had a grain elevator beside the railroad track just south of our house. That elevator was used to store the wheat that the farmers would bring in until it could be shipped by train. It was a big elevator for those days and very important to the community and the surrounding farmers. However, I never saw the elevator because I understood it had burned before I was born. It was never rebuilt and that part of the history of the town perhaps went up in smoke. I played on the rock foundation of that building, which I suppose is still there. I say "perhaps went up in smoke" because, subsequently, I have heard that the elevator was razed. I don't know the true story, but it was not uncommon for grain elevators to burn because of the highly combustible dry grain dust that was always present.

The biggest house ever in Ritchey was Captain J. M. Ritchey's house that stood on a little rise at the north edge of town, just northwest of where Ray's Store is now located. That house overlooked the town, had four acres of land and a large front lawn. It had three stories in the front and two in the back with 24 rooms and a full basement. It was the first modern house in Ritchey with indoor plumbing. Everyone called it the 'Ritchey Mansion,' and it was still called that long after the house was gone. I don't know when the house was built, but it burned in 1920. I remember playing on the foundation of this magnificent home destroyed by fire.

In the early years the school had a May Day event on what was the original large front yard of that old home. Poles were put up, and each class did an in-and-out skipping May Pole dance where we wound our colored crepe-paper streamers around the May Pole in a weaving pattern. Based on the grounds and pictures that mansion must have been elegant. It was the most historical house in Ritchey situated to overlook the village that Captain Ritchey's father, the original owner of our farm, had founded. The Ritchey mansion was never rebuilt. Again, fire had wiped from the face of the earth something that was architecturally very beautiful.

Fire also destroyed our hen house about the time I was born. That fire occurred during the night and, since there was no electrical storm or electrical appliances or heat in the hen house, the cause of

The Ritchey mansion. This house, built by Captain J. M. Ritchey, son of Judge Matthew H. Ritchey the founder of Ritchey, was the largest ever built in the village. It burned after the Civil War, some say as a result of Bushwacker action.

the fire was highly suspect. The building burned to ashes and afterwards the burned carcasses of the hens were counted. Although, the count could not be totally accurate, it was considerably less than the known number of hens in the house. Since stealing chickens sometimes occurred in those days, Dad always suspected that a bunch of chickens had been stolen during the night and the hen house set on fire to destroy any evidence. However, that could never be proven. That fire occurred before I was old enough to remember, so I only recall the replacement hen house that was built to the exact same design on the same foundation.

I do recall when our brooder house burned. It was located between the house and the barn, perhaps 80 or 100 feet east of the house. It was an un-insulated building and it was a cold night. The coal oil brooder stove was no doubt going full blast to keep the baby chicks warm. The fire probably started from the brooder stove and, with the dry straw litter on the floor, it was only a matter of minutes before the house and its contents of several hundred baby chicks were engulfed in flames. The fire occurred at night and I watched as a small child with a degree of horror from the east window of our bedroom. We didn't rebuild the brooder house and, instead, converted the existing smoke house to a brooder house for future chick raising.

Perhaps the fire with the greatest effect on us was when Grandma and Grandpa's house burned. They lived 10 miles east of us near Pierce City. At the time Grandpa was seriously ill in the hospital in Springfield and Grandma was up there with him. No one knows how the fire started. Uncle Willie, who lived across the street, was the first there and tried to save things. Grandpa had just bought a new innerspring mattress and Uncle Willie tried to save it as the newest purchase, but couldn't get it out of the upstairs window. As the fire closed in, he grabbed an armful of clothes from the closet, but couldn't get them because some of the hangers were hooked from the front and some from the back.

He couldn't just rip out an armload of clothes and throw them out the window, and he didn't have time to unhook them one by one. Uncle Willie and helpers did manage to save the old player-piano and some perforated paper rolls of player piano music. But all of the hand-worked lace and linens and other things from the Liste family in Germany that Grandma had so carefully protected were lost. Also, Dad's cherished large collection of books that he had accumulated as a boy was gone. We didn't have the space to store them in our home in Ritchey, so he had left the books with his parents for safekeeping.

I remember the telephone call informing Dad of that fire. We had just finished supper after our evening chores. We immediately got in the car and drove up there. All that was left were the hot coals, and the firemen from Pierce City were pumping water on those. It was a sad day for us all, particularly for Dad and poor Grandpa, who was very ill in the hospital. He wasn't told of the fire for sometime – until he was well on his way to recovery.

One of the most heart-stopping moments of my life occurred when I was in high school and got on the school bus at Midway High to come home. The bus driver, who had a rather sick sense of humor, told me our house had burned down, but no one was hurt. My spirit left my body as I thought of all of the personal things that were lost forever. I sank and my mind raced – and where would we live? Then the driver told me it was the vacant old house across the street, which Dad owned. I was relieved beyond belief. A comment on this event is covered separately in the essay, "Bedbugs."

The final fire that I will mention occurred after we all left home and Mother had sold the farm. Mother was no longer the owner, so it wasn't our monetary loss. I am glad she didn't see it burn. However, we had memories of the farm and the barn as did our children. They loved to visit their grandparents on the farm. The beautiful red barn with its curved arch roof and two big ventilators on the top of the roof, and cow and horse weather vanes on each end, was gone. We all knew every nook and cranny in that barn. It was heart breaking to learn of it. It was really the landmark of Ritchey and

The Smerdon barn and related buildings including the house on the right. The barn, a landmark in Ritchey, burned after Mother had sold the farm.

was situated right at the east edge of town, at the end of Main Street.

Apparently, the fire wasn't during a storm, so it couldn't have been lightning. And the loft was empty, eliminating spontaneous combustion as a likely cause. The cause was officially of undetermined origin. The loss was so great to me that for many years I did not want to return to Ritchey. Our family was no longer there, so why would I want to return? In one sense the barn was more important in my life than the house where I ate and slept and did my homework. The barn was the focus of our farm life, and it was where most of the daydreaming of my youth occurred.

I have returned to Ritchey several times since that barn, which Dad and helpers built during the winter of 1926-27, burned. But it isn't the same without that beautiful barn, and it never will be.

A barn burning at night.

WASH DAY MONDAY

Monday was always wash day. Who decreed this, I don't know, but Monday was wash day. We grew up with that knowledge from nursery rhymes. Tea towels sets embroidered with the various tasks for each day of the week depicted Monday as the day to wash clothes. On Monday, the job of washing was an all-day task: heating water, washing and rinsing several tub loads, hanging the clothes on the line and then taking them down, folding, ironing and putting them away. People in Ritchey didn't deviate from the Monday tradition because your day's work (and how well you had done it) was there hanging on the clothesline behind the house for all to see.

It was a day of hard work but, compared to some who washed their clothes by hand on a washboard in a washtub, Mother had a relatively good situation for laundering clothes. Early in their marriage, Dad bought her an electric Maytag washing machine. I think Helen may have been a baby when they got that electric model, with a wringer and an oscillating agitator in a square aluminum tub with rounded corners. In the inventory of their assets at the end of 1929, Dad estimated the value of everything he owned. He gave the value of that washing machine as $150, more than any mule or cow. No piece of farm equipment was valued so high with the binder and side delivery rake, both at $70. In fact, the washing machine was the most expensive thing they owned except the one-year old car (1929 Chevrolet @ $600 and the house and lots @ $1050). I have that inventory, written in Dad's hand, and dated January 1, 1930. He made two Maytag payments in 1929 totaling $20.54. Mother enjoyed cleanliness and was so proud of that washing machine. Before that machine, washing was done by hand using a wash board with a rippled metal washing surface. To get clothes clean with a wash board required hot water, strong lye soap — and a lot of 'elbow grease.'

The washing machine was the first major modern appliance that Mother had and to her it was the most important. It's very difficult to keep a farmer's work clothes clean. The clothes were always sweaty and frequently the overalls would be very dirty from working with cows, often in muddy cow lots. So a modern machine, with the agitator oscillat-

Washing clothes by hand on an old fashioned wash board.

ing in rotational motion and a wringer, was a real work saver for the farm wife.

Wash day started with heating wash water. Since we didn't have running water or a hot water heater in the house in the early days, the water was heated by a wood fire outside. We had a cast iron, round-bottom kettle that was about 30 inches in diameter. The kettle had three, stubby short legs and it was easy to build a fire under it. It was best to have the water very hot. So it might take an hour or more to heat it. On very cold days in the middle of winter or when it was raining, the water could be heated in a big elongated copper container on the wood cooking stove in the kitchen.

The setup for washing included the machine and two large rinse-water washtubs, a first rinse and a second rinse. These gal-

Typical wash day setup in the 1930's - a Maytag washing machine with wringer, identical to the one Mother had. The two washtubs are for rinsing the clothes.

vanized iron washtubs were about 30 inches in diameter. Referred to as a number 2 washtub, they had many other uses such as for the Saturday night baths, since we didn't have a bathroom. Another was to cool watermelons in the summer, where the tub could be filled with cool well water. Washtubs were handy for washing large quantities of vegetables during summer canning season and for all sorts of other things such as a container to hold meat during butchering.

We used hot water in the washing machine while the rinse waters were unheated. Mother used homemade lye soap which was cut in big bars that looked like giant, light-colored homemade brownies. The bars were about four inches square and two inches thick. Sometimes a child's job was to shave the soap in thin slices so it would quickly dissolve in the hot water in the machine.

The clothes were carefully sorted by color and degree of dirtiness. The white items were washed first. Next came the colored clothes and last were the work clothes, including the blue denim overalls and the blue cotton chambray work shirts. Generally, all the washing was done with the same wash water. The wash water and rinse waters became darker and soapier as the wash loads passed through. If the second rinse became too soapy and discolored, it would be replaced with clean water and then become the first rinse.

In the winter, washing was a cold job. The wash water was usually so hot initially that a wooden washing stick, a shortened old broom handle, would be used to fish the washed clothes from the machine so they could be fed through the wringer into the first rinse. After being agitated by hand to get the soap out in the cold first rinse, the clothes would again go through the wringer to the second cold rinse, where the final agitation by hand would remove the last bit of soap. The final step was wringing the water from the second rinse in the third and final pass through the wringer, with the damp clothes going into a clothes basket. For the white clothes, bluing could be added to the last rinse and the clothes were often starched. The clothes were then hung by hand on the metal clothes line.

The wringer position could be changed by swinging it on its mounting post, which was at one corner of the square tub washing machine. That way, all three wringing operations for each wash load were easily achieved. The wringer had two, counter-rotating, two-inch-diameter hard rubber rollers powered by the washing machine motor. You could get a finger or even an arm in the wringer if you weren't very careful. There was an emergency stop on the wringer so major harm usually didn't result when those accidents occurred. Salesmen would demonstrate the safety by putting a hand or forearm in the spring loaded wringer. Still, the women had to be very careful not to get loose fitting clothes they were wearing caught in the wringer. Only those who have observed women washing clothes with the old-style, wringer machine, can properly visualize the origins of the crude expression, 'she got her tit in the wringer,' indicating a most serious circumstance.

Hanging the washed clothes to dry on the long galvanized metal clothesline was no easy task. The line first had to be cleaned of oxidized metal that had accumulated on it since the last washing because it would leave a dark streak on the clothes. In the winter, when it was below freezing, hanging wet clothes was a very cold job. Mother couldn't handle the clothes and manage clothespins with gloves, without dropping some of the laundry on the dirty ground. So it was a bare handed job. The clothes were still hung outside in frigid weather because even though they would freeze, they would still dry. In the winter, drying might take more than one day. If it was raining, the clothes could be dried inside by the stove on a collapsible rack.

The ironing in the early days was done with heavy irons that were heated on the stove. The mass of the solid metal in the irons helped them hold their heat and you could iron continuously with three irons, one to iron with, while two were reheating. But you had to work fast. And the irons were very heavy. Again, the origin of the expression, 'she has too many irons in the fire,' no doubt came from wash day work.

Before ironing, the dry clothes would be sprinkled with water from a bottle, often a pop bottle that had a small sprinkler top. Sprinkled clothes left too long would mildew, so if ironing was delayed, they could be put in the refrigerator to prevent mildew and the necessary rewashing. The washing and ironing for a farm wife was a laborious task, even with an old-style, electric, wringer washing machine. There were no automatic washers with numerous wash and spin-dry cycles. There were no temperature-controlled tumble dryers to fluff clothes. There were no wash-and-wear fabrics. And there were no Teflon-coated, lightweight irons with accurate temperature controls and pushbutton spray or steam-iron features.

It's no wonder that people wore the same clothes for several days and changed only when they were 'dirty'. Dirty was defined as having visible dirt or a detectable odor, not because the garments had been on your body several times since last washed. We had school clothes, work clothes and Sunday-school clothes. We changed into work clothes as soon as we came home from school, in order to get several days wear between washings. Work clothes and school clothes were the same overalls and solid-color shirts, except the former might have visible soiled spots and been mended or patched more times.

It was during this time in the 1930's that soap companies, such as Proctor and Gamble, began to market their products by radio. Radios were becoming common in homes that had electricity, and these companies sponsored the on-going serials of the trials and tribulations of "Oxydol's Old Ma Perkins," "Stella Dallas," and others. Since they were promoting soap products such as Oxydol and Rinso, these radio shows became known as 'soap operas,' and the afternoon television shows remain so-called today, usually shortened to 'Soaps.' The advertisers chided housewives for having dirty, 'tattletale gray' sheets on the clothes line (all sheets were white then), and 'ring around the collar' on men's dress shirts (also only white). They claimed their products would make them 'white and bright.' The soap companies also advertised the gentleness of their product that would save housewife's hands from being red and rough.

Although our clothes were usually worn several days between washings and we didn't bathe daily, being clean was always stressed and being asked by Mother after washing up, "Did you wash behind your ears?" was a standard query. My answer was always "yes," but that didn't mean that after inspection I wouldn't be sent back to do the job again with the admonishment, "You better scrub with a washrag this time."

SATURDAY NIGHT BATH

Until early 1940, when we remodeled and greatly expanded our house, we lived in a small, four-room house. Each room was square and 14 feet on a side. The children's bedroom had two double beds and I slept with my older brother, John, in one and Helen slept with the baby, Glenn, in the other. In the kitchen there was an oak table in the middle and a large, black, cast iron, wood-burning cooking stove in one corner. There weren't any built-in kitchen cabinets, although there was one piece of kitchen furniture that Mother called the kitchen cabinet. I remember that it had some storage space and a bulk-flour bin in the upper part, with its own flour sifter. That was convenient, since Mother baked biscuits every morning and did other baking on many days.

Our round, sturdy, oak dining table was in the living room. As a small boy, I played under it, claiming that area as my own private sanctuary in the otherwise crowded house. During the winter there was a wood-burning heating stove in the living room. When it warmed up in the spring, the heating stove was removed to make more room. It came back in the fall, usually after a couple of cold snaps during which the only heat would be from the cooking stove, fired up with the oven door open to better heat the room. Normally, there were no stoves in the bedrooms, although each connected to the chimney.

I'm told that Dad put a heating stove in my parent's bedroom during the winter I was born at home. Good thing, too, because the temperature hit minus 31 degrees Fahrenheit on January 19, 1930, the night Dr. Lamson came out in a Model T Ford from Neosho to deliver me. That remains the record low temperature for Newton County to this day.

Our house, with about 800 square feet, was home for six people. It didn't have a bathroom. In the winter, the Maytag washing machine and washtubs were kept on the porch off the kitchen, and it could be moved into the kitchen for washing clothes on very cold days. The 30-inch galvanized, circular washtubs for rinsing the clothes were stored on hooks in the wall on the porch.

Mother believed that cleanliness was next to Godliness and she insisted on keeping us as clean as was possible for farm children. The wash pan was always handy by the kitchen sink, which Dad had installed with a single, cold-water faucet to provide running water. But the tea kettle on the cooking stove was always handy. In fact, Mother had two tea kettles. Normal washing was done with a fairly rough washcloth, which we called a washrag, using that 14-inch diameter, enameled wash pan, hot water and plenty of soap. Mother could scrub you all over with that wash rag, which the entire family used, and she was particularly rough when working on the elbows, neck and behind the ears. Boys fingernails were always dirty, and the only time that they really got soaked clean was during your weekly Saturday night bath.

Dad, being a farmer and working outdoors, didn't shave except on the weekend, unless he was going to a nearby town or there was some special event. He shaved at the wash pan in the kitchen, with a mirror propped up on the window sill over the sink. He kept the leather razor strop for sharpening the straight razor in the kitchen. Shaving nicks from that straight razor were common in those days, and a styptic pencil and small piece of tissue were the standard procedures to stop bleeding from the nicks.

We had our Saturday bath after supper. That way, we were clean for Sunday school and church the next day. The process was pretty much routine. Two teakettles of water were brought to a boil on the kitchen stove. The fire made the kitchen warm, so the kitchen table could be moved to the side and a circular washtub brought in and put on the linoleum floor close to the stove. The tub was filled about five inches deep with a mixture of hot and cold water to make the temperature just right. Everyone used the same tub of water starting with the youngest and proceeding to the oldest. As the water cooled, more hot water was added for each successive bather. Except for the very small children each person bathed in the privacy of the kitchen with the door closed.

The washtub worked fine for bathing the children, but no doubt posed a real challenge for the adults. I am confident that each developed his or her own style, since there was no way that a grown person could even approach submersion in that small, circular tub that was no more than 30-inches in diameter. We always used a washrag since we couldn't soak in the tub.

Washtub for the Saturday night bath.

In the summer, the baths were often taken on the back porch, on the southeast side of the house. It provided adequate privacy since no one lived in that direction. Since taking a bath at home in that small washtub was quite an ordeal, it's no wonder that many of the baths in the summer were down in Shoal Creek by the pasture. We used floating Ivory or Swan bar soap that wouldn't sink and be lost in the deep water.

Bathing on the porch led to an incident that I have heard Mother tell many times, always with almost uncontrolled laughter. One summer we had relatives visiting from Oklahoma, including our oldest cousin, Pauline Wyatt, who was a prankster. Mother also enjoyed a good trick, so she gladly went along with the prank.

We sold milk to some of the neighbors, which we bottled in a traditional milk bottle of that time that was topped with a waxed cardboard cap. One neighbor, Minnie English, lived a couple of blocks west of us and usually came after dark to pick up her daily quart of fresh milk, which was left on the porch. She carried a flashlight because there were no street lights, and you could always see Minnie coming by the bouncing beam of light on the ground ahead of her. As the relatives were visiting in the living room and Dad was on the back porch taking a bath, it occurred to Pauline that it would be funny if Mother took a flashlight and sneaked out the front door and walked around the house to the back porch with her bouncing beam of light just like Minnie English. Mother agreed to the prank.

Dad was a deep thinker and he was virtually oblivious to all around him when he was in deep thought. To hear Mother tell it, she assumed Dad would note the light and react when it was first in sight and Mother made sure the light beam occasionally glanced upward. Only at the last instant, as Mother was practically at the porch, did Dad register the situation. As Mother's light beam flashed up at him, he grabbed a towel and stood up like a gentleman in a lady's presence and said, "Hi'dy do, ma'm." His look must have been terribly funny and, although she was the only one to see it, Mother shared the story many times and without exception, erupted into uncontrollable laughter each time she recalled the event. Dad was a good sport and rather enjoyed the story himself as it was told later on. Mother never did tell us precisely what Dad might have said after his "Hi'dy do, ma'm," when he learned he'd been the victim of a prank. We can only guess.

In the winter of 1939-40 we started building a new house that was on the site of the old house. The new house would have about 1,200 square feet on the first floor and a floored upstairs where people could sleep, even if it was never finished. Most important, the house was to have a small bathroom with a built-in tub. During the winter, which turned out to be one of the coldest on record since the winter of 1929-30, we lived in the 20-foot square garage. Two mattresses upstairs in a shallow loft served as sleeping quarters for the four children. All of our heat was to come from the wood cooking stove, but when the temperatures dropped to about fifteen degrees below zero, Dad had to bring in the heating stove too, and rig the chimney for it. The carpenter, who was building the new house, lived with us and slept on a cot in the unheated smokehouse. He had to move into the heated garage for sleeping when the extreme cold spell hit. So we had three adults and four children in that small space. The Saturday-night baths continued in the same way, except a sheet was hung around the wash tub to assure some semblance of privacy.

We did much of the work of building the house ourselves. Money was in short supply, and we could not finish the upstairs, the built-in kitchen cabinets, or the bathroom at first. Some of that had to wait until more money was available. While we only had two exposed 100-watt bulb lights in the 14 by 28-foot living/dining room and were without many other amenities at first, we had more space and a bit of elbow room. Somehow, we obtained enough beds so each child had his/her own bed, and that, in itself, was a grand step forward.

Although the bathroom was not finished immediately, Dad did have the white, enameled, cast iron, built-in bathtub installed. I remember my first bath in that tub, which was in its place with the un-plastered walls on three sides and the wooden lath exposed. The water was still heated in a teakettle. But there was room to stretch out. No doubt, after nearly 20 years of marriage, having that tub where adults could stretch out and soak in a hot bath was a great source of satisfaction for my parents and helped relax tired muscles. In a couple of years, the bathroom was finished and hot running water was available. That ended the era of baths only on Saturday nights.

Bathing in Shoal Creek in the summer.

BUT HE'S A HARD WORKER!

Regardless of who you were, there was a measure of respect in Ritchey that could be earned by being judged a hard worker. It was a farming community, and our farm was right on the edge of town. In fact, it included nearly half of the original plat of Ritchey, all south of the railroad and all east of Jefferson Street which was never developed.

On the farm you knew down deep that your standard of living was related to farm production and that, in turn, on how hard you worked. While crop failure or other catastrophes could occur, the way to maximize the chance of success was simply to work hard and plan well. Anything less than your best was not acceptable. Dad, and Mom, too, always expected the best effort from us. Failure to accomplish something was acceptable if you had really done your best. Dad's words were, "Do your best. That is as good as anyone can do." Today, about 70 years after I first heard those words, they still ring in my ears.

Few people had the kinds of jobs that included paid vacations. The one exception in Ritchey was if you worked for the Frisco Railway Co. Ritchey was one of the towns that was home base to a section gang. The railroad provided a house along the tracks on the west edge of town for the foreman of the section gang. There was a section foreman and the workers who were called 'section hands.' Likewise, on the farm any person employed regularly was called 'a hand.' Being a good hired hand would bring respect. It didn't matter if you had little schooling.

The Ritchey railroad gang was responsible for safety inspections and maintenance on about six miles of track, maybe halfway to Granby to the west, which was about five railroad miles away, and east of Ritchey three miles towards Berwick. The gangs kept the tracks aligned and level, checked that the spikes anchoring the tracks to the ties weren't loose, replaced the creosoted wood ties when needed and checked the bridges and crossings. The gang also used hand scythes to cut the weeds along the right-of-way. These unwieldy and heavy tools had a long specially crooked handle with two hand grips, which could be adjusted to the height of the worker. A good hand, who kept the blade sharp, could cut a surprising amount of weeds with these ungainly devices.

The section gang also maintained the fence along the railroad because the Frisco Co. could be liable for any cattle, horses or mules that were killed by the trains. The only way a train could stop to avoid hitting livestock would be if it had already slowed for other reasons. Since stock on the tracks were a problem for the railroad and farmers, the railroad fences were the best around, usually with five or six barbed wires instead of the three normally used by farmers for cattle fencing.

Working on the Frisco was a highly sought after job. The pay was good for physical labor, maybe 50 cents an hour as opposed to the 25 or 30 that the farmers paid. And the work was steady. Also, a

Sharpening a scythe with a file.

vacation was automatic and if you stayed with it you would eventually earn a modest pension. However, I don't think most people thought of retirement then. You just worked as long as you could. People might have to slow down for health reasons but, except for the railroad workers, most wouldn't stop because there was little or no retirement income available. I suppose every boy growing up in Ritchey at one time dreamed of being a railroad hand.

The Ritchey section gang had three hands and a foreman. I don't recall seeing the foreman doing much physical work. To me, being a boss wasn't really work. The foreman was in charge and determined what was to be done and supervised the hands as they worked. Having what appeared to me to be a 'non-working' foreman was different from any farm work group that I had seen. Someone was always in charge, but they always worked too. In fact, the person in charge was usually one of the hardest workers, setting the pace for the others. I always thought if I were a section hand doing my best, I would probably resent the foreman standing around seemingly doing nothing except watching me.

We learned very early that being a hard worker brought praise and respect. Being honest, trustworthy and showing respect for elders was expected. Failing in those qualities automatically led to a warning or punishment. I suppose that down deep young people might think that they could goof off a bit at work and not get caught. But it wasn't a thing you would do once you were old enough to be depended on for real work. It was the right thing to do. We felt that the harder we worked, the more we contributed and the more we were respected.

I doubt if the work ethic in Ritchey was any different from most rural communities. It was probably the same ethic that hard working city people had. I now realize it all came from the principles set down by the country's founding fathers. Then hard work was essential for survival, but that wasn't the feeling I had as a boy. Survival never entered my mind.

Dad, by example, instilled a principle I have always tried to follow. We were not rewarded for how good we did the job, but we got praise for doing our best. As a small boy, I was always learning new tasks, some of which I had not mastered and could not yet do well. But Dad always knew if I'd done my best. And he unfailingly praised my best efforts, even if the outcome left much to be desired, at least in my mind. Half-hearted efforts wouldn't bring punishment like being untruthful or getting reprimanded at school, but Dad's looks of disappointment sent a more painful signal than any paddle.

Clearly, being a hard worker brought respect in the community. There were also things that lowered respect. For an adult, not tending to family responsibilities, not keeping a job, no matter how unsatisfying it might be, and drinking booze were frowned upon. The latter seemed to be especially important in this Southern Baptist setting. I guess it's not too surprising that drinking alcohol was generally frowned upon in that part of Missouri. After all, in the 1884 Newton County election the Anti-Bourbon candidate for Congress received 1,968 votes compared to 1,962 for the Democratic candidate. The only other Congressional candidate was from the Prohibition Party. With the Anti-

Bourbon and Prohibition Parties operating and the Women's Christian Temperance Union of Ritchey active in the early days well before my time, the settlers of that region had a firm temperance base. That tradition continued in Ritchey throughout my boyhood and may still exist among many of the sixty or so current residents.

I recall Mother, saying, "You know, he drinks!" That judgment said it all unless it was followed with something like, "- but he's a hard worker." Being a hard worker excused a lot. Mother maintained excellent relations with my paternal grandmother and grandfather. They were close to being perfect people, yet my German Grandma knew the medicinal benefits of whiskey and kept some in the deep recesses of a few cupboards and closets in the house – just in case. Grandpa, an Englishman who enjoyed a refreshing beer, more than once asked me as a boy if I'd like a taste, when we stopped at the 'beer joint' after I had accompanied him on errands. He, of course, always had beer. I always had a grape or orange Nehi soda, which came in a big 12 ounce bottle – much like a beer. If I'd tasted that beer, Mother would have known. I knew that. But Grandpa was a very hard worker and a highly responsible man – and he was family. That no doubt resulted in Mother overlooking his fondness for beer.

Many people in our community were poor. Some probably despaired, considering the challenges they faced. But most were committed to their families, were hard workers and wonderful people. And most that I know have achieved far more success than might have been expected. Committed hard workers usually succeed.

THE JOY OF RUBBER TIRES

Most people probably don't think much about rubber tires and whether they can bring joy. But if you'd worked on a farm when wagons had high wooden wheels wrapped in iron bands and implements rolled on steel wheels, you'd understand.

For many years, my father had two farm wagons with high wheels, not unlike the prairie schooners in western picture shows. The wheels were made of wood except for the iron bearing at the axle and the two-inch wide iron band on the outside that held it together. Those iron bands were called 'tires.' The wagons didn't have springs to soften the ride. You couldn't let the wheels dry out too much in the summer, because the wood would contract and the wheels would fall apart. If the wagons hadn't been used for some time and dried out, we poured water over the wheels to soak them for a day or two so the wood would expand and tighten the wheels. We liked to drive the wagons in the shallow part of the creek to facilitate this soaking and tightening of the wheels. When riding on one of these farm wagons, you felt the jolt of every rock and gully.

The wagon axles had to be greased with thick axle grease daily because the bearings were loose-fitting and metal to metal. The bearings were tapered, maybe four inches in diameter at the inside, tapering to two inches at the outside, which made greasing them easier. To grease the wagons you removed a large nut that held the wheel on the axle and tilted the wheel out to expose the inner part of the axle. Then you applied the thick axle grease from the inside. Since the axles were tapered, it was surprisingly easy to tilt the wheel of a heavy wagon. You didn't have to remove the wheel, but you had to be careful. Too much tilt and you might have the axle on the ground.

The wheels on the right side were held on by large nuts with right-handed threads, so the rotation of the wheels in forward motion of the wagon kept them tight. The left side had left-handed threads for similar reasons.

Subsequently, low-wheeled wagons that had all steel wheels came into use. The all-steel wheels were about two feet in diameter and the tread was about four inches wide. The low-wheeled wagons were nice because they were lower and easier to load, but the ride was even rougher than the high wheeled wagons because the wider steel wheels hit even more rocks. With steel wheels hitting the rocky road, the ride in all these wagons was noisy and bone jarring.

Early tractors also had steel wheels, with the large, rear-drive wheels having steel lugs bolted to them. They were very rough-riding and hard to steer. On hard packed gravel roads they also damaged the roads. They would quickly destroy an asphalt road. Fortunately, the used tractor, we purchased had rubber tires. But any new tractors that were available during WW II, had steel wheels because rubber tires weren't available. Tractors didn't have springs or shock absorbers, but the rubber tires

Farmall tractor with rough riding steel lug wheels. *Farmall tractor with smooth riding rubber tires.*

made the ride quite smooth.

In the late 1930s, more farmers accepted the fact that rubber tires could be used on the farm for tractors, wagons and implements. For a while, some farmers were reluctant, thinking that rubber tires on tractors wouldn't have enough traction to pull plows and other implements. Some of the first farm wagons with rubber tires were built using an old automobile chassis.

Because of a shortage of rubber, and tire rationing, we couldn't buy new tires for our implements during World War II. But farmers could usually put a big boot in a damaged tire and make it work. This was unsafe for cars at road speeds, but it would work well in the slow-speed operations on the farm. At the end of the war, rubber-tired wagons and other implements became common. They could be pulled faster with the newer tractors, which had a 'road gear,' that was four times faster than the highest field gears, but still less than 20 miles per hour. And the ride was quiet and smooth.

I can imagine the jolting ride of the early stagecoaches as they traveled on rocky trails over the mountainous West. My wife, Joanne, says that rough stagecoach rides may be why women of the West wore bustles. She would know more about that than I do.

Few people who haven't had first-hand experience with farming before the advent of rubber tires can appreciate the positive effect they had. You need to have had your innards jiggled and bounced all day to appreciate it. With rubber tires, there was less draft and tractors had better traction, to say nothing of the vastly increased comfort and reduced noise. I personally experienced the change and know the joy of rubber tires.

RHYTHM OF THE RAILROAD GANG

The Frisco railroad track followed Shoal Creek valley in a straight or gently curving line. It went straight east-west at the south edge of Ritchey and on through the middle of our farm. Our house, although at the edge of our farm, was also on a village lot at the southeast corner of Ritchey. In fact, our house was only a few hundred feet from the main track. It was so close that during dry weather when the wooden window frames were dry and loose in their window tracks, we could tell when a train was coming because the massive speeding train would vibrate the ground enough to rattle the windows. Although we got so used to it that we didn't notice, guests were sometimes startled when the windows suddenly started to rattle, often gasping wide-eyed, "What's that?" It was a little eerie to have the windows rattling before you could hear the train.

There was a siding track immediately adjacent to the main track near our house. It was more than a half-mile long and was regularly used as a temporary parking place so a train going in one direction could meet a train going the opposite way. The Frisco was a single-track line, so trains could only meet if one was on a siding. There was less than ten feet between trains when they passed. Freight trains were the norm, with only four passenger trains each day. One, named the Will Rogers, connected to cities in Oklahoma, including Claremore, where Will Rogers was born and where the monument to him is located. The Will Rogers went west about seven in the morning and returned going east about five in the afternoon. The Bluebonnet was the other passenger train, and it rolled to cities in Texas. The westbound train came through about 10 p.m. and the eastbound arrived sometime before dawn.

As these passenger trains whizzed by, I saw people relaxing in the dining cars and enjoying food on white, linen-covered tables. I envied them. The thought of traveling a long distance on a train was a dream. An even greater dream was making the trip in a Pullman sleeping coach.

Ritchey's first-class mail was delivered by the Will Rogers and the outgoing mail in a heavy-canvas mail sack was snatched by the speeding train from a special stand that held the sack near the tracks. A special arm in the mail car grabbed the sack as the train roared by. The incoming mail was thrown a distance from the speeding train so it wouldn't get sucked under the wheels. These heavy mail bags bounced and skidded along the gravel because this operation occurred with the train speeding past at 70 or more miles an hour. Postal workers in the mail car, which was near the front of the train, sorted the mail as the train traveled. The passenger trains always had the right-of-way. So, freight trains took the siding to make way for the much faster passenger trains, which tried to maintain their schedules.

There was another shorter side track that went behind the depot, maybe fifty feet south of the main-line track. This is shown on the plat of Ritchey surveyed in 1882. The longer freight trains didn't stop to deliver or take on merchandise in Ritchey. When freight was delivered it came by a short train that made local deliveries, called 'The Local.' It would stop on that side track long enough to unload. That side track

Railroad gang replacing railroad cross ties.

went by the stock pens and the tomato-canning factory, both of which existed when I was a boy. It also went past the grain elevator, which had burned or been dismantled long before I was born. In the early days, before long-haul trucking became popular, the railroad was Ritchey's link to the outside world and a box car would often be parked there waiting to be loaded or unloaded.

During my boyhood, that siding track was sometimes home to a special railroad gang that would come to town to repair the track. They would come with several cars, including one or more supply cars, sleeping cars, and a kitchen/dining car. These crews handled jobs that were too large for the regular three- or four-person local, section-hand crew to handle. Sometimes these special crews laid new, heavier steel rails on the main track. Dad told me at one time the track had 90-pound rails, meaning that the rails weighed 90 pounds per linear foot. I think that when I was born they had 110-pound rails and I remember when they put 140-pound rails in. As the freight trains and steam engines got heavier and faster, they had to have heavier rails to withstand the hammering and hold their alignment. Some of the freight trains had as many as a 100 railroad cars, but it was usually about 80.

Sometimes the special crews would come to replace the worn crossties in which the spikes holding the rails in place had loosened. The ties were impregnated with creosote to protect them from rotting in the ground. They would still split and deteriorate. At other times a crew would come to maintain the wooden trestles that crossed the creek or other streams.

I recall three different crews of specialists coming to town, a rail-laying crew, a tie-replacement crew and a bridge crew. These crews would maybe have 40 workers and they would have two sleeping cars, a dining/kitchen car. In addition they would have small, motorized, section cars, maybe eight of them, to transport the workers to the work site. The boxcars and flatcars contained supplies, such as wooden ties, bridge timbers or new rails. These railcars had wooden sides and were painted a dull, earth-toned red, about the same color as our barn. It was a totally self-contained little town parked on the side track and they might be there for several weeks. The cook would buy some supplies from local suppliers, but mostly they had a supply of staples with them.

When one of these crews came to town, they would be only a few hundred feet from our house. With the approval of Dad I would go over to the tracks and locate the head cook and check if they would like to buy milk or eggs, two farm commodities that we had in ample supply. I would agree to deliver these supplies to their kitchen car in the mornings before school. In those days we sold our milk fresh in ten-gallon, galvanized milk cans to a cheese factory or a condensed-milk processing plant. So we had plenty of fresh, whole, non-homogenized milk, from which they could skim rich cream after the cream had risen to the top overnight. The cook would use several dozen eggs and several quarts of milk each day. I don't recall how much we got for the eggs because my sister handled them, but I remember that I got a dime-a-quart for the milk. Dad let me keep this money and it was a small fortune for a boy.

These crews in the 1930's were comprised of African Americans from Alabama, Mississippi and neighboring southern states, with one exception – the foreman. He was always white and the person in front of the picture is the foreman. Since there were no African Americans in Ritchey and none in my school, this was the first time that I had the opportunity to see them work. They were certainly hard

Special railroad gang installing new, heavier rails. All workers are African Americans except the foreman, who is white and standing on a track in the foreground. Our farm is in the background.

workers and their muscular, shirtless bodies glistened with perspiration in the light. Of interest to me, they usually had a singer with them and they would work to the singer's rhythm.

For example, the rail-laying crew would put a new rail down and align it on its tie plates and the crew with large hammers would drive the six-inch-long railroad spikes to the cadence of the singer. The hammers looked like sledge hammers except the contact points of the head were about ten inches long and about two inches in diameter. This permitted driving a spike from either side of the rail. Three men would hit these spikes in sequence at less than a one-second interval, with precise timing. Although they did not have power hammers, they could drive a six-inch-long spike in about five seconds. Each tie plate had four spikes and they were set in a very short time.

Rail traffic didn't stop when rails or crossties were being replaced. So the crews, knowing the schedule of the trains, would remove only the sections of rail that could be replaced before the next train arrived. They worked fast and efficiently.

It was a marvelous example of teamwork by a highly efficient team. And they seemed to always be smiling and appeared to enjoy the comradeship of shared work. They were always singing and they worked with precision. It was like a drill team swinging in cadence to a marching song.

Buttermilk was the one thing that the head cook always wanted that I couldn't supply. We did make butter for our own use and Mother or Helen made biscuits with the buttermilk we had, but no one in our family drank it. Besides, we wouldn't have had enough to meet their needs. I always wished I could have supplied that item that the black workers longed for. It would have vastly increased my income when the gangs were there.

BAPTIZED IN SHOAL CREEK

Churches have always been an integral part of life in Ritchey. The town's first church was described in an 1888 history of Newton County as follows: "The public spirit is noticed in a fine cozy union church, in which the Methodists, Baptists, Presbyterians and Christians all worship. The building and furnishings cost the good people about $15,000."

Fifty years later, in the early 1930's, there were two churches, each constructed of wood, painted white and topped by a tall steeple for the church bell. The Baptist church was the largest, but it didn't always have a regular preacher. In earlier years it was sometimes served by a preacher who was there every second or third Sunday. A circuit preacher might cover two or more small towns on a regular, rotating basis. So in some weeks you would hear people say, "Preachin' this Sunday." On the Sundays without preachin', the various Sunday school classes were held and they generally lasted a little longer because you didn't have to break up for church. The deacons were very active in the Sunday school.

Ritchey Baptist Church.

When a church didn't have a full-time preacher, one could expect a good, long sermon from the circuit preacher. In some cases, it might be nearly twice the normal length. I didn't like the Sundays with preachin' because the service lasted so long. After you've heard all the bad things that you might do that would send you to Hell, it gets kind of boring. Daydreaming was more satisfying and that's what I did most of the time during preachin'. Dad had a very active mind and he was usually tired. Listening to 'Hell, fire and damnation' sermons, covering things he had heard before, would often cause him to doze. He wasn't a regular in church, but on those occasions when he went, he might doze if the preacher wasn't too interesting.

The Baptist Church also had a Sunday evening service. Therefore, on the Sundays when the preacher was there, the devout could get a big enough dose of the Word to carry them through the next two or more weeks until the next sermon. There also was the regular Wednesday night prayer meeting, which the deacons managed when a preacher wasn't available. The Baptist minister usually was not referred to as The Reverend so-and-so, but as The Preacher or Brother so-and-so, depending on his last name.

The Presbyterian Church in Ritchey was located adjacent to the school ground and about a half block from the Baptist Church. Actually, it was a Cumberland Presbyterian Church and was likely organized by settlers from the Tennessee/Kentucky region. More of the church-going people who lived in Ritchey went to the Baptist Church. When I was a boy, the Presbyterians only had service on the infrequent occasions when their circuit preacher was in town. The few members who attended those occasional services were mostly from the nearby rural areas. Actually, I wasn't motivated to learn very much about the Presbyterians since the clear message from the Baptist preacher was that if you weren't a Baptist you were in serious trouble and were probably headed for Hell. So why take the risk and even think about the other churches? One message was uppermost -- there was no shortage of things you could do to send you to Hell.

Ritchey Presbyterian Church with hitching rail in front.

When I was about ten or maybe even younger, the backers of the Holiness Church came to town one summer. They put up their tent across the street west of where the old hotel had stood on the south edge of town. The medicine show used the same area when it came to town. The tent was referred to as a 'tabernacle' and they had a lengthy service every evening for maybe two weeks. There wasn't much to do in town and not many ways that you could get in trouble if you were at anything associated with religion. So my parents let me satisfy my curiosity and go to the tabernacle meetings. People poured out of the surrounding hills for these meetings, and there was always a good crowd. I recall the pitch was somewhat different than at the week-long Baptist revivals that were also a summer activity. While the message, like the Baptists, pointed out the many easy paths to Hell, I sensed from the Holiness services – perhaps erroneously – a focus on the immediate payoff of getting the Lord on your side.

I remember the Holiness Preacher citing a case one evening in which a farmer and his wife were 'saved' and immediately the butterfat content of the milk from their cows jumped significantly. Since we were dairy farmers, and milk was priced according to its butterfat content in those days, an increase in butterfat would be money in your pocket. I was impressed and discussed this with Dad who, to say the least, was skeptical. That surprised me somewhat because if a preacher said it, it should be true. I hadn't thought that issue was negotiable. I have a different view today.

I recall there was a two-step process to salvation in the Holiness Church. First, you have to be 'saved' and then the next step was to follow the rules and good life and be 'sanctified.' I never really understood just what it all meant. This church group wasn't referred to as the Pentecostal Church, which they were. Some called them the 'Holy Rollers.' As the days of the tabernacle meeting passed,

I think I learned why. It turns out that they are a very participatory group. As the service progressed, people were invited to testify on the good things that had happened to them since they had been saved. There were some pretty impressive statements made about the tangible benefits. The last minutes of each evening, became more vocal, with more participating simultaneously. In the end, the crescendo of the worship reached such a pitch that it could be heard over much of the town.

A new church, called the 'Fire Baptized Holiness Church,' was organized in Ritchey as a result of those tabernacle services. An unused, rural, one-room school was moved to a small hill northeast of the Ritchey school ground, diagonally across the school yard from the Presbyterian Church. Those one-room schools had closed operations when the consolidated school district was formed and the pupils were bussed to Ritchey. Therefore, a nice structure was conveniently available to be moved. This Holiness Church was quite active, with several members from the local families as leaders. With a few exceptions, it appeared the women were the most active and the ankle-length, long-sleeved, high-buttoned collar, cotton dresses and black stockings became a common sight in Ritchey. No makeup whatsoever was to be found on the Holiness Church women and that was different from the Baptist Church, where the women would use powder and a touch of rouge and lipstick.

The Fire Baptized Holiness Church in Ritchey. This church is a former one-room country school building that was moved to Richey.

As I said, there wasn't much going on most summer evenings for entertainment, so we participated in anything that would help fill the hour or so from summer darkness to bedtime. Although I went to several tabernacle meetings that first summer, I was never in The Fire Baptized Holiness Church. More than once, however, my friends and I did sneak up near the church to listen more carefully to the rather loud vocal worship service as it ended.

Summer also regularly brought two events to Baptist Church activities. One was the Bible School, which probably lasted two weeks, with its morning instructional activities. Mother was active in the Baptist Church and helped as she could. Dad was as honest and moral a person as you will ever know, but his frustrations as a farmer led to a noticeable temper. His language around the barn would not normally be associated with a man of the church. The farmers had the easy excuse of work to do on Sunday morning, so the women often went to church alone. I worked on the farm during the week in the summers and never once attended the weekday morning Bible School.

The biggest summer event at the Baptist Church was the week-long evening revival. A powerful preacher would come to town and preach at the revival meeting every night for a week. At the end of each service, there would be a hymn or two sung softly while the preacher would call those uncommitted to the Lord or those who were backsliders to come forward and commit themselves to the Lord and the Baptist Church. That's how you became a member of the Church. You could do it at any Sunday service, but there was more hype at the revival. A young person was more likely to make that big decision at a revival after seeing several friends the same age take the step. That was the case for me. I did it on a Thursday evening, as I recall, and like the others who did so that week, I was to be baptized the following Sunday.

Shoal Creek was one of the most beautiful streams in the Ozarks. There is a small dam and grist mill on the creek. The water below the dam was mostly shallow, but about waist deep in deeper zones, with enough current to have small ripples. The streambed was covered with somewhat rounded pebbles the size of a half dollar or slightly larger. The water was cool because springs flow into the creek. That is where I was baptized.

I don't recall if the preacher kept his shoes on, but he waded out to his waist, fully clothed with dark trousers, white shirt and tie. Each person carefully walked out to the minister where the preacher prayed and said some nice things. I recall that the preacher said something like, "I baptize you in the name of the Father, the Son, and the Holy Ghost." While he was saying this each person was fully immersed to wash those sins away. When my turn came I was ready with my shoes off, but fully clothed otherwise. I don't remember the details of what the preacher said in the service of baptism, but I remember the water was cold. Somehow, I thought I should have felt different – more pure or lighter on my feet or something. I didn't, but I never told anybody. Actually, I never thought of myself as a particularly wicked person before the baptism. I was glad to have it behind me. On reflection, I pretty much think the sprinkling of water from a baptismal font, as was the case for our children, serves every bit as well

↑ *Baptism in a local creek.*

Bill O'Neal
of Newtonia

RAY'S STORE

At one time, Ritchey had several businesses including a bank, a bakery, a garage, blacksmith shop, hardware store and lumber yard, a hotel, a tavern, an ice house, three general stores, and even a grist mill and ice plant down on Shoal Creek. There were sawmills nearby. One of the general stores also housed the post office.

By the time I was born, most of these businesses had closed, and were converted to other uses, usually very inexpensive apartments or homes. By my teenage years, only one general store remained and it also was by then home to the Ritchey Post Office. That general store was owned by Ray Kistler. Its official name was Kistler's Grocery, but everyone just called it Ray's. It was actually a general store. It had groceries, a small selection of meats in a cooler, canned and boxed food on shelves behind the

Ritchey soon after the turn of the century.

display case with tobacco and candy. But it also had more. Ray had a small selection of cotton cloth, several bolts of different colors and patterns. He had sewing materials including threads, thimbles, needles, rickrack of assorted colors, and the like. He handled work gloves and Wolverine work shoes, rubber boots, and even some 100-pound sacks of feed for chickens and other animals. His shallow display counters were glass enclosed, with flat tops, and doors on the back. Kids with a nickel to buy candy would tap the nickel on the top of the counter as they impatiently waited for Ray to serve them.

When we children were sent shopping, we were told to go to Ray's and get this or that – and hurry. We were always told to hurry. Our parents knew our tendency to loiter. We were never asked to go to the store – there was only one that we used for groceries – it was, "Go to Ray's, and hurry."

Ray and Dad were longtime good friends. Ray may have been 10 or 15 years younger, but they had

Ray's store – Kistler's Grocery and the Ritchey Post Office.

a lot in common. Dad was an insatiable reader, probably very unusual for a southwest Missouri farmer, and Ray was probably the best person to discuss current events with. Many people in Ritchey didn't take a daily paper, but Ray and Dad did. It was delivered by mail, not by the early-morning paper boy. But any news you haven't heard is new news. They could discuss political issues and current events and probably did each time that Dad went to Ray's Store and had a few minutes.

Ray always asked Dad to help with the store's annual inventory, which was started after the store closed on New Year's Eve and went on into the wee hours of New Year's Day. Providing such help was a neighborly thing to do and, no doubt, provided intellectual stimulation for Dad and a welcome change from the milking, feeding and long days in the fields.

Ray's Store was typical of many country stores of that time, but it was far different from the stores of today. Ray was always in the store as its only worker, except for the 15 or 20 minutes he sometimes took to dash home for a sandwich at dinner (the noon meal in Ritchey). His wife, Mildred, would relieve him then. His hours in the store were long. He opened at 7 a.m. or before and closed between 9 and 10 p.m. He was in the store 14 hours a day, six days a week. He would also open for a couple of hours on Sunday before church, but dutifully closed when the Baptist service began (the church was only about 100 yards from the store.) Although I never saw Ray in church, I doubt if anyone in Ritchey would leave him off of a list of the five most honest and upright men in town. Ray, like his store, was a Ritchey institution.

In a village like Ritchey, the general store is the town social center if the owner permits it. Ray did. In the summer there was a wooden bench on the sidewalk right in front of the big front store window on the left side of the front door. Some called it the 'gossiping bench.' Although this was a simple bench with the seat and back made from a wide board, it was sufficiently comfortable for the 'town loafers,' who spent hours relaxing and gossiping there. The standard dress was blue-denim, bib overalls (usually pronounced 'overhalls'), a work shirt and ankle-high, leather work shoes, all of which could be brought at Ray's. While they probably didn't have much money, most denizens of Ray's benches would carry a good quality pocketknife, which they often used to whittle on a soft piece of wood. Lacking that wood, they were sometimes seen carving initials or simply whittling on the seat of the very bench they were sitting on. I remember the unpainted benches in front of Ray's as being well-carved, with some deep notches whittled in the front edge of the seat.

Ray seemed oblivious to it all and, while I never saw him socialize with the loafers as they spent hours outside his store, he accepted them as a part of Ritchey's social culture. When it was cold, I think he welcomed them inside to sit around the big pot-belly stove at the back of the store.

People who stopped in to buy a sack of flour, some sugar or whatever would also pick up the latest news about happenings around the town. We lived on the edge of town, and it was a short walk to the store. However, people from the country would drive a few miles for supplies. Those without cars would come by horse-drawn wagon, or maybe by buggy. They would generally stock up before returning home since the spur-of-the-moment, "Go to Ray's and hurry," which my parents enjoyed, was not an option for them.

There was a convenient hitching post a short distance from the store for clientele that came by horse. In the evening, after supper, you'd usually find a handful of people visiting after their purchases were made, or maybe they'd just be in to visit without buying anything. Some would stay until closing. After all, there was no indoor social center, so in the winter Ray's served this need. But the weather had to be pretty cool to keep the regulars off the benches in front of the store.

Much of Ray's business was on credit. No charge cards or anything like that existed. Ray had individual 3-by-5 yellow sales pads for each of his credit customers with their name printed in ink on the spine. He knew his customers and would automatically pick up the correct pad when they entered the store. As they told him what they wanted, he would get it and place it on the counter, item-by-item. Seldom did they have to say, "Charge it." That was understood. No one signed a credit slip. With many poor people around Ritchey, there must have been a few customers who didn't pay their bill before leaving town. I understand that some customers, who were too far behind in paying their grocery bill, would be restricted to basic staple foods and not permitted to charge such luxuries as soda pop or candy.

Dad usually charged the groceries, perhaps for the convenience of sending the kids to Ray's without money, but in many cases it likely was because he was short of cash. But the bill was always paid promptly when the milk check came in. We looked forward to Dad paying the bill because Ray would send home a small brown paper sack with candy for the family. We would each get one or two small pieces, and if we were lucky one of them would be a chocolate covered sugar candy that was our favorite, and, no doubt, terrible for our teeth.

Businesses such as Ray's couldn't exist today. He was part of the community – an institution. He would not idly stand by and see people go hungry. But he would be sure that what they got on credit were basics. I suspect that every small village in rural areas had a store like Ray's.

RALEIGH MAN AND THE MEDICINE SHOW

name was Bluyler?

Healthcare in the 1930's was a far cry from what it is today. We only went to the doctor for rather serious illnesses. And going to the hospital was viewed as the last resort. If you were taken to the hospital it was generally recognized that there was a fair chance that you wouldn't come back. When I was growing up, no one in our family ever went to the hospital, except on one occasion. That was when my mother was very, very sick. I was quite small, and my grandmother was staying at our house and taking care of Mother. Things were very hush-hush, and I didn't know what was wrong with her, but I knew she was very sick. Everyone whispered when I was around. I realized just how sick she was when an ambulance came to take her to the hospital. The ambulances in the larger towns in rural areas were mostly associated with the funeral homes, and the one that came for Mother was from a funeral home in Pierce City, 12 miles to the east. It took Mother to St. John's Hospital in Joplin, which was 35 miles away.

Although nobody told me, I feared that my mother would probably die, since she had gone to the hospital. But a miracle occurred, and she got well. Afterward, I remember Dad smiling and saying under his breath that the funeral home had charged him almost nothing for the ambulance trip to the hospital, presumably because they thought they would recover the costs with the funeral expenses. Fortunately, that funeral didn't occur for more than 40 years. Medical care as we know it today was essentially non-existent in the early days.

In many cases, the medicines used by rural people came from cure-all potions and ointments that were ordered by mail or, perhaps, bought at a medicine show. Advertisements of such remedies in newspapers were common. In the 1930's, Ritchey was periodically visited in the summer by a traveling medicine show. The show was free and held outdoors on a grassy area at the south edge of town. Folding canvas benches were set up for the audience and temporary lights strung up. The show consisted of a few vaudeville acts, which were the drawing card that brought the rural people out of the hills. These acts often included a juggler, trained dog acts and maybe a slapstick comedian. Between acts, a salesman would bark the wonders of various tonics and lotions as assistants went through the audience taking customer's money and providing the elixirs. I was always amazed at the number of people who would buy up a good supply of these patent medicines. The salesman was persuasive and, if you had an ailment, the potion he was hawking would provide a cure for it.

Those medicine shows would travel to the little towns throughout the region and return to Ritchey once a year. The show was outside, so they skipped all but the summer months. Customers came from miles around and apparently accepted these wonder cures at face value. We went to the show for entertainment, but our parents seldom, if ever, bought any of the medicines. I think Dad was suspicious of such traveling troupes and their cure-all potions. Also, he said, if you believed it would work, the same stuff would be cheaper at the store.

The newspaper ads for mail-order medicines made promises similar to those made by the medicine show barker. Here's an example of a cure for catarrh from an early local newspaper ad:

A Simple, Safe, Reliable Way, and It Costs Nothing to Try

>Those who suffer from catarrh knows its miseries. There is no need for this suffering. You can get rid of it by a simple, safe, inexpensive home treatment discovered by Doctor Blosser, who for over thirty-five years has been treating catarrh successfully.
>
>His treatment is unlike any other. It is not a spray, douche, salve, cream, or inhaler, but a more direct and thorough treatment than any of these. It cleans out the head, nose, throat and lungs so you again can breathe freely and sleep without that stopped-up feeling that all catarrh sufferers have. It heals the diseased mucous membranes and arrests the foul discharge, so that you will not be constantly blowing your nose and spitting, and at the same time it does not poison the system and ruin the stomach, as internal medicines do.
>
>If you want to test this treatment without cost, send your address to Dr. J. W. Blosser, 321 Walton Street, Atlanta, Ga., and he will send you by return mail enough of the medicine to satisfy you that it is all he claims for it as a remedy for catarrh, catarrhal headaches, catarrhal deafness, asthma, bronchitis, colds and all catarrhal complications. He will also send you free an illustrated booklet. Write him immediately.

The Raleigh Man was a traveling salesman who provided spices and other cooking condiments, sewing supplies and some standard medicines and liniments. This man no doubt had a name, but to us he was simply the 'Raleigh Man' because he distributed Raleigh products. He traveled to the small towns and farms on a regular basis. He stopped by individual homes and would take orders for products to be delivered on the next trip. I remember his vehicle, which was a Model A Ford that had been equipped to carry his numerous samples. Each item had its place, including some items that were carried in special containers attached to the running boards of the car.

The Raleigh Man was gregarious and made friends easily. Apparently, he sometimes arranged for lodging with certain families along his routes so he didn't have to return home each night. Although Ritchey at one time had a hotel, it had closed many years before and, when I was a boy, the building was the permanent home for several families. After we expanded our four-room house to a much larger one in 1940, our house was one of the places where the Raleigh Man spent the night because I recall him staying with us once or twice.

He was a good conversationalist, and Dad no doubt found having him with us to be an opportunity for a different conversation and a break from the silence of working in the fields. He brought news, since he visited many homes in the region. Mother seemed to look forward to his visits and the new supplies of spices and other things for the kitchen. She felt his products were good and the selection of some items better than from the small Kistler's Grocery in town. The Raleigh Man continued to come to Ritchey until in the late 1940s. Considering everything, his business must have earned a very modest income. When his health prevented him from continuing, the business died. I imagine the Raleigh Man was one-of-a-kind to his many customers. I've heard others my age who grew up in small rural communities in other states speak of their Raleigh Man.

There were other traveling acts that occasionally came to Ritchey besides the medicine show. One that I will always remember was the trained mule act that advertised Mule Beer. A small covered truck with an announcement of the act emblazoned on its sides would drive around town and it would be noticed. People accustomed to very little traffic always looked when a car or truck went by to see who it was. The truck stopped at the edge of a street near the downtown. A crowd soon gathered as the mule was unloaded down a portable ramp. The act consisted of various tricks by the mule, including wild shaking or nodding of its head in answer to various carefully worded questions. I distinctly remember the mule being asked the age of an early teenage boy in the crowd. The mule answered by pawing one of its front feet on the ground the proper number of times. The mule got the answer right, and the crowd was amazed. I know I was. People were impressed by smart animals.

The final part of the act came when the handler thanked the mule for a wonderful show and offered him a beer as a reward for his performance. The mule would gesture in a positive way when hearing he was about to get a bottle of beer. The handler would hold up a longneck bottle of a competing brand, Falstaff Beer, not Mule Beer, and the mule would take a big swig. Then almost instantaneously he would spit it out, frown and wildly shake his head. The handler would ask what was wrong – would he like a Mule Beer? The mule made big, affirmative nods. The handler then held up a longneck bottle of Mule Beer and the mule would down it in two or three gulps. Then he would look at the crowd and give a big smile. That was the end of the show, except for the young people hanging around to pet the mule and the adults lingering to talk with a degree of wonder about the mule.

I don't know where Mule Beer was brewed or how long the brewery existed. Nor do I know if the act improved sales of Mule Beer, but I will never forget Mule Beer advertising with its traveling, trained mule. I don't remember this ever returning to Ritchey.

No doubt most readers who grew up in the age of television have difficulty understanding the hunger for entertainment that rural people of my generation had. We always had a radio. But some without electricity didn't even have that. Some, like our neighbor, Mrs. Marion, couldn't read. The newspaper came by mail, but few in town subscribed. While people knew how to entertain themselves, they craved the opportunity for any kind of outside entertainment – and that entertainment didn't have to be very sophisticated.

PARTY LINE – THE ORIGINAL AOL

In 1930 when I was born, there was one telephone in Ritchey. It was in Largen's Store, where the post office was at that time. The wooden phone was mounted on the wall, with the device you spoke into mounted on the front. It could be adjusted up or down a little, but a short woman might have to stand on tiptoes to speak into it. The earpiece was about four inches long, and it hung on a yoke on the left side of the phone. A crank on the right was used to ring up someone. Two round bells, sort of like owl eyes, sat at the top on the front of the phone and would ring when a call came in.

There wasn't any local service. A normal call, which was always long distance, would be three minutes and all calls were expensive. After three minutes the rates went up markedly. All calls from Largen's involved an operator. You would ring the operator and give her (operators were all women) the number and city you were calling. The operator would work through appropriate other operators to route your call. When the connection was made, she would advise you to go ahead. After the call was completed, you stayed on the line to find out the charges, or if the connection was broken, you would re-ring the operator to get the charges. Then you would advise Mr. Largen of the charges and pay him. I believe his phone was connected to a switchboard in Granby, a small town to the west, and the phone line was along the railroad tracks.

Farmer on a rural phone line.

Mr. Largen provided an important service to Ritchey in those days. But it had its downside for him. If there was an emergency and someone needed to make a call during the night, they would have to go to Largen's home, a block west of his store, wake him up if he was asleep, explain the emergency and ask him to go unlock his store so they could make a call. I don't think it happened too often because people didn't call except in a true emergency, but it did on occasion. The most serious case would be to call a doctor. We children were all delivered at home by an M.D., Dr. Lamson, but many babies were delivered at home by a midwife in the area.

On one occasion, Dad had to call the doctor during the cold wintry night of January 18, 1930. With snow on the ground and the temperature well below zero – and destined to set a record for the coldest night ever in that county, my father went to Mr. Largen's home and woke him to say that he needed to call Dr. Lamson in the county seat. Mother was in labor and the doctor needed to come right away. Dad made that call, and Dr. Lamson came the 13 miles from Neosho to Ritchey in a Model T Ford. I arrived after midnight on January 19, the night after the record cold temperature in Neosho. Dad said the thermometer on the back porch dipped to 32 degrees below zero. I am personally grateful for Mr. Largen's phone.

About ten years later, there was a phone company in Berwick, about six miles east of Ritchey that brought a single-wire phone line to Ritchey. The line followed the road. A single-wire phone meant that there was one copper wire and the phone circuit was completed through the earth. Each phone had a ground wire that was attached to a metal rod driven deeply into the ground. The signals were often weak, with a lot of static, particularly in dry weather. But it was phone service. I've heard that when the connection was bad people would pour water on the soil near the ground wire to improve the electrical contact with the earth and, thereby, reduce static.

Since my grandparents were close to Berwick and Dad could call his parents at less cost, he signed up for a party line. We had our own phone and, like the one in Largen's Store, it was a large, wooden, wall mounted phone. There were maybe ten other phones on that party line and each had its distinctive coded ring.

The rings to indicate who was being called were not unlike the dot and dash Morse code, with the signals either a short ring or a long ring. A short ring was maybe one second long and a long ring was two seconds or a bit longer. Our call was two shorts and a long, like - - ---. Everyone on the party line heard the rings and knew when you received a call. Moreover, if you were the curious, snoopy

Eavesdropping – getting information for gossiping.

type, you could go to the phone, gently lift the receiver and quietly listen to your neighbor's conversation. There was a problem, however. You could generally tell when someone picked up to listen by a slight click on the line. Also, if more than one joined the eavesdropping party, the signal got progressively weaker, sometimes to the point where you couldn't hear. Usually, you had a good idea who the eavesdroppers were and when you couldn't hear there was no harm in loudly saying, "Mabel, please get off the line. I can't hear." I'm told that often you would hear one or more clicks and then have a much improved signal.

No prudent person would share a deeply held secret on a party line. These phones enriched the gossip that was so essential to the communication in these small communities that had no TV, or, in some cases, radio, and certainly no scandal magazines at the grocery checkout counter. In fact, Largen's or Ray's stores didn't sell magazines or newspapers, let alone The National Enquirer, which probably didn't exist then. Gossip was a form of entertainment as well as information exchange, although the accuracy of the stories was often questionable. The party line had the potential to put all party line holders in rural America on line – the original America On Line.

Although Dad was a farmer, he had learned about physics and basic electricity in his two years at the University of Missouri. He knew the principles of how phones work. I remember when better phones came in and Dad was talking about them, mentioning that they had an all metallic circuit. That meant that instead of depending of the earth to complete the circuit, there were two copper lines and this led to much improved reception.

Before I went to college, we got an improved phone with no party line and the old wooden wall phone was relegated to the attic. Now you have to go to a museum to see these old phones. But they served the rural communities well. In a true emergency, the doctor was only a phone call away. I am personally glad that Mr. Largen had a phone on that cold January night in 1930 when Dr. Lamson was needed, and a messenger didn't have to be sent by car or horse to fetch the doctor.

Today, even as an engineer, I marvel at how pervasive the phone has become. The cell phone, optical circuits and satellites have given us instant communication everywhere. Most young people can't imagine a time when phones were only used in emergencies. In college in the late 1940's, I communicated with my parents by writing, for the cost of a three-cent stamp and some time. I doubt if I called home more that a half dozen times in my four years as an undergraduate. Technology has indeed put most of us on the information superhighway.

QUILTING BEES AND BRAIDED RUGS

There weren't many things more beautiful to a rural woman than a handmade patch work quilt. They appreciated the untold hours of labor that went into these works of art. First, a quilt maker would save cloth scraps of various colors and patterns. These remnants were saved from other sewing projects such as a dress or a shirt. The small pieces were then sewn together to create a quilt pattern. This was not a haphazard process. If the quilt didn't have proper balance of color and pattern combinations, it would be second-rate. In the early days, the patches that made the top of the quilt were sewn together by hand, but Mother had a Singer sewing machine that could, under her skilled hand, perform that task.

No scraps of colorful cloth were thrown away because they could be used in quilts or braided rugs. The bottom of the quilt was made of solid cotton cloth sewn together to make a piece the size of the quilt. Cotton batting provided the insulation and it went between the solid cloth bottom and the colorful patchwork top. The quilting held the batting in place so it didn't lump when washed.

Quilting required a special quilting frame that was adjustable to the size of the quilt. The frame was made of straight, narrow boards that had holes drilled along their entire length on about two-inch centers. The frame could be adjusted into a rectangle of any size for the quilt. The un-quilted top and bottom with the batting in between was then stretched on the frame. The holes were used for lacing the quilt into its stretched position. The whole apparatus looked a little like a colorful trampoline.

The assembled device was placed on small sawhorses or the back of a chair about chest high for a woman sitting in a chair. The quilters would sit in the chairs along the long sides and start the process of sewing the top and bottom together with very small hand stitches. These ladies worked with one

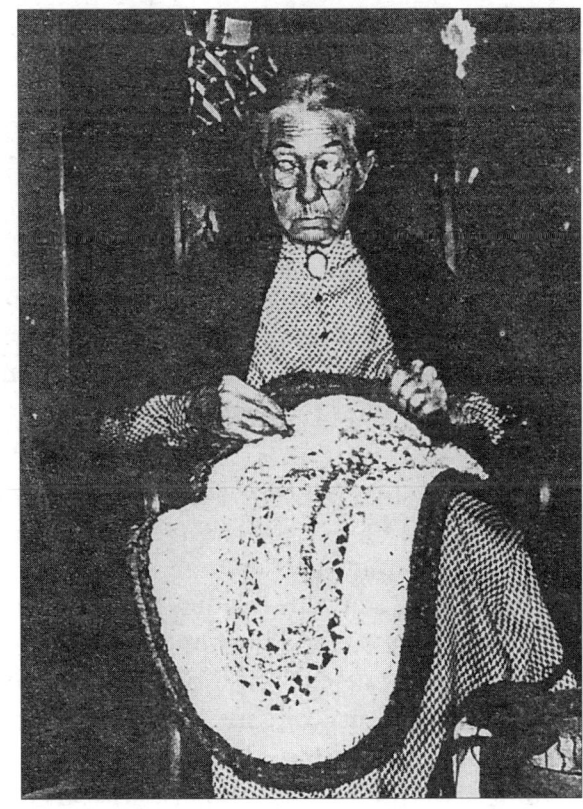

Working on a rag rug before bedtime.

Women quilting for a good cause at a quilting bee.

hand above the quilt and the other below. They could work on one side at a time, or on both if there were enough workers. They would stitch in as far as they could conveniently reach. Then the long stretcher frame boards on the sides would be used to roll up the stitched part of the quilt and bring unstitched areas within reach. The process of quilting and rolling was repeated until the entire quilt was finished.

The stitching wasn't just random rows of stitched thread. Those lines of quilted thread also had to have an artistic pattern that was keyed to the patterns of the patchwork top. The beauty of the quilt came from three things: The colors and quality of the cloth, the mosaic patterns formed when it was cut and combined, and, finally, the line patterns and quality of the quilting stitches themselves. Large stitches, known by quilters as 'toe-nail catchers,' were to be avoided and were the sign of careless work.

Mother often had the quilting frames up in the winter in the living room, the only place with enough space for them. During the day she could do a little quilting if she had time and she could also do some during the winter evenings. An hour or two a day for several weeks would accomplish much. I remember that when the quilts were started and the frame was expanded to its maximum size, there was little space at the sides of the frame. The most convenient way to get through the room was to crawl under the quilt. That was always the path that a child would choose. The quilting frame was put in the west end of our living/dining room. None of the bedrooms were large enough for a bed and quilting frame.

Sometimes a group of ladies would get together to make a quilt. It might be a gift for a newly married couple or for a host of other reasons. This social affair was called a 'quilting bee.' I call it a social affair because it was a time when the women could visit and be brought up to date on families, the community, or general gossip. This tedious quilting work must have gone a lot faster when there was conversation. Mother had a lot of work to contend with, including caring for chickens, helping with the chores, preparing meals and tending to the needs of the family. For her, quilting was usually more for utilitarian purposes than for the artistic value of the quilts. Still, it was art and it was common for women to enter quilts they had made in county fairs and other festivals. But, to my knowledge, Mother never did that. However, I think she enjoyed quilting, particularly when she could do it with other women and visit while she worked.

I remember the large oval braided rug, also called a rag rug, which we had in the children's bedroom of the old house between the two double beds. Since that room wasn't heated, it would be freezing in there and on the coldest winter nights and we would stack four or five quilts on our bed. The wooden floors were very cold. That thick, cotton, braided rug, with its spiraling patterns of braided-cotton scraps sewn together, provided good insulation from the cold floor. Eventually these homemade rugs became rather dingy, since they were very hard to wash and we didn't have a vacuum cleaner. Nonetheless, they were warm and functional. This was another use for scraps of cloth that would be wasted otherwise, and these rugs were virtually indestructible.

We had several braided rugs that Mother had made. However, I don't think she liked them very much since they were hard to keep clean. Smaller, store-bought, cotton rugs could be more easily washed and looked cleaner. However, they never lasted as long as a home-made braided rug. No doubt, if you live with things you have made because you have no choice, you long for manufactured things. I think that was the case with Mother. However, I wish I had that old braided rug that sat between the children's beds in our old house. I'd put it by my bed now to show off its handcrafted beauty.

JOBS FOR THE WOMEN

There weren't many jobs for women in Ritchey that paid a living wage. Most women did not drive, nor did they have access to a car. So they couldn't look for work in neighboring towns. Nearby Neosho had a couple of condensed milk plants–Pet Milk and Carnation Company–but they didn't have many jobs for women. And most people were too poor to employ maids or cooks. Education stopped with a high school diploma, if that, for almost all women living in small, rural towns. There just wasn't much opportunity for work outside the home. So, women helped with farm work, gardening, and drying and canning food for the winter. Above all, they cared for the children, made most of their clothes, and were the primary early educator for them.

Our wonderful neighbor, Mrs. Marion, appeared to me to be the major bread winner in her family. In the summer, she worked in her large garden, pushing a small cultivator to keep the weeds down. She had three dairy cows that she kept in a pasture rented from Mr. Largen. She milked those cows and her husband delivered fresh milk and butter to the neighbors. One son, Roy, was a nearby farmer, and he would put hay and feed in the small barn in back of her house so the cows had feed in the winter. Roy would plant some sorghum cane for his mother and used his tractor to power a roller cane press to squeeze the juice out of the raw cane. In the fall, Mrs. Marion would fire up her special molasses cooker and make sorghum molasses. She would sell the molasses in one-gallon, shiny, tin, molasses buckets the size and shape of a gallon paint bucket. This enterprise provided some income, but its operation only lasted a few weeks in the late summer or early fall. It is described in another essay.

Some of the women would do sewing if they had a sewing machine, but many didn't own one. Others might make quilts to sell because they were sewn by hand. There were some very beautiful quilts made in that part of the world. In the 1930's, a woman would be lucky if she could make 15 to 25 cents an hour.

In and around Ritchey there were two seasonal enterprises that gave women a chance to earn money. One was picking strawberries in the spring. Southwest Missouri, particularly in the rocky hill country, was good for growing strawberries and these were picked in the spring. I think most of these went to berry sheds, where they were put in strawberry boxes and shipped by rail to cities. The pickers had a wooden tray that would hold six, quart boxes of strawberries. The pickers would go down a row stooped over, picking the fresh strawberries, and, when they turned them in they received a stamped aluminum token for each box. Those tokens were worth a few cents each. At the end of the day they would cash in their tokens and take home a few dollars for their day of stoop labor.

Both women and children picked strawberries during the short harvesting season. One problem was that it was tempting for children large enough to pick strawberries to stay out of school to earn some money. I never picked strawberries for pay because we had work on our farm to be done, but I envied those who could earn ready cash that way. My sister Helen did pick strawberries, but only on Saturday. Our parents would never permit any of us to skip school to work, regardless of how pressing the work might be.

For several years during my boyhood, there was a tomato canning factory just south of the railroad tracks and west of the depot. It conveniently straddled The Branch, a small stream that flowed through Ritchey, and tomato peels and other waste could be dumped in it. After each rain that material would be carried a short distance from Ritchey to Shoal Creek. The canning factory season was during the late summer and early fall when tomatoes were in good supply.

The farmers on small, rocky hill farms would plant a few acres of tomatoes timed to come into production during the canning factory season. This was a good opportunity for those small farmers in the hills to raise a cash crop. Picking the tomatoes was labor intensive and, like picking strawberries, was stoop labor. But growing tomatoes definitely could bring needed cash to the family.

Dad didn't normally raise tomatoes for the factory and depended on dairy cows, pigs and chickens as the source of income. But one year, he decided to plant five acres of tomatoes for the canning factory. During the preceding winter, we made tomato crates using a pattern he probably obtained from the county agent. They were made of oak slats the size of a wooden lath, about a quarter-inch thick and an inch-and-a-half wide. They were nailed together by hand, with a space between each slat for air circulation. I don't know how many crates we made, but it was a lot. I got more experience in nailing than I wanted, although I usually enjoyed building things.

We set out thousands of tomato plants in our tomato field. We fertilized them and they grew well and in August they produced an abundance of fruit, several tons at least. Dad didn't hire tomato pickers. That was left to the family – himself, Mother, John, Helen and me. I don't recall if Glenn was old enough for the task, but, if he had been, he would have had his share of stoop labor picking tomatoes and loading them on horse-drawn wagons for the trip to the factory.

The canning factory employed dozens of women during its roughly six-week season. The tomatoes were washed and scalded and then moved on a conveyor past a long bench of women. They used a special spoon-shaped tomato knife to remove the scalded skins and core the tomatoes. Then they'd put them in shiny tin cans that moved on another conveyor to a capper and on to large cooking racks that would be hoisted, swung over the cooking vat, and then lowered into the boiling water that was heated by a large furnace. After cooking, the tomatoes would be hoisted out of the cooking vat and sent on to the area where the cans were dried, labeled and packed into boxes for ultimate shipping by rail. The canning factory was the one major production enterprise in the village. It required a lot of labor and most of that was provided by the local women.

This was a good source of income for women during its short season. But like most things in the village, its days were numbered. The canning factory closed around 1940, never to open again. Since I disliked the stoop labor of picking tomatoes, I was not sorry to see it go. But it was a sad day for the many women, who needed the extra cash they earned at the canning factory.

GAMES

There weren't any specialty toy stores in Ritchey or even in the county seat, Neosho. However, the Neosho dime store on the court house square had a small toy section with inexpensive toys and trinkets. Sponge-rubber balls, inexpensive games, toy guns, and dolls were available for anywhere from 15 cents to a dollar. Larger toys, such as tricycles and wagons were at the hardware store or in the Sears & Roebuck catalog. Toys were generally purchased only at two times during the year, at Christmas and for birthdays. No one had many store-bought toys and children or their dad made most of their toys. Still, I have no doubt that children had just as much fun in the 1930's as they do today with their electronic games. None of our toys had batteries and computer chips were unknown.

We learned to use our imagination to create things. If we played cowboys and Indians, all we needed was a toy pistol, a crooked stick or your pointed forefinger for a gun. A chicken's tail feather attached to a string made a headband for an Indian costume. A farmer's red handkerchief was the bandanna bank robber's mask. The plot for the game played tended to mimic the storyline in the latest Hopalong Cassidy, Gene Autry or Roy Rogers moving picture we'd seen.

There was always a lot of running and hiding involved in children's play. These were not games for 'couch potatoes.' To be a cowboy required a broom-handle horse and a good imagination. Holding the broom handle at one end and straddling it gave us our imaginary version of Roy Rogers' famous horse 'Trigger,' Gene Autry's 'Champion,' or the Lone Ranger's 'Silver.' Your horse was as fast as your legs. A cowboy hat added reality and the fifty-nine cent straw hat from last summer worked well. The variations possible in these games were limited only by our imaginations. The Tarzan movies were also sources of make-believe games, with an opportunity for us to compete as the best imitator of the yell of Tarzan of the Jungle.

The games represented the prejudices of the day. Seldom if ever were the Indians the good guys. They were the attackers of covered wagons and they scalped the innocents. The one exception that I recall was Tonto, the faithful Indian companion of the Lone Ranger. The youngest children were generally relegated to the less desirable roles of Indian or outlaw. In the end, the cowboy movie idol was always the winner, with the outlaws and Indians always ending up captured and in jail – or dead. The accuracy of those toy pistols was remarkable with the shots always being fatal after a shout of, "Bang, you're dead."

For young children, the total enjoyment from play seemed correlated with the amount of running involved, whether it was 'ante-over' played with a rubber ball or one of the tag games like 'Dare Base' or 'Blackman.' The latter was another example of the latent, but unacknowledged, prejudice in these Ozark hills, where there were few African Americans.

Ante over was a game for all ages. The equipment was a dime-store sponge rubber ball, the size of a tennis ball, and a house or other building with a simple roof and no gutters. It had to have an unobstructed path around it. Two team leaders chose sides. Any size group could play and adults joined the children. The teams would go to opposite sides of the house. The one with the ball would call out, "ante over," and then threw the ball over the house. If a person on the opposite team caught the ball on the fly, that entire team would silently run around building each acting like they had the ball to confuse the opposition. The opposing team would take off around the other end of the house. The player who had caught the ball would try to hit an opposing player with the ball. If successful, the player who was hit was captured and had to join the team that had caught the ball. If no player was hit the game would continue with the player who caught the ball, yelling, "ante over," and throwing this time.

If the ball was not caught on the fly, the ante over process would continue in the opposite direction. The only time the teams exchanged sides was when the ball was caught. The team with the most players when the game ended was the winner. The game also ended when the players' energy ran out, time available expired, or when virtually all the players had been captured by one team.

Common homemade toys included stilts, a slingshot or beanie flipper (which was often referred to as a nigger flipper, again an indication of the terrible prejudices of the area at that time), rolling hoops, whistles, and even tin cans, which served in several games. Stilts were simply long poles to which blocks of wood were attached at anywhere from 18 inches or more off the ground. The poles extended about five feet above the blocks. The trick was to be able to walk with one's feet on the blocks and hands on the handles above. It was really a competition and the kid who could stay up longer or walk on the tallest stilts was the acknowledged winner. While it might appear easy, it took a lot of talent and practice to be a good walker on high stilts. My older brother, John, was always quite good on stilts.

Every boy had a slingshot, which was made by cutting a forked, Y-shaped branch from a small limb. The base of the Y needed to be about three-quarters-of-an-inch in diameter and perhaps four inches long. The upper arms were also about four inches long. Strips of rubber about a half-inch wide or a little wider and about a foot long were cut from an old automobile inner tube. That was when all auto tires had separate inner tubes. Now you'd have to use bicycle inner tubes to make sling shots since virtually all of today's tires are tubeless. A piece of thin, flexible leather was needed for the pocket where the stone was placed. This was usually made from the tongue of a worn-out shoe.

The ends of the rubber strips were attached to the arms of the forked shaped branch that had been cut and stripped of its bark. The other ends were fastened to each end of the leather stone holder, which was usually a one-by-three-inch rectangle, with the corners rounded. To have a good slingshot, the rubber from the inner tube needed to be very elastic. A slingshot, which could be carried easily in a hip pocket, was a handy thing for a boy to hunt with, although few birds or rabbits were felled by its stones. A lot of them no doubt were startled as the stones whizzed by. Perhaps the greatest pleasure came from the fun and anticipation of hunting with the slingshot you'd made yourself. You also could challenge a playmate, who also had a slingshot, to see who could knock a tin can off a post the most times with ten shots at twenty paces.

Our whistles were made from a straight section of a soft maple branch that had been cut when the sap was flowing in the spring or summer. We tapered one end for the mouthpiece and cut around the wood just through the bark about four inches from the mouthpiece end. Our trusty jackknife was all that we needed for the job. By gently tapping the bark with the back of the knife handle, you could loosen it so it would slip off over the mouthpiece. A small notch for the whistle hole was cut about three-quarters-of-an-inch from the mouthpiece and then the bark slipped off. A whistle cavity was then cut with the size of the cavity controlling the tone. Finally, the top of the branch from the cavity to the mouthpiece was shaved to provide an air passage from the mouthpiece to the whistle notch and sound cavity. The bark was then slipped back in place and you had a whistle.

Each whistle had a different tone, and you could make one with a variable tone by cutting the cavity completely through the branch and sliding the end away from the mouthpiece back and forth while you blew. But these fancy whistles were not so durable and didn't work well when the bark dried. So more often we made the simple whistles. Whistles were extremely convenient for signaling when boys were playing games where hiding was involved, since each whistle had its characteristic tone.

Tin cans provided hours of fun. This was before the days of thin aluminum cans and the tin-coated, iron cans were quite durable. Besides the various versions of Kick-the-Can, there was a version of hockey played with sticks and a tin-can puck. This game was largely unsanctioned by the parents and usually didn't last too long because someone would eventually get a stick whacked across their shin, causing considerable pain. If no blood flowed the victim might be shamed into staying to keep the game going.

Another game involved stomping your shoe in the middle of an old style iron drink can laid on its side so the ends came together affixing it to your shoe sole. I recall that this was done more by girls than by boys. On reflection, it's hard to see why this was fun, but I recall several girls walking down the street with tin cans attached to their shoes, laughing and giggling as they went. Short stilts, without handles, could be made by punching holes in each side of two cans and fastening them to your shoes with a heavy string or baling wire. The string or wire could be extended so it could be held taut with your hands to hold the cans against your shoe soles. The object was to walk on the contraptions without falling and, like most games, this was a competition. Whatever you did, you wanted to do it better than your friends.

Strange as it may sound, I remember amusing myself by swatting flies and later learning to catch then with cunning and quickness of hand. Since we had dairy cattle, and even separated the cream from the milk on the back porch of the old house until about 1940, there were lots of flies around. Since no one liked flies, we would kill them any way we could. We used homemade fly traps, used sticky flypaper, and fly spray in the house and the barn. Still, there were always flies on the porch in the summer. They would walk around sampling dried milk that had spilled on the unpainted floor. Even if you hosed the porch, the milk soaked into the wood and attracted flies.

The fly-swatting game I played was to watch them congregate and then see how many I could kill with one swat. I recall frequently getting a half dozen on a single swat, and maybe as many as ten on a few occasions. It didn't make any difference how many you killed, there were always more with the breeding ground of the cow lots nearby. Catching flies with your bare hand was another thing. Since the fly always flew as your quickly moving hand neared it, the trick was to judge where the fly would be when your hand arrived. Also, you needed to concentrate on the fly's eyes and get it looking at you and not your poised hand. I was good enough at it that I would challenge all comers to fly-catching contests. You might be sitting someplace and a fly would appear. Since you can't always carry a fly swatter, fly-catching skills came in handy – and it was fun.

A greenish, shiny, flying bug we called the June bug usually came in the late spring or early summer. It was a beautiful, green beetle, with a crusty back and a sturdy character. They didn't bite or sting. It didn't seem possible that these creatures could come from the white grubs that live in the soil, which to me were not pretty at all. While the June Bugs were with us, we used to catch them and tie a thread around one of their legs. Although they were tethered to you, they would fly their hearts out as little, temporary pets. You could run and follow your June bug as it tried to escape. When our parents were alive and lived on the farm in Ritchey, we taught our children the art of catching and tethering June Bugs when they visited their grandparent's farm.

Games frequently played by two or three children, included marbles, jacks, mumbly peg, jump rope

Our daughter and a niece with their tethered June bugs on their noses.

and washer (or penny) pitching. Marbles and jacks were played outdoors in the summer and indoors on the floor in the winter. There were other indoor games in the winter like 'Hide the Thimble,' and some table games that were inexpensive, such as dominoes, checkers, various card games and Chinese checkers. Dad made a Chinese-checkers board and all that was needed was an appropriate number of marbles of the correct colors.

The most popular marbles game involved simply drawing a circle with a stick on a clean, smooth patch of soil that was bare and packed. Then we'd place the marbles in the center. It was a boys' game. Each shooter had his personal shooting marble called a 'taw.' Since the shooting was done by bending the thumb inside the closed fingers and holding the marble with the forefinger against the thumb knuckle and accurately shooting it at the target with a flip of the thumb, the taw had to be just the right size and surface texture. Our marbles were mostly glass and a bag of maybe three dozen or more could be bought for a dime or a little more. However, we also used steel ball bearings, which we would get when a ball bearing would go bad in a piece of farm machinery or down at Dink's garage when he replaced a wheel bearing of a car. These were called 'steelies.' Sometimes the taw was called an 'agate,' but I don't think any of our playing marbles were real agate. Shooting at steelies was a bit hazardous because there was a danger that your taw would break, usually popping in two hemispherical sections of equal size.

There were a lot of variations in the game of marbles besides the one, where you tried to shoot as many marbles as possible out of the circle. You shot from the edge of the circle, and if you knocked a marble out and kept your taw in the circle, you shot again from that spot. A good shooter could nearly clean the ring if he waited until the end to go after the large marbles and more dense steelies. The heavier marbles would cause the taw to bounce back out of the ring instead of stopping at the point of impact when the hit was perfect. There was a lesson in physics here. The winner was the one with the most marbles in his pocket when the ring was cleaned. If you were a gambler, you could play 'keeps' which meant each participant put the same number of marbles in the ring and you kept all the marbles you knocked out. Mother wouldn't let us play 'keeps' if she knew about it, because she viewed it as gambling.

Other variations of marble games were ones where four-inch holes were dug in the bare ground at various locations and you built an obstacle course to be negotiated in the same manner as miniature golf. Using your taw only, each player shot alternately. If you went in the hole, you could shoot again toward the next hole. The winner was the first one in the final hole. Another variation, which was good indoors or outdoors, was to line several marbles in a row on the floor and shoot at them from a distance of about ten feet. If you hit one, you got it and could shoot again from the original shooting location. The winner was the one with the most marbles after all marbles in the line had been hit. In a sense, this was a little like duck-pin bowling, except all that we needed were a few glass marbles that you could buy four-for-a-penny.

The marbles were beautiful because they came in all colors and combinations of colors. Some had rainbow-like striations inside the nearly clear glass. I guess there must have been an infinite variation in the color combinations and internal light reflecting properties of marbles.

Not only are marbles colorful, but this is an international game for boys. Boys seem to play marbles in even the most poverty stricken villages. In a village in the Himalayan Mountains of Northern India,

Marbles.

I have seen boys playing marbles in the dirt, except the shooting technique was totally different. Here the marble was catapulted by placing the taw at the end of one forefinger, and while holding it with the thumb and forefinger of the other hand the catapulting forefinger was pulled back and released to send that taw zinging with uncanny accuracy. In India, I have also seen a shooting technique where the taw was placed between the thumb and forefinger and popped out with a pinching action much like popping out watermelon seeds. While the velocity of the marble was not so great, the accuracy that some of the children obtained was amazing and indicated untold hours of practice.

Incidentally, spitting or blowing watermelon seeds was also a contest we enjoyed while eating watermelons during their delightful summer season. Seedless watermelons had yet to be developed. Then, all had big black seeds. By curling the tongue or pursing the lips in a small circle and using a blow-gun action, we could get good distances.

Pitching pennies was a game that I didn't play much and I never told my folks about it on the few occasions when I did. I like to compete, but I am not a real-money gambler at heart. Pitching pennies was real-money gambling. You drew a line, which the players stood behind when pitching the pennies. Another line about fifteen feet away was the target. There were no sidewalks in Ritchey except for a short block by Ray's Store downtown, where the seams in the sidewalk could be used for pitching pennies. The rules were simple. The player whose penny was closest to the target line on any given toss took the pennies from all participants. The game ended when one player had all of the pennies. Sometimes we played the game with washers from Dad's supply in the workbench area in the barn.

Horseshoes was another favorite game. We usually played with real iron horseshoes – the ones that were made by the blacksmith in town. The iron stakes for this game were usually made from old Model T Ford axles. Children sometimes played horseshoes, but it was more often played by men on leisurely Sunday afternoons.

A hoop was another popular home made toy. Any iron hoop could be used. One of the best was the demountable iron rim from a truck tire rim. These are not used now. It was smooth, narrow and about 20 inches in diameter. A boy would take a stick of his choosing and roll the hoop ahead of him. Any size smooth, circular piece of iron would do, including some that were less than a foot in diameter. It just depended on what you could find. The large ones were easier to control than the small ones. Also, the stick sometimes had a crosspiece nailed to one end to help control the hoop. The goal was to be in total control of the hoop as you ran. If you had a hoop and had to run an errand, it was logical to take the hoop and practice on the way. If you were really good, you could roll your hoop over a small target or across the railroad tracks and not lose control. Rolling old auto tires was also fun and provided another use for the tires in addition to making tire swings or cutting them in half like a bagel and making shallow containers for watering chickens.

A boy's pocketknife was very useful. Besides making slingshots, whistles and simply whittling or carving on a soft piece of wood, you could use the knife to play mumbly peg. The small blade of the typical two-bladed jackknife was fully opened and the longer blade was half opened. This meant the

Mumbly peg.

small blade pointed out from the end of the knife handle and the long blade was at a right angle to the handle. The long blade was stuck slightly into the ground and the end of the handle was placed on your forefinger, which was resting on the ground. You flipped your finger up, giving the knife a spinning motion. If the knife stuck into the ground on only the short blade when it landed, that was four points. If it came to rest only on both blades, you got three points. Two points were scored if the knife stuck on the long blade only, and you got one point when it ended up resting on the long blade and the end of the handle. No points were scored if the knife fell over, which was the most common occurrence. The players alternated flips and the game went to 21 points. Scores were kept by scratching marks in the dirt for each point. The dirt had to be moist and soft to play this game.

Mother in her sixties showing her grand children how to play jacks.

The winner cut a short piece of a small stick, usually a wooden match stick, to a half-inch length and stuck it slightly into the ground. Then while holding the fully opened long blade and using the back of the knife handle as a hammer, the victor closed his eyes, or was tightly blindfolded, and had one chance to drive the short stick into the dirt. Most losers wanted the blindfold to be used to keep the winner from peeking. The loser had to root around and get the stick out of the ground with his teeth. The loser always hoped the winner would miss the stick in an overzealous attempt to hit it very hard and drive it deep into the dirt. Mother never understood why boys liked to play this game and discouraged it. But it was still quite popular with young boys.

Girls played jacks. Although I have seen boys try to play jacks, it was never more than an effort to prove an ill-advised claim that anyone could do it. The girls developed uncanny skill and dexterity in playing jacks on the floor and any boy who thought he could do better got his comeuppance when he attempted to prove his claim. I remember Mother, well into her sixties at the time, teaching her granddaughters how to play jacks. They had never seen grandmother sitting on the wood floor with a small rubber ball and handful of jacks. They were surprised at how good she was. Obviously, Mother spent a good bit of time in her childhood playing the game in the early 1900's.

Our school didn't have much playground equipment. The grade-school children had a swing and a teeter-totter (seesaw), both made locally, and nothing else. So, during the 30-minute recess, the teachers would get the children involved in group games that featured enough running to burn off the excess energy that most of the kids had. The games were designed so everyone ran, not just the athletically gifted. These games included jump rope, London Bridge, hopscotch and May I? (these four were mainly for girls), dodgeball, red rover, and a host of tag games such as dare base, and, I regret to say, blackman.

Dodgeball required only a volley ball. A large circle at least 30 feet in diameter was scratched in the dirt with a stick and all of the children, except one, got in it. The object was simply not to get hit. The thrower stayed on the outside of the large circle and threw at someone inside. When a player was hit he or she left the circle and then participated in throwing. The light volleyball could be thrown directly or finessed with a spin bounce, making the ball jump off line to hit someone. The last person in the ring was the winner. Surviving to the end took quickness and agility.

Jump rope only required a length of jute rope, usually with a knot tied in each end to prevent it from unraveling. A single-person jump rope might be seven feet long. A girl would hold an end of the rope in each hand and swing the rope over her head and jump each time the rope came toward her feet. Girls developed fancy jump steps. The rope would come forward over her head in front of her to the ground. Or it could be rotated in the opposite direction, which required a bit more practice to become adept. Since the jumper controlled the rope, she could time her jumps fairly easily.

A second method required a longer rope of perhaps 20 feet, held by two girls one at each end. They would stand maybe 15 feet apart and swing the rope so it made a loop higher than the tallest girl. Girls would line up at an angle and enter the rotating looping rope and jump maybe twenty times and then exit without stopping the rope. The objective was to always jump at the right time so the rope didn't hit your feet. Sometimes two or three girls would get in and jump at the same time. Fancy jump steps added to the fun. The rate of rotating the rope might be at one second intervals, but if a girl called for 'hot pepper' the girls on the rope would speed up until the jumping girl could no longer keep pace.

Hopscotch is a game in which a figure, usually a series of squares in a pattern like a two T's placed top-to-top with one square between, is scratched on the ground or laid out on a sidewalk with chalk. A girl tosses a small stone to the first square and hops through the course and back, picking up the stone on the return. The next time the girl tosses the stone to the next, more-distant square and repeats the process. If the stone does not stay in the target square, she loses her turn and her competitor tries. The winner is the one who first completes the course by having tossed the stone to all squares and hopped the course.

Red rover was a game in which the class divided into two groups of equal size. The groups stood in lines parallel to one another about 60 feet apart. The object was to capture other players and the team with the most players at the end of recess was the winner. One team started by holding hands as tightly as possible and stretching the line as far as possible while holding hands. That team picked an opposing player that it thought it could capture, say Mary. Then it called to the other team, "Red rover, red rover, let Mary come over."

Mary's task was simple. She decided which link in the human chain she thought she could break. She then ran as fast as she could crashing her body into the tightly held hands at the chosen point. If she broke the grip and went through, she had captured one of the two players whose grip had failed and could take the captured boy or girl to her side. If the grips held, she was snared and she had to join the opposing team. The game continued with alternate teams calling, "red rover, red rover, let (the name of the one chosen) come over." The winning team was usually the one that could most effectively apply the double-wrist grip so that even small players who had small hands and weak grips could be protected by stronger players on either side. To my knowledge, no one ever had an arm jerked out of its socket in this game, although, on reflection, it seems that must have been a possibility. But the players were small children, less than ten years old.

Crack-the-whip was another running game. I don't recall that the teachers encouraged this game, but it was played nevertheless. It was similar to red rover in that the players tightly held hands, and a strong grip was essential. A very strong player, usually a boy, would be at one end of a chain of boys and girls who were all holding hands. He was the 'whip cracker.' The group would run in a line while holding hands until at some unannounced point the whip cracker would suddenly stop and pull hard starting a whip-cracking action that could send the player at the end flying off the chain. The trick to staying on was a strong grip. It was no game for sissies because the end person or two often went tumbling and skidding along the ground if they lost their grip. I suppose part of the fun was seeing the predicament of your unfortunate playmates. A good whip cracker could snap several off the running human chain. Children from farms who had developed strong grips by milking cows were good at this game.

Dare base and blackman were both forms of tag. In dare base, as I recall, two parallel lines were scratched in the dirt, maybe 60 feet apart. These lines comprised bases and one couldn't be caught while on a base. One person was chosen to be 'it' and this was usually a boy. He went to the middle area between the lines. He could then dare someone to leave the base and that person had to run to the opposite base and, hopefully avoid being tagged. Once tagged, the person went to the middle and became a tagger or catcher. Blackman was similar, but more frustrating to the person who was in the middle at the beginning. Here, the participants could leave the base at will and oftentimes the poor person in the middle, called 'the blackman,' could be rather harried before he caught that first person to join him in the middle to become the second 'blackman.' Those small or relatively slow couldn't be forced to leave the safe haven of the base, as was the case in dare base.

In Ritchey, most children were healthy because both work and play involved a lot of exercise. There were no fast food places, and childhood obesity was rare. We didn't have many store bought toys, but that didn't stop us from having fun. As we grew older, we played organized games like softball, volleyball and basketball. All of them, including basketball, were outdoor sports since we didn't have an indoor gymnasium at our grade school.

The games we played as children had four characteristics. First, expensive equipment wasn't needed. In some cases they were tag games or hopscotch, which required no equipment at all. Others required only an inexpensive ball. Second, they were virtually all action games with a lot of running. To some degree, they helped us develop dexterity and hand-eye coordination. Third, all in class without a physical handicap participated. No one could opt to sit on the sidelines. Finally, in many games we made the rules. As long as all played by the same rules, that was fine. Computer and TV games were far in the future, as were the widespread child obesity problems that are plaguing the country today.

We didn't have any African Americans in our community, and I suppose most would have said we weren't prejudiced. But it is clear to me now that there was prejudice. Why else, when we were in the third and fourth grades, would we play a game at school called 'blackman' or call our slingshot a 'nigger flipper?' Or why didn't the Indians ever turn out to be the good guys in the cowboys and Indians games? While I am embarrassed to mention those names for the games, that was what they were called in the 1930's in Ritchey. I suspect the same is true in many other communities in the Ozarks, as well. It's a part of our history, and we need to acknowledge the past and learn from it.

TELLING GHOST STORIES

Ritchey had quite a few raconteurs, but that isn't a word that most villagers would have recognized. I never heard the word used, but if it had been, someone might have demanded an apology, thinking that a raconteur might be someone who was crossways with the law – like John Dillinger or Al Capone.

French words weren't used in Ritchey. But most locals learned to spin a good yarn almost as soon as they could talk. Gossipers usually embellish the facts a bit as stories are retold over and over. Oftentimes, stories were manufactured on the spot. So the story was told slowly to buy more time to think about the story line. One thing for sure, you had to verbally create the setting. If it was a ghost story, the setting could be in a cemetery or an old, abandoned house that was 'haunted.' A word picture of the dirty, cobweb-filled, dark, dank cellar where the original owner had been buried under the dirt floor and his ghost would return at night – and so on – was created. Many movies at the time were horror films and scary and Alfred Hitchcock films were always very much so. Some of these movies were a source of ideas.

The best ghost stories were told in totally darkened rooms or outside on cloudy, moonless nights. Bats were good additions – vampire bats, of course, to bring blood sucking into the picture. Living in the country, we all knew about real bats and some were very much afraid of them.

In telling ghost stories, we tried our best to set the imagination racing, which often meant that parents later had to spend some time trying to calm children so they could sleep. Telling ghost stories seemed to be a favorite pastime of school children when they would get together after dark and had some time to kill. These stories might not have parent approval, but verbal communication skills were improved.

Death was very scary, of course, so involving undertakers was good. We soon learned who the brave ones among us were because some youngsters were just too frightened to listen to these ghostly tales. Calmly sitting through a creepy ghost story was thought to be a mark of courage. We must have told other stories, but I mostly remember the ghost stories. Halloween was the best time for them.

There was an old, vacant, two-story, concrete house out on Highway 60 near Ritchey, that everyone called the 'haunted house.' I don't know who originally lived there and when, but it was not occupied until after World War II, when a veteran friend of the family bought the house and property and for a short time operated a small convenience store and gas station beside the highway. That didn't last long, and the business closed. I doubt if that house was ever occupied again. Even though it must have been difficult to tear down those concrete walls, it's now gone like so many other things we knew. I actually slept in that house after the friend moved in after the war. It was probably in about 1946. Ten years earlier I would never have imagined sleeping in the 'haunted house.'

Joanne's father came from a story-telling family in Tennessee. And they were letter writers. Not only did they tell stories when they were at the annual family get-togethers but they would tell stories in chain letters that followed a circuit among the ten siblings. When that envelope arrived with ten long-hand letters, perhaps four pages each, a person would be brought up-to-date on how things were in all of the siblings' families. That envelope would contain perhaps 20 pages of long-hand letters written on the front and back. The process was each sibling would take out his/her last letter and add a new one. If each sibling had kept all of those letters, it would comprise a valuable personal history of that family's life.

The chain letter would cycle maybe every two or three months. It is now hard to imagine waiting that long for news. If any member did not participate the communication link would be broken. That chain letter continued for decades until some of the family started dying and the telephone became the means of staying in touch. But the communication capacity we have today with the internet and cell phones was inconceivable back then.

Some stories involving the dead were intended to scare. Others were to be humorous. To show the nature of the latter type, I heard this one when I was a young boy.

An old, skinny man with sunken jaws who lived alone in the country had died sitting up in his chair. By the time he was discovered, rigor mortis had firmly set in. The mortician had difficulty getting the body flat so he could get it in the casket for viewing after the funeral. Lacking a better plan, the undertaker rigged a setup with straps attached to a straight, stiff board that held the body flat.

After a lengthy funeral service, the casket was opened for viewing. Several had dutifully walked slowly by for a last glimpse. Then suddenly, with a snap, the chest straps failed and the body sprang upright. The corpse was sitting up in the casket! People panicked, scrambled for the door, and sprinted from the church in every direction – some for a great distance. One man who was subsequently leaving the church in his car noted a trembling participant sitting on a rock by the side of the road a mile from the church. He was still shaking and gasping for breath. The man stopped his car and asked the individual what he thought of the funeral service. Breathing hard and still shaking, the winded person breathlessly responded, "Damned a church with only one door."

THE SWIMMIN' HOLE

Ritchey didn't have a swimming pool. Most likely the only town in Newton County with a swimming pool in the 1930's was Neosho, the county seat. I doubt that most of us in Ritchey had been in a swimming pool more than twice by the time we graduated from high school. However, we had ample swimming opportunities in the summer. The town was located on the north edge of Shoal Creek valley. In that area, the creek runs along the south side of the valley, right at the edge of a wooded, steep hill. The Ritchey mill was directly south of town and its dam impounded water to drive the turbine powering the grist meal. The area just above the dam, once called Mirror Lake, was called the 'mill pond' during my childhood. The current was very slow at the mill pond, and any suspended sediment in the stream settled to the bottom. Therefore, the mill pond had a mud bottom, but the water, while

Swimming below the Ritchey bridge.

murky, wasn't muddy. With one exception that I will mention later, few people swam in the mill pond because of the mud bottom and, except for right at the dam, it was impossible to reach by car.

Below the mill's dam, the water was blue-green, with a gravel bottom, and it was a better place to swim. Ritcheyites would picnic there on Sunday's. Except for a few deep holes, the water wasn't over chest deep to a man and you had to be careful if you were tempted to dive in. When I was growing up, but still rather small, the place where we went swimming was called 'The Bend.' It was located about a quarter mile below the mill and, as the name implies, it was at a bend in the meandering stream. The Bend was a few hundred yards below the old single-lane, iron truss bridge that carried all traffic to the south of Ritchey. However, one could drive to The Bend right along the creek in Largen's field, so it was accessible by car. Roy Marion farmed that field, and he was very tolerant regarding the crop damage caused by auto traffic to Ritchey's most-used swimmin' hole.

As discussed in the essay entitled "Saturday Night Bath," we didn't have a bathroom in our house until about 1941. Most in the town also didn't have indoor plumbing. Therefore, by necessity, not choice, we used an outdoor privy, which some called 'the outhouse.' We simply called it 'the toilet.' We used this facility, rain or shine, and regardless of how cold it was. The toilet paper in the privy was usually last year's Sears & Roebuck catalog. Fortunately, that was when catalog paper had the texture of newsprint and before the days of slick paper catalogs with color pictures. We didn't enjoy the luxury of soft toilet tissues.

When we were small and would on occasion have to urinate or otherwise have to relieve ourselves during the night, we had a chamber pot with a lid on it under the bed. That pot saved us from going out in sub-freezing weather with a flashlight to use one of the two holes in the two-holer toilet – and where any misdirected stream would certainly freeze, providing indisputable evidence of a poor aim. Poor aim was particularly annoying to the girls, and the frozen evidence was hard to hide.

In the winter, when people weren't working in the fields and getting dirty with a lot of sweat, the weekly Saturday night bath was acceptable. But it was another story in the summer. The creek provided an opportunity for a swim and to clean up. This was important to men, who may have been working in itchy grain chaff or hay dust.

At The Bend you entered the water from the north on the inside of the curved meander of the creek where water was shallow. It increased in depth as you crossed the creek, getting to be waist deep on an adult at the south bank and possibly deeper in some scour holes. The current progressively increased as one waded out into deeper water. Children could safely wade and play in the shallow water.

Swimming suits in those days were 100 percent wool. Dad had a one-piece black swimming suit that had straps over his shoulders to hold it up. It was a man's suit with thin straps scarcely covering his chest. He had probably had it since he was married, and it no doubt had a few moth holes that had been repaired. My hand-me-down navy blue wool swimming trunks were used for many years. It also had some patched moth holes. After we went swimming, we would hang the swimming suits on the clothesline to dry. The wool suits wouldn't completely dry in 24 hours and the next day the swimming trunks would still be damp.

The Bend was a charming area on beautiful Shoal Creek, with large, overhanging trees along the banks. The bed of the creek was gravelly, with rounded river-washed stones from three-quarters to three inches in size. These stones weren't sharp, but anyone who didn't go bare-footed in the summer and had tender feet would walk gingerly into the water. As you entered deeper water and buoyancy lightened the weight on your feet, the uneven stones were less of a problem.

Crawfish, which we called 'crawdads,' would hide under the larger stones and we would catch them and carefully try to avoid their pinching claws. On occasion, we would feel a crawdad at our feet and a pinch. It was only startling, never serious. The creek also had leeches and occasionally one of those bloodsucking creatures would latch onto us. That, too, was not serious and a burning match held to the leach's body would cause it to quickly release its hold.

There were several other areas along Shoal Creek that teenagers would use for swimming. The Bend was a good place where parents could take small children and be sure that they wouldn't step off in deep water. Still, excited children could wander out into water over their heads and watchful parents had to be alert to prevent that. Children also could swim, or play in the water, with relative safety in the area below the dam where the water was shallow virtually everywhere. The areas where the teenagers would swim had no shallow areas and were definitely off limits for young children and those who couldn't swim.

There were a few places on the outside of the meanders where the water at the creek bank was deep enough for diving and a wooden plank diving board could be mounted on the bank. One of those places was east of Ritchey at the Turner Bridge on Highway 60. There was another place east of the mill pond in our pasture where my younger brother, Glenn, in his teenage years built a diving board for use by himself and his friends. However, the most common way of entering the deep water was not by a diving board, but by swinging from a rope tied to a large tree limb overhanging the creek. The rope would have some knots tied in it for a better grip. A teenager would climb out partway on the limb and get the rope and then, Tarzan like, swing out over the water and release with a great Tarzan yell, hoping to enter the water in a somewhat dignified manner. It was great fun, and, with a limb extending a good distance out over the creek, it was possible to get a big swing and release eight or more feet above the water. Most of our efforts wouldn't have won any style points.

A swing rope was tied to an overhanging limb at the swimmin' hole that Glenn developed. There was also one just below the iron bridge west of the mill. For a boy to take a mid-afternoon dip to cool off meant that any swimming trunks he might own would be at home. Many probably didn't own trunks. The common way to solve the problem was to skinny dip. The boys would swim without clothes below the bridge, making sure to be in the water when a car approached. This swimming hole had no shallow water so it couldn't be used by small children or those just learning to swim.

Yet another swimmin' hole, popular with teenage boys, was on the south side of the mill pond about two hundred yards above the dam. It was used by boys in Ritchey who were older, perhaps the age of John. To get there you had to carefully walk across the dam and then follow a path upstream to a very large overhanging tree that had the rope swing. This was an out-of-the-way place and I never saw boys swimming there use a bathing suit. Boys could climb out of the water with the aid of large, exposed tree roots along the bank. These roots permitted the swimmers to exit the mud bottom mill pond without being dirty. You could tell when the swimmers were there by the shouts and yells they made as they dropped from the swinging rope into the water. Girls learned to avoid that area when the teenage swimmers were there.

Our summer afternoons weren't spent at the swimmin' holes. On the farm, there were always jobs to be done. The brief swims were for cooling off and for cleaning up. We lived on a beautiful stream, and we went swimming in it on occasion. However, we didn't routinely go to the swimmin' hole for an afternoon of relaxation and a tan. We could get a tan working in the fields. To some degree, our swims were like those of the cowboys of the Old West, where the swims were for refreshment and to a large degree to wash off the sweat and grime.

THE TRAVELING OUTDOOR PICTURE SHOW

Perhaps more than half of the families who lived in Ritchey or nearby didn't have an automobile in the 1930's. They were dependent on walking or using animals to travel where they needed to go. Some didn't have electricity and, therefore, no radio. This was before the days of transistors and radios then had energy devouring vacuum tubes that generated a lot of heat. While there were radios that operated from a 6-volt, lead-acid, car battery, the battery life was short and they were quite expensive. Since Ritchey didn't have a movie house, for many there was little opportunity for any professional entertainment. Life wasn't easy for these hardworking people, who had little money for luxuries. So, in most cases, what entertainment they had they generated themselves.

The nearest movie house to Ritchey was six miles away in Granby, where there was a poorly maintained theater. The wooden seats in the Club Theater were unpadded and the quality of the projector and screen weren't good. Neosho, the county seat, and only 12 miles from Ritchey, had three movie theaters. But only the Orpheum could be classed as being first-rate. The others, like the Club Theater in Granby, were shabby and run down. The picture shows (movies were then always referred to as picture shows) in all these theaters except the Orpheum, were B-grade, but the price wasn't bad. An adult ticket to the B-grade picture shows was 25 cents, and a ticket to the top of the group Orpheum Theater was 40 cents. A child's ticket was maybe half that amount. While these prices were reasonable, they were much too expensive for some people except on special occasions. Since Dad's farming business often took him to Neosho, the picture shows we attended most often were there. However, we were the exception among Ritchey residents, because we had a car and transportation wasn't a major problem.

The first movie I ever saw in Ritchey wasn't an outdoor presentation, but at our school house in the winter. I presume some special arrangement had been made with the Ritchey School Board to have this shown in the school house. This picture show was a silent, flickery film shown on a temporary screen. The audience sat at the pupil's desks or in chairs. I scarcely recall the film or details, but it may have been in 1935. Seeing a picture show was unusual for anyone in Ritchey at that time, and it might have been the adult's excitement over the event that caused me to remember that silent film. But I do remember seeing my first picture show, even if I don't recall the plot, actors or any other details. These incidentals are long since gone.

For those in and around Ritchey who seldom, if ever, had the opportunity to go to a picture show in Granby or Neosho, Abe's Traveling Outdoor Picture Show was a godsend. During the warm season, late spring to early fall, this traveling outdoor picture show came to Ritchey once a week. That traveling show made a circuit, stopping in a different small town or outpost, such as Smackout east of

Ritchey, each night of the week. How could a store and filling station on the highway get the name, Smackout? I don't know! Rumor had it that potential customers came to this unnamed trading post and requested some item. The normal response of the proprietor was, "Sorry, I am smack out of it." The name, 'Smackout,' stuck so the tale goes.

It was only a filling station and associated small store on Highway 60, but to the rural people nearby, it was a place to congregate for a picture show. Abe's show came the same night each week and for Ritchey that was Thursday night for several years and then, for some unknown reason, shifted to Monday night.

When Abe's show came to town, it was with a sixteen millimeter, sound, black-and-white, full-length feature, a cartoon, an episode of a serial and a preview of next week's show. Abe had a small, covered truck, not unlike a small U-Haul rental truck. The truck carried a portable screen that could be hung from a tree, two speakers (also hung from a tree) and enough folding canvas benches without backs to seat perhaps 150 to 200 men, women and children, two or three on a seat. Half or more of the audience would be children. The truck also carried roles of canvas with eight-foot-long stiffeners to be stretched among trees and buildings to provide a temporary 8-foot-high wall around this starlight theater.

In Ritchey, the picture show was set up between two buildings on a smooth, flat area that was normally the croquet court. That was okay, because no one would play croquet on picture-show night. The original Largen's hardware store, where Blackie English and his family lived, and Dink Crow's Garage formed two sides. The front canvas wall was stretched from one building to the tree where the screen was hung and on to the other building. The canvas wall at the back was stretched from one building to a tree by the projector truck, which was backed up to the proper spot for projecting the film, and on to the other wall. The entrance was between the truck and the tree. That was convenient because the 11-cent admission charge for children was handled by Abe's wife at the truck. I'm sure the charge for adults was higher, but probably only a quarter.

Like the drive-in theater of later years, the picture show started when it got dark. The show was only cancelled if it was raining steadily. People would tolerate a canvas seat that was damp from a shower in order not to miss the show.

On picture-show night, the horse-drawn wagons with loads of rural families would start rolling into town in the late afternoon, children laughing in excitement. They would arrive maybe an hour-and-a-half before dusk with makings for a picnic supper. A festive atmosphere enveloped the place. Ray's Store did a big business in soda pop and bologna for sandwiches. Although his store was only a hundred yards from the outdoor theater, he kept it open and never closed to watch the film himself. His store stayed open until his normal closing time or until after the show ended.

During the summer, our farm work and evening chores lasted until well after dark on most days. But on picture-show night we planned ahead to get at the chores early so we could make the show. Still, we were usually rushing frantically to finish washing milking utensils and grabbing a bite to eat in order to get to town, only one block away, before the cartoon started. If we missed the cartoon, we felt cheated by a penny or two of our 11-cent admission.

This was not a continuous show as in regular theaters, where you could stay and see the cartoons the next time around. If we did not have time to wash up much, it was no big deal, because, after all, it was an outdoor theater and dark. Also, others would be there without bathing, so the source of any sweaty odor would be uncertain.

On occasion the show would have not one, but two, early-vintage, black-and-white cartoons – a real bonus. Next was always an episode of a serial, which usually continued for about 13 weeks. The hero or heroine was always left in the most precarious of circumstances at the end of each week's episode. It would seem impossible that death could be averted as the train bore down on the heroine tied to the tracks or as the hero went flying over a cliff as his horse stumbled. We were left hanging until the next time when a miraculous escape would occur. In the end, good always prevailed over evil, and the hero or heroine remained in good health. I remember one serial titled, "The Perils of Pauline." And Pauline managed to escape unscathed from some very perilous circumstances.

The main feature was a full-length, three-reel film. We knew it was a three-reel film because Abe only had one projector in the truck. The feature would stop at the end of each reel, when Abe would rewind that reel and put on a new one. It gave people a chance to stretch after sitting on the crowded backless seats. Sometimes the projector bulb would burn out. That, too, caused a delay until Abe could replace it.

The picture was generally a Western starring such stars as Tom Mix or Hopalong Cassidy. I believe it was before the time of the more popular singing cowboys, Gene Autry and Roy Rogers. Sometimes the film was a Bowery Boys feature, very slapstick comedy with virtually no storyline. Although most seemed to enjoy the film as much as if it were, "Gone with the Wind", I doubt if any of the films could be rated above C. Film ratings in those days related to the quality of the actors and the story. They had nothing to do with violence, sexual content, or nudity. While there might be implied sexual content, it was indirect and there was never any nudity. But the children got their 11 cents worth, no doubt about that.

The conversation around town the following week would be on the plight of the serial star. Some would be sure that this time his faithful Indian companion, Tonto, would not be able to save the Lone Ranger from certain death or that Pauline would indeed succumb to her peril this time.

I suspect that the only films that several around Ritchey ever saw during the year were at Abe's Traveling Outdoor Picture Show. The events seemed real, and make believe and drama weren't things that most people in Ritchey thought about. Abe provided a wonderful escape from a hard life for these Ritchey people, and the film always had a happy ending, even the serial at the end of its 13 gut-wrenching episodes.

There were a few in Ritchey who stopped going to the outdoor picture shows after they were converted to the Holiness religion during a revival one summer. The Fire Baptized Holiness Church, organized after a major tent revival, taught that moving picture shows were bad. I fear that the devout among the Holy Rollers and their children missed out on the entertainment that Abe provided.

SUNDAY AFTERNOON BASEBALL

There weren't many things to do in Ritchey on Sunday afternoons in the summer. Television didn't yet exist and the town didn't have a local movie theater. Ritchey also didn't have a city park or swimming pool, although there were several swimmin' holes down at the creek. We could listen to the St. Louis Cardinals baseball game on the radio, but we could also do that on week nights. We often listened to the broadcast of Cardinals night games on the small radio in the barn while we were milking. It made milking go faster.

Baseball was a favorite sport and Missouri had two major-league baseball teams, both in St. Louis, the Browns in the American League and the Cardinals in the National League. Both teams played in the same ball park, old Sportsman's Park, located a short distance from downtown St. Louis. In fact, in those days, before expansion of the big leagues, there weren't any teams in the United States west of St. Louis. Many eastern cities, besides St. Louis, had two teams, such as Chicago, Philadelphia, Boston, and New York. One was in the National League and one in the American League.

There were two minor-league professional teams in southwest Missouri. The Springfield Cardinals, a farm club of the St. Louis Cardinals, and the Joplin Miners, a New York Yankees farm team. Ft. Smith Arkansas had a farm team in the same league. Missouri also had the Kansas City Blues, a Yankee farm club, which was just below the majors. Kentucky's Louisville Cardinals was another Cardinal farm team just one step removed from the major leagues.

One of the biggest trills I remember was going to a professional baseball game, and the Joplin Miners was the only team near enough for us to consider. We made it to a professional minor-league game only once or twice during the season, and that was always a twilight double-header. Two-games-for-the-price-of-one was the incentive that made it time and cost effective, both important to Dad. On those rare occasions when we were going to a game 35 miles away in Joplin, we would do our chores early -- really early. We would milk the cows maybe three hours before the normal milking time and rush to wash the milking equipment and leave for the games, having a bite to eat in the car. Mother prepared food for us, but she didn't go to the games. The first game of the double-header was always seven innings and the second game a full nine innings. We seldom made it there for the start, but we would enjoy a lot of baseball during the evening. Regardless of how lopsided the score might be, we always stayed until the last out to get the full measure of value for our money.

In those games, we had the chance to see some of the great ballplayers as they passed through the minor leagues on the way to the majors. I had a chance to see Stan Musial in two games in Joplin when he played briefly for the Springfield Cardinals. It so happens that within a very short time after those games Stan was called up to Louisville, and, after being there for about six weeks, he was moved up to St. Louis. I remember seeing him hit a towering home run over the scoreboard near centerfield in Joplin's Miner Stadium. I was a St. Louis Cardinal fan and I became a worshiper of 'Stan the Man' Musial. During the War (World War II) he entered the service, but he returned after the war to have a great career, and I followed his progress religiously, always checking his batting average in the morning paper.

I later had an opportunity to see Stan-the-Man play a few times in St. Louis, and I enjoyed it immensely. In 1946, between my junior and senior years in high school, Mom and Dad let me join a friend, and we hitchhiked to Columbia, where we made preliminary arrangements for enrolling at the University. Then we hitchhiked on to St. Louis for a Friday-night Cardinal game, stayed over for a Saturday game, and a Sunday doubleheader, and finally caught a night train home in a chair car. The Cardinals played the Brooklyn Dodgers in that series. That was the first year ever that two teams tied for the National League championship – the Cardinals and the Dodgers. St. Louis won the one-game playoff and went on to defeat the Boston Red Sox in the World Series. So that summer I saw Stan play on the 1946 World Championship team. What a thrill!

I remember many details of Stan's career, but none more vividly than the flight of that baseball in that home run high over the tall scoreboard I witnessed in Joplin when I was about eleven. As a footnote, when I was working on my Ph.D. degree at the University of Missouri in 1958, my wife, Joanne, and I were in St. Louis. We were poor graduate students on the GI Bill with two small children, Tommy and Kathy, who we had left with friends in Columbia. We decided to really splurge and go to dinner at a famous St. Louis restaurant, Stan Musial's and Biggies. As fate would have it, my hero, who was then retired from baseball, came in. He was greeting guests and autographing 8- by 10-inch black-and-white photographs. I asked him to autograph one for our son Tommy, who was three years old. Quick-witted Joanne asked him to autograph one for Kathy, who was less than two, although Joanne didn't mention that fact. The photograph was really for me, but I couldn't tell that to Stan the Man. The real thrill for me was being within inches of Stan the Man, my childhood baseball hero.

Although trips to see the Joplin Miners were rare, we still saw plenty of baseball right in our backyards. Most towns had an amateur team, and Ritchey was no exception, I don't remember if the team had a name like 'The Ritchey Tigers' or even a sponsor, but they did have uniforms and played on Sunday afternoons. Their uniforms were mismatched and had seen a few seasons, but they all had 'Ritchey' across the back. The Ritchey home games were played at a baseball diamond at the west end of one of our fields, just south of the depot. So, the baseball field was on our farm. I am sure that Dad provided the space for baseball more out of community spirit than anything else. There was a backstop screen, built of chicken wire, behind the plate. Bleachers sat behind the backstop and for maybe 50 feet along both sides. They were made of rough-sawn, oak lumber and three rows deep. I would guess that nearly two hundred people typically came to the games. There was no admission, but a hat was passed for donations to help buy baseballs, bats and to cover other expenses. I'll bet if they collected more than 20 dollars at one of those games, they were elated.

The games had only one umpire. He was a local and wore street clothes, but no protective equipment. So, he stood behind the pitcher and called the balls and strikes from there. He also had a good view of the bases to make the calls on base runners. A good catcher could finesse a lot of strike calls by quickly moving his mitt as he caught the ball, stopping it just over the edge of the plate. It was an art that went out of baseball when the plate umpire moved behind the catcher.

I really don't remember much about the players, except for two who stood out. One was 'Shorty' Marion. He was a son of our neighbors, Mrs. Marion and Alec, and short, like his father. Shorty was a good shortstop, had a good glove, and was a dependable hitter. He almost always managed to get the bat on the ball. There was a big league player named Marion, Marty Marion of the St. Louis Cardinals, but he wasn't the one that played in Ritchey or even any relation. This Marty, also a shortstop, was tall and lanky, not short, and was known as 'Slats Marion.' Our Shorty Marion wasn't big league material, but he was a good player for the amateur league Ritchey was in.

Pitcher Lefty Oxendine was the heart of Ritchey's team. He was lanky and had a relaxed, loosey-goosey motion, with good control. He was hard to hit. Lefty worked in the lead and zinc mines, so he was underground during the work week. As a result, his skin was pale, compared to others who worked outdoors. When Lefty was pitching, Ritchey had a good chance to win. Local people felt that Lefty had big league potential. I was convinced that he could play for the Cardinals, if he had been given a chance. We'll never know, because Lefty had to work in the mines to support his family, and any dream of being a big leaguer, which he must have had, took second place to supporting his family. The Ritchey team played for the joy of the game.

When I was old enough to play baseball, Ritchey no longer had a team. The Ritchey baseball field was back in dad's crop rotation. The last Ritchey team was fielded before World War II. I played some baseball in high school, and even briefly played on an American Legion team from the small town of Stark City, seven miles south of Ritchey. I was pretty good with the glove, but not a very good hitter of curve balls. However, I did once hit a home run. It wouldn't have been a home run in any park with fences. But if you play in a pasture and hit it between two outfielders, it can roll on-and-on, and you sometimes can round the bases for a home run. My one home run actually rolled just beyond a barbed wire fence. If I'd thought for a moment about the reluctance of most players to risk tearing their uniforms on barbed wire, I could have rounded the bases at a more leisurely pace.

When the Ritchey team was playing, fans came from the surrounding hills to see the games, not just the parents and relatives of the players. It was good entertainment, and those lazy Sunday afternoons at the local ballpark in our field are among my fond memories of growing up in Ritchey.

A CIRCUS COMES TO TOWN

Occasionally we would see a circus train pass through town. We could tell they were circus trains because the boxcars were yellow, with "Ringling Bros. and Barnum & Bailey Circus" painted in large, red letters across the sides. But they never stopped in Ritchey.

Although Ritchey could put together a crowd of maybe 300 people for special events, with its 200 or so inhabitants and people in from the surrounding farms and small villages, that wasn't enough to attract the circus.

But Ritchey did have one advantage over most small towns. Circuses traveled by train in those days. Ritchey had a loading chute for cattle next to the Frisco railroad side track, where a circus could unload its animals, and a small circus did come to town once when I was a boy. There might have been other circuses that stopped during the town's early years, but I never heard about them.

I was about seven years old at the time, and don't remember the name of this small circus, but I do remember the excitement it caused. Once the town kids and those in the country learned the circus was coming, it was hard for them to think of anything else. Many of these kids were from poor families that didn't own cars. So there was no way they could travel 35 miles to Joplin, a city of 35,000 to see the Ringling Brothers Circus. Most had never seen a circus and could only imagine what it was like from the descriptions brought back from Joplin by those who had been lucky enough to go.

My family had a car, but the trip to Joplin still was a major expedition. With our chores and the other farm work, it was difficult to get there. When we did go, usually only once a year, it was pure magic for us kids and we talked for weeks afterwards about the big-cat trainer and his ferocious lions and tigers, as well as about the glamorous Great Wallenda trapeze artists, dressed in silky white, and their daring feats high above the ring.

The circus that stopped in Ritchey could have been a small offshoot company of one of the bigger circuses, or one of the lesser companies, like the Curtis Brothers Circus. Whatever it was, it was plenty big enough to cause a lot of excitement in Ritchey.

The circus arrived in two, colorfully painted box cars. I imagine the performers, who doubled as circus hands during the tent set-up, rode in the caboose, but some could have ridden with the animals. The two yellow circus cars were hooked to a short train, pulled by a small engine, that we called 'the local.' It left the circus cars on the siding by the loading chute so the animals could be unloaded. The one-ring tent was set up just south of the depot on the corner of one of our fields and just across the road east of the tomato canning factory. It was on the same spot where Dad provided land for the Ritchey baseball team. Just like in the movies, the one elephant provided the draft power to raise the tent. The portable stands were erected and the calliope cranked up. The circus was set up in an afternoon, with the show in the evening. The tent and stands came down during the night. By the next morning our circus was ready to move on to the next town, where there would be another one-night performance bringing joy to another batch of kids.

There had to be some kind of advance publicity, because the people came with their teams and wagons loaded with children from the hills all around Ritchey. It was a festive, picnicking time. It seemed to me that there were a lot of people there, even if it was only a few hundred. I suppose I must have known that the circus was coming, but, if I did, that memory is foggy now and all I clearly remember is the yellow boxcars on the siding tracks and suddenly knowing that the circus was really in town.

A three-ring circus is overwhelming, because you can only watch one ring at a time. But at a one-ring circus, like the ones popular in Europe and that very small Ritchey circus, you can focus on everything.

Except for passing through on a train, I doubt there has been an elephant in Ritchey since that glorious day in the mid-1930's when a small circus came to town. But there are at least a few 80 year old-kids today who remember when the elephant and its circus came to Ritchey.

THE BARNSTORMERS

I remember the first time a barnstormer landed in Ritchey. He flew low over town, and, of course, everyone looked up to see his plane. Even if he hadn't been flying low, we would have looked up because airplanes weren't common in the 1930s, and just seeing one fly over was a major event of sorts – certainly something out of the ordinary in our day-to-day existence.

We'd sometimes see DC-3s, which were the new, 21-seat passenger planes manufactured by Douglas Aircraft Co., or we might see an open-cockpit biplane or a small, high-wing monoplane that had two seats, one behind the other. Many times, these planes were following the Frisco railroad tracks that ran pretty much in a straight line from St. Louis to Springfield to Tulsa. Pilots usually flew when visibility was good and would visually navigate between cities by following rail lines, or what the pilots called the 'iron beam,' as contrasted to a radio beam.

Like most kids during the 1930s, my brothers and I were fascinated by aviation, and maybe that's why my two brothers became pilots. Older brother, John, learned in the Navy and younger brother, Glenn, earned his wings in the Army.

Airplane shows were common at county fairs, with aerobatics, wing walkers, and parachute jumps. Many times, the wing walkers were securely fastened to the plane wing so it could even fly inverted. But at other times they would do daring stunts, such as transferring from one plane wing to another when they were flying close, with their wings nearly touching, or one below the other. Remember, these planes were bi-winged planes with struts and cables between the wings. The daredevil wing walker could hold onto these. All of this was done in flight, with no parachute apparent, although one was likely concealed under the wing walker's jacket. The movies also reflected our romance with aviation, and few weeks went by when some movie didn't feature airplanes doing daring stunts like those in Howard Hughes film "Hell's Angels."

The fields on our farm were in the bottom, running east-west, parallel to the creek and fairly long. Since we were near town, this was an ideal landing field for the pilot in a yellow Piper Cub, who landed in a nearby field. We watched excitedly as this plane throttled back and floated down onto our recently harvested hayfield after circling the town very low a couple of times.

Mother, Dad, all of us children, and nearly everyone else in town rushed out to the field to see the plane. The pilot asked who owned the farm, and when Dad said it was his, the pilot offered to take Mother for a free ride. She'd never flown before, but gamely climbed in behind the pilot and buckled up, which was an unusual experience in itself because this was long before cars had seat belts.

The plane taxied to the end of the field, revved the engine and then rolled along and lifted majestically into the air. We were transfixed, particularly because we could see Mother's broad grin, as the

A wing walker.

plane sailed overhead and soared west, before circling back over town and our farm.

Later, Mother laughed as she recalled the flight and told this story on herself. She was excited, and maybe even a little scared, and as she looked down at the farm buildings, she saw tiny white chickens in the yard. "Gracious, I left the brooder house door open and all the baby chicks got out," she shouted to the pilot. That would be bad because the chicks were too young to be out in the cold air and many would probably get pneumonia and might die. The pilot chuckled and told her that those were fully grown chickens down there in the chicken yard, not chicks, and they only looked small because the plane was high in the air.

I can't remember if anyone else took a flight that day, or if the pilot made any money. I certainly didn't go up because the flight cost $5, which was a lot of money in those days, and far more than I ever had at one time. Other barnstormers used our field after that, but it wasn't a common occurrence.

My first long airplane ride was between my junior and senior year in high school in the summer of 1946. Brother, John, was a Navy dive-bomber pilot, and his aircraft carrier was being deployed to the Mediterranean. He planned to have his wife, Frances, and their baby, Johnny, come to Missouri and stay at our house while he was at sea. He asked me if I would come to Jacksonville, Florida and drive back with Frances and my baby nephew, Johnny. He bought me a plane ticket, and I was thrilled. I had never been more than 100 miles from Ritchey, except to visit my maternal grandparents in Oklahoma and relatives in Kansas City,

The flight was in a DC-3 and it stopped in every decent sized city on its route. My flight wasn't non-stop by a long shot: Joplin to Tulsa (change planes), Tulsa to Ft. Smith to Little Rock to Memphis to Birmingham to Atlanta (change planes), Atlanta to Savannah to Jacksonville. There were eight legs on that flight and, in that DC-3 that cruised at about 180 miles per hour, the trip took from early morning to late in the evening. I enjoyed every minute of it and my eyes were glued to the window to see the countryside below.

Since I was 16 and had a driver's license, I anticipated helping with the driving. But it was not to be, as Frances did all of the driving. I tended to baby Johnny, a new experience for me. It was my first long, cross-country trip and I thoroughly enjoyed it. I clearly remember it.

Small Piper Cub airplane like the one in Mother's first flight.

JACK ARMSTRONG – THE ALL AMERICAN BOY

Our floor-model radio was a beautiful piece of furniture. It had a walnut cabinet about three feet tall and sat against the wall, near one end of our combination living and dining room. It was attractive, with its large, illuminated dial and two knobs, one for tuning and the other an on-off switch and volume control. The lower half had a wooden lattice backed by metal cloth over a single, ten-inch speaker. The radio electrical works weighed perhaps 20 pounds and had a dozen or so vacuum tubes of different sizes, some four inches tall. The power transformer was heavy and comprised much of the radio's weight. The vacuum tubes would sometimes burn out. If the radio stopped working, we'd take the tubes to the county seat to be checked by a radio shop.

The radio didn't have a built in antenna. So it was connected to a long metal wire that was either strung up in the attic or fed out through the window and along the roof of the house. A good antenna was essential for decent reception. The nearest radio station was about 30 miles away in Joplin, but we usually listened to KWTO in Springfield, which was about 65 miles away. The announcer said that KWTO stood for Keep Watching the Ozarks. When there were thunderstorms and lighting nearby, the reception was terrible, with loud static making it difficult to hear the station. But that didn't occur too often, and most of the time we could get good reception on a few stations. This was before FM broadcasting, and the power of small, local AM stations was limited, maybe 500 watts, to avoid interference with other stations.

As a boy, I spent many hours lying on the floor near that radio listening to adventure series such as, 'Jack Armstrong, The All American Boy,' or 'The Lone Ranger.' In the evening after supper, particularly in the winter, we would listen to other radio programs.

Although our radio was a large floor model, table-model radios were available in the 1930's. These also had wooden cases, often with rounded wooden tops, and were about eighteen inches tall. The controls were at the top and the smaller 8-inch speaker was at the bottom. There were even battery-powered radios for those who lived in the country and didn't have electricity. These radios looked similar, but were powered by 6-volt, rechargeable car batteries. Cars had 6-volt ignition systems in those days. Since these radios used heat generating vacuum tubes and had a large power drain, the batteries had to frequently be charged. This discouraged the rural people without electricity from listening to the radio for long hours or leaving it on when not listening to it.

Sometimes in those days, people used crystal radio sets that didn't require a battery. But I didn't know anyone it Ritchey who had a crystal set.

I would come home from school each day at 4:30 p.m. and change into my work clothes. But before I went to do my chores, I always pleaded with Mother to let me listen to the adventures of 'Jack Armstrong, The All American Boy.' That 30-minute program came on at 5 p.m.

As I listened I imagined myself as Jack Armstrong in all of those exciting adventures. In my mind I could visualize the things that happened as if it were on a giant TV screen, although this was many years before anyone had TV. As I did my chores, I daydreamed and relived Jack Armstrong's adventures. I ate the advertised Wheaties that Jack ate, and I sent the box tops in with a quarter to get my magic ring or bottle of invisible ink so I could write secret messages. Radio could take me anywhere in the world, even though I was a young boy confined to a farm in the Ozarks.

Those who liked mystery theater had a large selection, such as 'The Shadow,' 'The Thin Man,' and 'The Inner Sanctum.' The comedies and the musical variety shows were among my favorites. Bob Hope, Jack Benny, George Burns & Gracie Allen, and Phil Silvers were all popular comedians long before television. These radio comedians entertained us with jokes and monologues, and large bands, with popular singers, and gave us the latest in music. 'The Hit Parade' on Saturday night, with Perry Como and other singers, was sponsored by Chesterfield Cigarettes, and featured the top ten tunes each week. It was almost as important to know which song was number one as it was to know which baseball teams were leading the two major leagues. 'Fibber McGee and Molly' was a wholesome, if somewhat slapstick comedy, and 'Amos and Andy' seemed an innocent enough program. However, we now realize that the program had significant racial overtones. But these were the days of Al Jolson and minstrel shows, and sensitivities were not yet attuned to prejudice and racial issues as they are now.

Harry Carrey started broadcasting the St. Louis Cardinal baseball games in the early 1940's, as I recall. He went on to become one of the all-time favorite baseball broadcasters until his death in 1998, when he was still broadcasting Chicago Cubs games. His graphic description of the plays made it possible for radio listeners to see the flight of a home run ball: Harry would excitedly say, "He slams a towering fly to center field – it might be – it could be — it is a home run."

Early in his career, Harry Carrey didn't travel with the team for road games. He did a slightly delayed radio broadcast from a studio in St. Louis, using a ticker tape report of the game. There were sound effects of the crowd, the crack of the bat, and, of course, Harry's colorful commentary. No doubt there were many other great radio broadcasters, but Harry was the one that I listened to.

The farmer's work, with its long hours in the field, was usually boring, but, of course, no more boring than the long hours of the housewife doing work when the children were away at school. But with the radio, the housewife could be entertained as she worked. And she listened to the early radio soap operas of the time. The marketing people knew that this afternoon radio audience was dominated by housewives. The continuing radio dramas were always sponsored by the soap companies. There was 'Oxydol's Old Ma Perkins,' 'Stella Dallas' and others for a total of maybe three hours daily in the afternoon. The women could listen to the drama and in the advertisements hear how, if they used this particular soap, they would never have to deal with red and rough hands from their laundering and dishwashing, or 'ring around the collar,' or 'tattletale gray' in the clothes they laundered.

I didn't listen to the soaps unless I was sick and had to stay home from school. I don't remember much about them, but, as I recall, the story line usually involved family settings and relations with relatives and neighbors, with, perhaps, a hint of inappropriate love affairs. But you had to use your imagination and you could take the story in any direction that suited you as far as the subtleties were concerned. There were no graphic descriptions or harsh language as in today's TV soaps.

Radio let your imagination generate the excitement. There was no need for the graphic violence seen today in movies and TV programs. But sound effects were very important.

During World War II, Americans got their war news from three sources: Through radio and the reports of the war correspondents, newspapers and newsmagazines, and the weekly Movietone News reels shown in movie theaters. Life Magazine was a photo news magazine that did a dramatic job of showing pictorially the horrors of war. But most of the timely news was on the radio. President, Franklin D. Roosevelt, regularly reported to the public with his radio 'Fireside Chats.' Most Americans didn't know he was confined to a wheelchair, as a result of polio. They didn't see the President in unguarded moments as is the case now with TV. But they knew Roosevelt's views from his radio addresses and what they read in the newspaper, and they elected him President four times, the last time when he wasn't in good health, but we were still at war. The radio was his power base.

Yes, the radio in the 1930's and early 1940's was a favorite piece of furniture. We rallied around the radio to be excited by adventures we could visualize in our minds, to be entertained with the latest in comedy and music, to enjoy the daytime drama of the soap operas, and to get the latest news and weather reports. We were never short of entertainment, even if television was still a decade or more away. The radio communicated with all the family and all radio programs were suitable for the entire family. In fact, there was no need for a rating system to protect children from abusive language or excessive violence. The radio broadcasts relied on the power of the imagination. Children imagined childlike adventure from Jack Armstrong and the Lone Ranger – and adults could imagine adult adventure from the Ma Perkins and Stella Dallas programs. And all escaped the drudgeries and hardships of the time with the comedy antics of Bob Hope, Jack Benny, Fibber McGee and Molly, and many others.

STEALING WATERMELONS

During watermelon season the older boys would sometimes tell stories about stealing watermelons from a local farmer's patch. I don't know if these tales described real events or only imagined ones. But more than 60 years later, I suspect it was the latter more often than not, but these stories did generate excitement and daring as we imagined the illicit thrill of stolen fruit. Boys weren't the only ones that told 'watermelon stories.' Uncle Willie told one on a cold, winter Sunday afternoon when several relatives were visiting Uncle Curt and Aunt Grace. They lived on a farm about eight miles east of us.

Before I get to Uncle Willie's story, you need to understand the role that stories filled in our households back in the "30s and '40s. They were part of the self-made entertainment that people relied on in lieu of Sunday afternoon TV football, video games, stereos, trips to the mall, and the many other diversions that we have today.

On this cold winter Sunday, we were sitting around the heating stove telling stories. Some of the plots were a little thin, but a good storyteller can varnish over that and still create an interesting yarn. This storytelling and gossip could go on for hours.

Looking back over the decades, I now realize that all these stories about farmers lurking with a shotgun in the shadows of their watermelon fields were probably just fantasies. I never once heard of anyone getting shot or even threatened. But to us boys, the thought of facing a 12-guage shotgun or getting our behinds peppered with no. 8 lead pellets was enough to set our imaginations racing.

Mother was good at telling stories. She told a Halloween story that involved a farmer and a shotgun. This was back in Western Oklahoma in the early 1900s.

Teenaged boys planned to overturn a farmer's outhouse, but had heard that the farmer was quick on the trigger and ready to deal with Halloween pranksters. So they carefully planned their strategy. To get a better view, some of the boys silently climbed a tree to act as lookouts while the others turned the privy over.

Suddenly, the farmer appeared in his nightshirt, shotgun in hand. Those at the privy ran for dear life. To scare the boys, the farmer fired into the air toward the tree where, unknown to him, the lookouts were stationed. Fortunately, no one was hit, but the terrified boys dropped out of the tree, probably scaring the farmer out of his wits. The boys hit the ground running got away unhurt, the privy sat undisturbed on its foundation, and the farmer was thankful he wasn't being hauled off by the sheriff. I heard the story more than once when Mother told the story to different people. Every time Mother told it, she would start laughing so much she could hardly finish. Likely, she visualized the frightened look on the boys' faces as they dropped out of the tree, as well as the startled look of the farmer.

Uncle Willie's story was of two old maids in the country who had a watermelon patch that was a few hundred yards from a country road. A field of corn sat between the road and the patch. The corn rows ran from the road to the watermelon patch. These sisters were known to wear light-colored, print, cotton dresses and starched sunbonnets. They were never without their sunbonnets. When the watermelons were ripe, the corn would be at least chest high and would provide good cover to sneak from the road to the patch. The old maid sisters were thought to protect their watermelons, and rumor had it that they did it with their shotguns.

Two neighboring teenage farm boys knew of the watermelon patch and planned the assault when the watermelons were ripe. On a moonlit night, they quietly made

A watermelon patch.

their way up the corn rows from the road to the patch. Arriving there, according to Uncle Willie, they were just letting their eyes adjust while surveying the patch and looking for large watermelons in the moonlight. Suddenly, two figures wearing light-colored, print dresses and sunbonnets stepped out of the shadows of the moon. Startled and scared, both boys ran as fast as they could from the patch to the road. No shots were fired as the boys had feared. The only problem was that one of the boys happened to get started on his escape straddling one of the rows of corn. The story goes that he ran this entire distance to the road straddle this row of corn, probably anticipating the loud report of a shotgun and the sting of the pellets on his backside.

Running that distance at maximum speed straddling a row of corn would create an unforgettable impression on your inner thighs and other unmentionable parts of your body, and Uncle Willie's listeners roared with laughter at the thought of those boys hightailing across that cornfield. Uncle Willie was a good story teller. The old maids probably didn't even own a gun, and, even if they did, would not have used it. I would love to hear their version of the story, if, in fact, this incident actually happened.

My personal watermelon story occurred in the early fall of 1945 during my junior year in high school. Two men in Newtonia, a small town a half-mile north of the high school, had a watermelon patch at the west edge of this small village. Five of us high school boys planned to raid that patch one evening well after dark. All of us were juniors except one senior, Ray Ferguson, who had a beat-up, 1937 Ford. The plan was that we would go by car to near the patch and sneak up a ditch, two from the east and two from the west. We planned to get two watermelons and hide with them in the ditch. Then, Ray would drive by the patch and we would quickly load the melons, jump in the car and be off for our watermelon feast. A classmate, Frank Myers, and I were to approach the patch from the west and two others would come from the east. Frank was a tall, gangly kid who had very long arms and long fingers. He was three or four inches taller than I was and his arms also were that much longer than mine.

Frank and I crawled up the ditch, which was infested with weeds we called beggar's lice. These little prickly seeds would stick to your socks, clothes and even your hair. We were both loaded with these burrs when we got to the edge of the patch. We climbed over the fence and were inside the patch trying to adjust our eyes in the starlight and sense where our schoolmates were. Suddenly, to our stark surprise, two figures stood up immediately in front of us with a blinding flashlight beam in our eyes and one said in a gruff, loud voice, "Stick 'em up or I will blow your guts out."

Instantly, we complied, no doubt with a terrified looks on our faces. But Frank's knees buckled and here he was beside me on his knees with his long arms reaching to the stars. They were almost as high as mine. Our schoolmates approaching from the east saw and heard the developments and were gone in a flash. I can still hear their feet pounding the road as they ran at top speed to safety to let Ray know that Frank and I had been caught.

Finally – and it then seemed like a very long time, but it must have been less than five minutes – our captors could no longer keep from laughing. To our surprise they identified themselves and said, "Now that you're here, let's have some watermelon." They picked one from their own patch, and said, "Invite your friends to join us." Since they didn't have guns and it was a great adult joke to them to catch these teenagers, Frank and I complied. Our compatriots had run the full half-mile to Ray's car, told him of our plight, since they had seen the flashlight and heard our capture. The three made a high-speed pass by the patch in Ray's old dilapidated Ford to survey the situation. They subsequently returned and stopped a distance away, well out of shotgun range, and we communicated with them.

Our compatriots couldn't be convinced it wasn't a trap. They wouldn't come closer and were instead planning on how to tell our parents and, perhaps, how to get us out of the county jail. In the meantime, our captors, who had brought a knife, had cut a watermelon and Frank and I were enjoying it. Finally, after we had had our fill and realized that our partners in crime weren't going to come close, one of the men said, "We've had our fun. Let's go home." They departed chuckling, no doubt thinking they would have still more fun with this. Frank and I climbed over the fence and walked to Ray's car, where Ray, Charles and Don were waiting. When they realized that they could have shared in the watermelon, they were irritated. But what could Frank and I do?

The story doesn't end there. My sister, Helen, worked at the Army base, Camp Crowder, just outside of Neosho. She stayed in a rooming house in Neosho. One of our captors also worked at Camp Crowder and he knew Helen. The next morning he told Helen that her brother, Ernest, was in jail in Neosho because he was caught stealing watermelons. I'm sure he said this completely straight faced. He'd demonstrated that he could do that when he scared the daylights out of Frank and me the night before. Helen, bless her heart, must have fretted as to what she should do. But finally she was told the whole story – I'm sure much to her relief. The owners of the watermelon patch had enjoyed more fun than they could have hoped for. I expect they told this story many times to their friends. And it was probably embellished a bit each time it was told.

I don't think my parents ever heard of this incident. I certainly didn't tell them and my loyal sister, Helen, would never have done so. If they had heard the story, Mother would have fretted and worried. Dad would have smiled internally, and while he would not have approved, he would have thought, "Boys will be boys."

A final comment on "stealing" watermelons: None of us in that group had ever stolen anything of value, and none had a record of any criminal activity. At least two of my compatriots are now dead. I suspect that our captors are also gone. I'm also sure that all of us, particularly our captors, had a lot of fun telling and retelling this story. Both Frank and I lived on a farm, me being the son of a farmer and the school board president, and he, the son of part-time farmer and full-time school teacher. It would be nice if the temptations young people encounter today were as innocent as those we faced.

SHIVAREE

When a couple gets married in southwest Missouri the odds are that they will be shivareed by their close friends. At least that was the case up until a few decades ago. One definition of a shivaree is: "a noisy mock serenade to a newly married couple." However accurate that might be, it does not tell the whole story of the shivarees we had in Ritchey. First of all, you always hoped that the newlywed couple would be in bed when the shivaree started at around bedtime. It was also important to try to silently sneak up under the newlyweds' bedroom window to start the process as loudly as possible with the blast of a large firecracker or the report of one or more shotguns fired in the air. Surprise was most desirable. And, of course, it would be ideal if the couple were caught in a compromising situation. But we never knew about that – only hoped.

A 12-guage shotgun was the standard noisemaker used by the men, which ostensibly could be safely fired in the air. Women used metal dishpans and large metal cooking spoons to bang away and create noise. I always kept a store of firecrackers saved from the Fourth-of-July celebrations for shivarees.

I was told of a shivaree for a local miner and his bride, which had special sound effects created by dynamite ignited while tied to a low-hanging limb of a nearby tree. The story, which no doubt is true given the many mines in the area, is that one side of the tree was blown away, but the shivaree was successful. We never thought of the shivaree as a dangerous event, but with shotguns, let alone dynamite, it wasn't child's play. It was a celebration, and, in fact, an act of friendship and respect by your friends to go to all the trouble of planning and executing a good shivaree.

Although the newlyweds couldn't know when a shivaree might occur, they had to be prepared with treats for all of the revelers – cigars for the men and candy for the women and children. When the shivaree started, the newlyweds had to find their clothes, often in the dark if it was summer and the windows were open and the blinds were up to permit air circulation. The noise would continue until the newlyweds appeared at the door to invite the celebrants in. Often that invitation did not come for several minutes.

Once invited in, the women and children would be offered candy, which could be homemade fudge or a box of candy bars stored away for the occasion. A man could choose candy, but it was not considered manly to take both candy and a cigar. It would be unheard of in Ritchey for a female to select a cigar. A non-smoking male might prefer the candy, but he'd be looked on as kind of a sissy. As a result, a lot of non-smoking men passed up the candy and took home a cigar that would grow stale on the dresser or wherever the pockets were emptied. Some non-smokers would light up to be macho, only to regret it later.

After the candy and cigars, the newlyweds were usually asked to do something to 'demonstrate their love.' Typically, this might mean the recent bridegroom would be asked to wheel his bride in a wheelbarrow around the block, if in town, or to some distant point and back if the couple happened to live in the country. Singing and cheering by the revelers accompanied this trip in the wheelbarrow. A potentially embarrassing situation could be when a small man married a 'stout' woman and had difficulty managing the wheelbarrow and its burden. You can imagine the conversation and chiding. On occasion, the bridegroom might be thrown into a pond or stock tank, if he had been 'uncooperative' or had ignored the revelers for too long before inviting them in for treats.

Some participants usually had special tasks to perform when the couple was out on their wheelbarrow excursion. This included such things as short-sheeting the bed, putting salt in the bed and removing bed slats or adjusting them so the bed would collapse if action in it later in the night became too intense.

To be shivareed was an honor, and it meant that you were respected and loved by genuine friends. If you were not, that could suggest lack of respect for you by your so-called friends. I don't know of any couple who have been shivareed who do not reflect on the event with fond memories.

I have a keen personal recollection of one shivaree that demonstrated the potential danger of mixing shotguns and a shivaree. When I was a junior in high school, a classmate, Abby Adams, got married. It was appropriate to shivaree her. Our classmates, all 17 of us, planned the shivaree. Frank Myers came by in his father's car to pick me up. He had a shotgun in the car and asked me if I was planning to bring one. I said no, I had a shoebox full of firecrackers. We proceeded to rendezvous with our classmates and then to the home of Abby's parents, where the newlyweds were staying. However, the word of the planned shivaree had leaked, and Abby and her new husband were not at home.

We learned that they had escaped to a neighbor's house. We decided to go there, only to meet the couple in their car on a country road. We managed to corner them and we started the shivaree right there on that country road, with the cars of the revelers surrounding the car of the newlyweds. Shotguns started firing as I was getting my firecrackers ready to ignite under the couple's car. A country road was an unusual location for a shivaree, but we were well on our way to a noisy celebration. Then it happened.

I felt something hit my shoulder. There was no pain but I knew something had hit me. I walked over in front of one car's headlights and looked at my shoulder. My shirt was soaked with blood. I'd felt no pain, but I instinctively said, "I've been shot." In an instant, the word spread, the noise stopped, and people rushed to me. Someone shouted, "Get him to a doctor." Seven other people and I piled in Don Turner's 1939 Mercury convertible, which was a nice car but had a small exhaust leak that let fumes into the car as he drove. If I was going to pass out, I would have in that fume-laden car. We were only about five miles from Pierce City, and we found the house of Pierce City's only physician, only to learn that he wasn't home. As we pondered what to do, someone noted that one of Don's tires was leaking fast and almost flat. As the entire troupe had followed, I transferred to another car, and we proceeded to Monett, the next town about five miles further east. There was a small Catholic hospital there, so that's where we headed.

We arrived there about 10 p.m. to find two nurses, both Roman Catholic Sisters, on duty. Everyone followed me in to tell them that I had a gunshot wound, which happened at a shivaree. One nurse was from New York City and the other from Philadelphia, and neither of them had ever heard of a shivaree. There we were, a group of scraggly looking 15 to 17 year-olds claiming the gunshot wound occurred at an event those nurses had never heard of.

The next thing I knew the police arrived. Fortunately, they were locals and had heard of a shivaree and the suspicion that we were another 'Pretty Boy Floyd' bank-robbing gang was allayed. A doctor was called. The bleeding had stopped, and I felt okay. Strangely, I hadn't had a queasy moment. I was not yet 16 at the time and, since my life was not at risk, the physician said that my parents must give their okay before he would remove whatever it was in my shoulder that had caused the bleeding, presumably something to do with a shotgun blast.

My close friend, Chuck Hailey, telephoned my parents to give them the news. It was 1945 and my brother, John, a Navy pilot flying high-performance military aircraft was on active duty. Mother answered the phone since Dad was taking a bath at the time. Chuck had a simple message which was, "Mrs. Smerdon, I'm at the Monett Hospital and Ernest has been shot." Mother immediately screamed and then fainted.

It so happens that we had the carpenter who was building cabinets in the kitchen staying with us at the time, and he was in the living room where Mother had answered the phone. He summoned Dad to come to the phone immediately, even if he was dripping wet. Dad had a hearing deficiency that sometimes made it difficult to hear on the phone. He assumed that something had happened to my brother John, the Navy flyer. He tried to field the conversation from Chuck, who was only trying to say that I had been hurt at a shivaree. Mother revived and Dad finally understood. They rushed to get dressed and in the car to come to the Monett Hospital. Fortunately, before they could depart, the doctor called and calmly explained the situation, including the fact that I was doing okay, but they needed to come and sign some papers, since I was legally a minor.

As we waited for Mom and Dad to arrive I was interrogated by a police officer, a necessary procedure in the case of a gunshot wound. Fortunately, he knew what a shivaree was. I had done nothing wrong unless going to a shivaree and standing in the wrong place was a crime. After the doctor removed a piece of shrapnel from my shoulder, I had to spend the night at the hospital on a cot in the hallway, since all the rooms were occupied. The shrapnel turned out to be a piece of the gun barrel. The police speculated that the end of the shotgun barrel exploded because it had mud in it.

I remember the physician telling me that I had been hit in the shoulder four inches to the left of my jugular vein. If it had been four inches to my right, I would never have made it to the hospital. I told him if the shrapnel had been four inches further left I wouldn't have had to be there at all because the piece of barrel would have missed me. That twisted piece of barrel was more than an inch long and about a half-inch wide. It went through my leather jacket and its lining, the tip of my wing-like sport shirt collar that was fashionable in 1945, and the shirt itself. Fortunately, its energy was somewhat spent when it hit me and, although the shrapnel lodged against the bone, it didn't damage it. I was back in school after one day and back at full speed in almost no time. I only missed one game of basketball. On reflection, I was very lucky because Abby's shivaree could have cost me my life.

I recall numerous shivarees, but I remember three in particular. My first was Ralph and Zelda Nimmo's shivaree when I was about seven. The previous Christmas I had received a toy, spring-loaded shotgun that would pop corks and made a decent bang for a child. I was very proud of that gun. Zelda was a distant cousin and I took my toy shotgun to her shivaree. To my regret the spring broke and it would no longer make the popping sound. That's when I lost interest in taking shotguns to shivarees and decided to use firecrackers instead. The second shivaree that I will never forget was Abby's. And the third was our own in Ritchey.

Joanne and I were married in June 1951, immediately after I graduated from the University of Missouri in Columbia. I was 21 and she was 19. I had received a commission as a second lieutenant in the Air Force. After a short honeymoon at the Lake of the Ozarks, we spent a couple of weeks in Ritchey with my parents before I reported to Lackland Air Force Base in San Antonio for active duty. My younger brother, Glenn, orchestrated the surprise shivaree, and it was a grand occasion. We were close to a compromising position when the first firecracker went off under our open window that June. But we were prepared and had our cigars and candy, and I got to wheel Joanne in a wheelbarrow around the block and through the single main street of Ritchey.

    As a footnote, in 2001 we had our 50th wedding anniversary celebration at The Lodge in Roaring River State Park, near my childhood home in southwest Missouri. Our children had arranged a beautiful dinner for the 80 friends and relatives. They prepared a slide show with music depicting our lives together. Our oldest son had brought a decorated wheel barrow all the way from Ohio for me to wheel Joanne around the Lodge in. The children also had cigars for the men and candy for the women. It was a great memory of the real event in Ritchey in June 1951.

THE JOLLY WORKERS

Small rural villages like Ritchey didn't have service clubs. There weren't enough people for such a club, and people didn't have the time or the spare money to go to dinner (we called the noon meal dinner and the evening meal supper). In fact, there was no place to have such a meal because the town didn't have a restaurant. I don't know if the county seat had a Rotary, Kiwanis, or Lions club, but I suspect that one or more of the men's service clubs would be active there.

There were fraternal lodges like the Masonic Lodge and Dad became a Mason before he married at the age of 25. He was a member of the Masonic Lodge in Pierce City, where he went to school, 12 miles east of Ritchey. Dad might have attended the Lodge meetings a few times after he married, but I don't recall him going to a Lodge meeting. Nor did he ever mention such activity when I was growing up.

Although Dad was busy, he was not too busy for service activities. At one time he was the Justice of the Peace in Ritchey, but I don't recall him doing that after I was old enough to remember such things. I do recall Mother telling us of the time when Dad married a young couple who were from the hills close to Ritchey. I guess they had obtained the marriage license if one was required and had arranged with Dad, the Justice of the Peace, to marry them. They were married in our house. Mother put on her nicest table linens, prepared some refreshments and she and Dad put on their best go-to-meeting clothes. I sort of recall that Mother said the couple were poor and probably didn't have any but their ordinary clothes. But they got married just like most couples of that time did. I hope they had a happy life. Mother was an official witness to the marriage and both she and Dad signed the marriage certificate. I think that was the only marriage that Dad performed as the Justice of the Peace.

The service activity that Dad was most involved in was as a member of the Ritchey School Board. Dad was well-read and one of the most educated people in the school district, having spent two years at the University of Missouri from about 1915 to 1917. He knew the state education laws well and was a great resource for the school board. He was elected to the school board soon after he moved to Ritchey and served continuously until his death, well after the last of us children had graduated from high school in 1953. His period of service was from 1931 until he died in August, 1963. The 1964 Midway School annual yearbook was dedicated to him for his service. It had his picture and this memorial:

John Erle Smerdon – In Memoriam
In memory of John Erle Smerdon, our friend and loyal supporter, President of the
Board of Education, and member for 32 years, we express our gratitude for the many
hours of time devoted to our school and community.

I didn't attend public school a single day when Dad was not the president of the school board. My younger brother and sister could make the same statement and perhaps my older brother, too.

The teachers were, no doubt, aware that our Dad was president of the school board. I can't say whether that helped us or not, but I can honestly say that I don't think it did. We all made good grades. We benefitted greatly from our work ethic and knowledge that Dad expected us to apply ourselves and do our best. His constant admonition, "Do your best. That is as good as anyone can do." always was in the back of my mind and I never forgot it. I do know that if we were punished or reprimanded in school (spankings in school were acceptable then), we never told Dad. If we were spanked in school and he knew about it, we would get another one at home – just for doing whatever we did to justify punishment at school. No doubt about it! Silence on such matters was the best approach.

I remember one occasion, when there was a vacant teacher position, we were in the fields working and we saw a man, dressed up in a white shirt and tie, walking out to us in the field. Mother had directed the teacher applicant to Dad. He interviewed the teacher in the field asking about his transcript, how many credit hours he had, his experience, inquire who his references were and the like. I stood idly by, but couldn't help hearing the conversation. I didn't know about college credit hours then, so that question was puzzling to me. Moreover, I didn't know how much our teachers were paid, and Dad would never share such information with me. But when pay came up, my keen ears could catch the $75 per month. I recall that grade-school teachers were paid about that much in the late 1930s.

From Dad's records, Ritchey School had eight teachers in 1932-33. The monthly pay of the four grade school teachers with two years of college and a state teaching certificate, ranged from $50 to $70 per month depending on education and experience. The three high school teachers, all with a baccalaureate degree, ranged from $75 to $120 per month, with the highest pay to the school superintendent. There were a total of 222 pupils in school and the library had 309 volumes. See Appendix IV for the excerpts from the complete school survey dated December 2, 1932.

When the Ritchey School closed because it didn't have enough pupils, it joined with the larger Midway School six miles to the south, and Dad became a member of that new school board. Again, he was elected president. He was always interested in education and encouraged us at every chance.

The only paying work outside of the farm that Dad ever did was to work in helping farmers develop a 'Balanced Farming Plan' and soil conservation practices. This was after WW II, in the late 1940s, and he worked with aerial photographs of the farms taken from a small plane. Dad understood agriculture and good farming practices, such as crop rotations, soil testing, soil maps, etc., and he was good at this task. In fact, he had been selected as the outstanding farmer in the county in the 1950s. He was a great help to all the farmers in the region, and they often sought his advice.

Mother was always active in a local women's club, organized by the county home demonstration agent, who worked for the Agricultural Extension Service of the University of Missouri. These clubs would meet monthly in the afternoon, always in the home of a member. The hostess would spruce up the place and provide refreshments. Each meeting had a project or some educational activity, usually related to homemaking. The club selected its own name and the club in Ritchey chose, 'The Jolly Workers.' They were certainly hard workers and they were jolly – they made any task fun. Their educational tasks were usually important community services. For example, they might hold a health and hygiene clinic in which they could help the community members learn about these important things.

Or they might prepare food for some event where people would gather, or help with elections. During WW II, there was a big push for all Americans to raise food in gardens and can it for use in the winter. These wartime gardens were called 'Victory Gardens.' However, most families in the rural areas already had gardens, but many needed to learn about preserving food. This included learning about pressure cookers, which assured that the canned food was brought to a sufficiently high temperature

Women in a sewing club making dresses.

to kill any dangerous organisms in the food. The Jolly Workers conducted these educational sessions and helped women learn when a jar of canned food might be bad and cause acute botulism food poisoning. Several projects taught young people to sew and make clothes. It was practical and related to homemaking, but it was also a needed social function in which the women could get together and visit – and gossip if they were so inclined. And they usually were.

At the beginning of each club year, the women drew names for their 'secret pal' for the year. This person would remember her pal's birthdays and holidays with little gifts, often handmade, but never reveal her identity to her pal. The club was a circle of friendship that was of great support to women who had little to look forward to in their daily lives except hard work and inadequate appreciation.

Most of The Jolly Workers were also members of the Ritchey Baptist Church, the largest church in the area. So, essentially the same group would prepare food for the various church social functions. The Jolly Workers Club, being a state-sanctioned organization, would be open to anyone interested. But I don't know if any of the women from the two smaller churches, the Fire Baptized Holiness Church and the Cumberland Presbyterian Church, were involved. I don't remember any. So the Jolly Workers may have been a bit of a clique.

THE '35 OLDSMOBILE

I suspect that everyone has one particular car that they remember better than any other – sometimes fondly, perhaps sometimes not. For me it is the '35 Oldsmobile that Dad bought in 1937. That car was the source of a lot of happiness – and a lot of frustration. It was the car that I first drove on the highway at the age of fourteen. It was the car I took on my first date. It turned out to be a real workhorse of a car and, through the years, its looks showed that.

The very first car that I remember Mother and Dad driving was a 1929 Chevrolet. They had had a Model T Ford before that. The '29 Chevrolet didn't have a self starter or a heater – and, of course, no radio. It didn't have a trunk and its spare tire was mounted on the outside at the rear of the car. It was a fairly cantankerous vehicle, as I recall. When we went on trips in the winter, we children rode in the backseat and used a heavy wool blanket called a 'lap robe' to keep our legs and feet from freezing. Of course, we wore our winter coats, gloves and caps as well. Still, we would get awfully cold in a fairly short time. Sometimes, when it was real cold, Dad had to crank very hard to get it started. We didn't have a garage for that car.

I don't know if Dad was considering buying a new car or not when a used car salesman drove by one summer Sunday afternoon in 1937. He was in this good-looking, tan, 1935 Olds. It was a sleek-looking car and the salesman took us for a ride in it. It had a self starter, heater, radio, hydraulic brakes and a knee-action front suspension, instead of the common, solid front axle. There was also a trunk which housed the spare tire and still had room for other things.

Apparently the salesmen in those days would get in a used car they wanted to market and drive around showing it to people, hoping to make a sale. Whether Dad was thinking of getting another car or not, the salesman's timing was good, and he did show up with this nice car. We children were all urging Dad to buy it. While in 1937 most in town didn't have a car, it seemed to me that we had the oldest car in town. I don't think that mattered much to Dad, but it did to us kids. All he wanted was dependable transportation.

I doubt if our pressure had much effect on Dad's attitude, but no doubt he was interested. Mother stayed on the sidelines and let him handle all of the talk with the salesman. They got to the point where the car was obviously acceptable because they were bartering on the price. I don't recall the price they decided on with our Chevy trade-in, but I think the salesman was asking $700 at first. The price agreed to was likely less than that.

That was a beautiful car, and it served us well for a while. Later, we did have more than our share of trouble with it. It may have been that the relatively untrained mechanics that worked on it in Ritchey weren't the best. Most of the work was done by Dink Crow at Dink's Garage, which was about a block

A 1935 Oldsmobile.

down the street from us. Dink was an older bachelor and enjoyed his beer. I understand he usually 'hung one on,' to use local parlance, on Saturday night at Carrie Armstrong's Tavern. Apparently, when he had had a bit too much to drink he became cantankerous and sometimes wouldn't pass up a fight if another drunk challenged him. Or he might be the challenger. I only heard these stories of fights. You never knew if the skinned knuckles you saw on Dink's hands were from a slipped wrench or from a Saturday night skirmish at Carrie's.

I remember Dad's first experience with the hydraulic brakes quite well, because their response was quite different compared to the old '29 Chevy. On the Chevy, which had mechanical brakes, you had to push down hard on the brake pedal. The same pressure on the Olds would lock the wheels and send unsuspecting passengers flying. There were no seat belts in those days. So, until Dad got used to the brakes, passengers had to stay alert. I also remember the softer ride. This car had coil springs on all four wheels, which was a rather new innovation for a 1935 car. The shock absorbers soon were worn enough that their damping effect was gone and you would get a bit of a roller-coaster effect when you drove through a dip in the road or stopped suddenly.

World War II started four years after we got that car. When gas rationing came, we got a Class B ration card which, provided gas for farming, which was essential to the war effort. I believe a Class A card permitted you to buy four gallons per week. I don't recall that we were ever short of gas because we generally only made necessary trips. I do remember that repair parts were hard to get or maybe Dad just put off buying them because of the cost or inconvenience. The muffler on that car never seemed to last more than a year. Most of the time the car had a hole in the muffler, and there was a low roar from its powerful six-cylinder, in-line engine.

That noise turned out to provide a nice early warning for us children when the folks were gone and we were supposed to be doing chores, but instead were horsing around with cob fights or similar mischief. We could hear the car when it was about a quarter-mile away, and that was generally enough warning for us to get at the business of chores and make respectable progress on the work during the time it took our parents to get home and change into work clothes before coming to join us.

At the age of 13, I learned to drive the car in the fields, where it was often taken when we went to look at the crops. However, I didn't drive on the highway, only on the nearby country roads. But Dad asked me to drive on the highway on February 15, 1944, one month after my 14th birthday. I remember the exact date because it was the day after my Grandma Smerdon died.

As was the practice at the time, men came to the home of the deceased and 'sat up' with the body all night. Dad had been up most of the night and when we were to drive home from Grandpa's, he asked me if I wanted to drive because he was a bit drowsy. That was the start of a lot of driving for me long before the age of 16 when I would get a driver's license. On the farm, young boys usually drove cars and trucks well before the age of 16 because they needed to help. After all, I had a year's experience driving our tractor in the fields, and no license was needed for that.

The steering tie rod connectors on that car were deficient by today's standards. When they were quite worn and loose, the wear on the front tires could really be bad. Also, if a front tire was not well balanced, or had a boot in it as was sometimes the case with scarce tires during the war, the car would shimmy. I recall the speed limit was 45 mph, and the car would warn you with shimmying if you tried to drive above the limit. If you tried to drive a shimmying car, it would literally shake the front fenders loose since they were bolted on in those days.

The real scare came when a worn tie rod dropped off while you were driving. One front wheel couldn't be steered and the car tended to dart to one side. If that happened, you had to be lightning fast on the brakes to avoid flying into the ditch. More than once, we wired the tie rods up with baling wire until we could get replacements. Most of the time, we got the new tie rod ends at Myers Motor Supply in Joplin because it was the biggest parts-supply store in the region, and it wasn't easy to find parts for that model car.

We would do our own wheel alignment using two, short, straight boards. We would overlap the boards to create a sliding gauge. Then we would measure the distance between the front of the front tires by touching the opposing ends of each board to the tire. We'd note how far the boards overlapped and then measure the distance between the back of the tires, again noting the overlap. The object was to make this overlap the same for both the front and back of the wheels. In this way, we could be sure the wheels were parallel. Actually, we made the front spacing a tiny bit smaller to create a slight toe-in, which was said to be ideal for handling and tire wear. This may sound crude compared to the sophisticated machinery now used at tire stores. But it worked on the Olds. Of course, we weren't driving down freeways at 80 mph.

The emergency brake on that car never seemed to work after the first few years. It was mechanical and seemed to never be in adjustment. The regular brakes were hydraulic, but didn't have the dual hydraulic system now required on all cars. So if the brakes sprung a leak, you were in trouble. For a tiny leak you might pump the brakes to get good stopping power, but that would be gone soon unless the leak was repaired and the hydraulic brake line bled to remove air bubbles and the fluid replenished. Most often, the leaks were in the wheel cylinders or in the master cylinder because the material for seals wasn't good in those days and occasionally failed.

We eventually perfected a technique for stopping the car without brakes using the stick shift to gear down to low and then shut the engine off. If we drove the car without brakes, we had to be very cautious and good at gearing down. This required some double clutching, since the low gear of the three-speed manual transmission didn't have synchromesh gears and would grind if you weren't good at the task. I remember coming home from a ball game at high school on a recently graded, gravel road when the brakes went out. I drove with one wheel on the ridge of loose gravel at the edge of the road that had been left by the road grader.

Driving with one wheel on soft gravel helped slow the car while I geared down to stop. I'll now admit that I was going a little too fast approaching the intersection of this gravel road and paved U. S. Highway 60, and I needed to employ all methods available to stop.

As I look back and think about the problems we had with that car, brake failure is not the one I remember most. The brakes did fail on occasion, and we did have to replace the tie rods periodically, but it was basically a good six-cylinder car and it ran well – after you got it started.

On cold winter days, we had a terrible time getting that car started. We didn't drive a lot, and the battery always seemed to be low. If the engine didn't catch after a few turns, that was it. Jumper cables weren't of any use, since we only had one car and there were no others nearby. But you can start a manual transmission car by pushing it. Several people had to push the car to start it. For the first few years after cars came with self starters, manufacturers also provided a hand crank that could be used to turn the engine over and start it by hand. Our '29 Chevy had a hand crank. But this 'modern' 1935 Olds couldn't be started that way. First, we would push the car by hand and try to get it started, and we were usually successful except in the winter. If we weren't successful before we got too tired, we would use a team of horses, or, in later years, the tractor to pull the car and start it. That was a pain in the neck in the winter, though, because it was hard to get antifreeze during the war. So we didn't keep antifreeze in the tractor and, instead, drained the radiator at night. We'd have to fill the tractor radiator with water before it could be used. We usually put warm water in the tractor, because we had to crank it by hand, and it started easier when it was warm. We never had trouble starting the tractor. It had a simple magneto spark engine and may have been a better design for cold weather starting.

Dad had a bit of a temper and I don't think anything made him madder than to be dressed up to go to town and then not be able to get that damned car started – to use his words. Frankly, his words were usually even stronger. When I took the car to high school events, I usually had a carload of riders, and they all knew that if they rode with me they might have to push the car to get it started after the event. It always started well when it was warm and the engine usually stayed warm enough from the driving so it would start easily after a picture show or a ball game.

However, when I was dating I had to be careful because it wouldn't be gentlemanly to ask my date to push the car, and, anyway, it was too heavy for one person to push. I developed a sure-fire way to start the car when I was taking a girl to the picture show. We generally went to Neosho or Monett to the show. Both towns had some hills within a couple of blocks of the theatre. I would simply park on a hill a few blocks away, next to a driveway or on the corner so I wouldn't get penned in. If the car didn't start right off, I would put it in second gear and depress the clutch to let it coast. When it reached the speed of a fast walk I would release the clutch. The momentum of the car would turn the engine over to start it. The procedure never failed. Doing that never bothered me much except when I was dating Maxine Hayden from Wheaton. Her father owned an auto-repair garage and his car was always in top shape. I knew Maxine's father could have had that Olds purring like a kitten.

Despite the problems through the World War II years, the car served us well. We used it like a pickup to haul things, and that '35 Olds generally had hard treatment. The trunk, and even the back seat on occasion, was used to haul chicken feed from the large feed store in Neosho. We didn't have a pickup, and that was the only vehicle we had for hauling things. So the car was hard to keep clean. The trunk was always dusty from feed that had filtered through cloth feed sacks. Eventually the fenders got banged up and those dents were never repaired, so the car took on its own character.

The car was only involved in one accident, and that was relatively minor. My brother, John, was home from the Navy and several of us were going to the picture show in Monett. We'd had an icy spell with freezing rain, but it had thawed and the highways were clear, at least we thought so. The car was full, and John was driving east on Highway 60. About five miles west of Monett there was an icy patch as slick as any road you will ever find. The car spun around and was skidding on the icy pavement backwards when it went into the ditch and turned over on its side. No one was hurt and little damage was done except for some bent fenders. There wasn't even any broken glass until the glass in the back door window on the bottom was broken by someone standing on it as we climbed out through the door on the top.

Those dents were never fixed and for some time we had cardboard in the back door where the window was out. The car ran about the same with the dents. Eventually, the front bumper was broken and came off when we were trying to start it by towing it with the tractor. The tractor driver kept going when the car driver stopped and the heavy log chain we were using ripped the bumper off the car. That also didn't change the way the car drove.

We kept this car not so much because we wanted to, but because new cars weren't available during the war. After the war when a few cars were available for civilians, you had to sign up on a waiting list to get a new car. Dad had his name on the waiting list for a new Chevrolet both in Monett and Neosho, but cars weren't produced for the public until the end of the war in 1945. We didn't know when we would get a new car, so we had to keep the old one going. I don't think Dad considered another used car because his luck had not been the best with the Oldsmobile. In 1946, Dad's name finally reached the top of a waiting list for a new car. It would be a Chevrolet Coupe. At about that same time, our Grandfather Smerdon died and Dad got his 1942 Chevrolet, which had been one of the last new cars delivered before the war.

Since John, now married was still in the Navy and needed a car, Dad let him buy the coupe and we drove the '42 Chevy. That Chevy was a very good car and it never failed to start, nor did the brakes fail. So it was a joy, and my parents kept that car until they bought a sleek, new, white 1951, Chevrolet, four-door sedan that had a rakish, sloping back. Dad had also bought a 1947 Chevrolet pickup, the first and only one he ever owned. That pickup was a nice vehicle, and I used it on some dates when it was new. Eventually, the farm work took its toll, and the pickup became a strictly utility farm vehicle.

We sold the '35 Oldsmobile in 1946 after we got the '42 Chevy. We had it for nine years. At the time, there was a problem with the old car's brakes and also with the transmission. The stick shift could be moved to a given gear position, but it might not be in gear. This made stopping the car by gearing down a risky proposition. Dad thought about selling it for junk, but someone wanted to buy it and fix it up. The buyer offered very little for the car and was told that he could come get it. We thought he would tow it away, but he said he would drive it. He was given fair warning about the hazards. I remember when that man left with that car. A lot of memories went with it, both good and bad. But mostly they were good memories.

As far as we know, the new owner of the '35 Oldsmobile made it safely to his destination, which as I recall was Joplin. Anyway, we didn't read about an accident in the paper, so we assumed the best.

HOLIDAYS AND BIRTHDAY SPANKINGS

The holidays that had special meaning to us as children, were the Fourth of July, Thanksgiving, Christmas, Easter and Halloween. Birthdays were also special, but not celebrated in my family with a birthday party. The only school holidays were Thanksgiving and Christmas. We were, of course, off on Easter Sunday, but we went to school on Good Friday. We certainly knew about Armistice Day (the name we used before it was changed to Veterans Day in 1954), Memorial Day (then called Decoration Day, since graves were decorated with real flowers from Mother's garden), Valentines Day, Washington's and Lincoln's birthdays (again before the advent of President's Day). But these were not real holidays since school went on and nothing special happened. The Fourth of July (we didn't call it Independence Day), Thanksgiving and Christmas were different. Something very special occurred on those days.

Fourth of July. We planned for this celebration for weeks. We had to decide which firecrackers to buy with the money we had saved and the dollar that Dad gave each of us for fireworks. How to spend that money involved some major decisions. We had to decide whether to go for the large, expensive firecrackers that generated the most noise or the smaller, less noisy ones that would give us more bangs for the buck.

We usually spent the July Fourth evening with our grandparents, and they would give us sparklers, Roman candles and skyrockets. This made the decision on what to buy a bit easier. Since we anticipated getting fireworks from Grandpa and Grandma we would get some less expensive, but less loud, firecrackers, which meant that we could spend more of our money on some heavy artillery.

Three- and four-inch salutes were expensive, as were torpedoes that you could trigger by throwing against a wall or the pavement, but their report was very loud. Still, they were so expensive that a dollar or so would only provide entertainment for a short time. So I bought only a few of them to save for a special time when we could demonstrate our daring to friends by lighting these dangerous devices. Most of the money went for the standard flash crackers and even a few lady fingers, which maximized the pops per unit cost. It was said that a lady finger could go off in your hand and not hurt you. I never tested that theory. A flash cracker under a tin can would give a pop and send the can 10 to 20 feet in the air. The can was generally no worse for the wear.

A three- or four-inch salute under a can was another matter. The explosion was loud, with a powerful 'phrooom' sound, somewhat muffled by the can covering it. The can would fly 30 or 40 feet in the air. We rushed to recover the can to see if the seams had failed. Generally, the closed end of the can was rounded by the blast and the seams of the can showed stretch marks and occasionally total failure. The excitement I am sure was because we had been warned that if one of these three- or four-inch salutes went off in your hand you would surely lose a finger or a thumb. This was daring stuff.

We usually didn't plan on working in the fields on the Fourth. Of course, if the weather had been bad with spring floods delaying the corn planting or if other farming problems had occurred, we might end up cultivating corn or putting up hay. The weather controlled how much farm work might be planned for the Fourth of July. But there was always milking, gathering eggs, feeding and other chores. Every day was the same in that regard. If field work was planned, the day was a little shorter, but there was time to shoot the firecrackers. In fact, when I went to the pasture to get the cows for the evening milking, I would take a few firecrackers and throw one at the cows that were the stragglers. These gentle stragglers, like Mert, who was always at the rear of the group soon learned that the bang of a flash cracker was no big deal and ignored them. Gentle milk cows pretty much moved at their own pace with a slow walk, their hind legs sort of apart to keep the legs from jostling their large milk laden udder.

Watermelons and soda pop were synonymous with the Fourth of July. We never had soft drinks in the refrigerator and to have a soda pop was a special event. Coca-Cola in those days came in an 8-oz., hour-glass shaped classic Coke bottles. Grapette was popular among some of the older girls and it came in 6-oz. bottles. All soda pop cost 5-cents a bottle, and you could get Nehi drinks in grape, orange, strawberry and other flavors or RC Cola in 12-oz. bottles for that same nickel. Dad would buy a case of 24 bottles of assorted pop for the family on the Fourth. I recall that the 24-bottle case cost 90 cents at Ray's Store. That was probably close to Ray's cost, but it was his way of helping families celebrate the Fourth. There was no deposit on the bottles that had to be returned and no written record kept of who had them. But we returned all of the empties in the wooden partitioned, reusable pop case. I suspect that Ray would have remembered if they hadn't been returned.

The week before the Fourth, Ray always bought several watermelons at the vegetable market on his weekly buying trip to Joplin. Before the Fourth was about the only time Ray had watermelon. They were invariably large, Black Diamond watermelons that were shipped in from Texas or maybe southwestern Oklahoma. We would cool the watermelon in a washtub full of cool well water. No ice was ever used to cool a melon, and the refrigerator didn't have room for a large 30-pound watermelon. But they were very sweet and tasty. We generally cut the melon just before we started the evening chores. We were allowed to eat all we wanted, since that was quite a long time before bedtime. Watermelon was cut in semicircular-shaped pieces about an inch-and-a-quarter thick, and we always ate it outside. We all developed great skill in spitting watermelon seeds for distance during the inevitable contests to see who could spit one the farthest.

Dinner (the noon meal) on the Fourth was always a big meal with fried chicken and a lot of garden fresh vegetables. The fryers were often the first of the season and were killed and dressed that morning. Sometimes, on the morning of the Fourth, some of the neighbors would come and buy one of Mother's young fryers. We would catch the largest young rooster that we could get and tie his feet together with binder twine. Mother had a portable spring scale that had a hook at the bottom to hook the twine at the chicken's legs and she would hold it out and let the buyer read the weight. A live fryer might go for 20 cents a pound, pretty high for those days. But fried chicken was a treat that many of the Ritchey townspeople didn't have very often.

Since Mother hatched her own chickens in the spring to restock the laying flock, we had a lot of young roosters around in the summer. These were white leghorns, an egg-laying breed, as opposed to the larger meat breeds used by the commercial broiler producers. So they weren't large. Mother would generally kill and dress two for the Fourth. This involved heating water to boiling on the stove and then catching the roosters. We would wring their heads or chop them off and when they quit flopping around, we would dip them into the scalding water two or three times to loosen the feathers so they could be plucked. The cats usually got the chicken heads and scurried off to some out-of-the-way place to work on their own Fourth of July feast.

The chicken plucking was usually something the kids were asked to do. We could get all of the large feathers, but there were always some fuzzy, tiny feathers that were very difficult to get. Mother would loosely roll up an old newspaper and set it on fire in one hand while she held the plucked, headless chicken by the feet in the other hand and then she would twist the chicken above the flame to singe the fuzzy pin feathers away. After that, the chicken was washed, dressed and cut up for frying.

You could see what the chicken had been eating by examining the gizzard. The entrails and feet went in the slop bucket for the hogs, and the rest of the chicken, including the gizzard and liver was fried. I always liked the gizzard and usually got it since no one else argued for it. I don't think I have had a chicken gizzard since I was a boy. The fried chicken made the Fourth of July a feast, but there was more to preparing it in those days than most young people of today realize. Now, you just go to the supermarket and buy a dressed and precut fryer at a cost far less than what they cost then, when all factors including inflation are considered.

After finishing the evening chores, which we did earlier than usual on this holiday, we had supper and prepared for the evening fireworks. We were usually with our Grandma and Grandpa Smerdon, Uncle Willie and Aunt Edith, and Cousins Bill, Bob and Jack. One year we would go up to their place near Pierce City, and the alternate year they would come to our place in Ritchey. Skyrockets and Roman candles had to be pointed toward the garden or an open field, never toward the barn and its dry hay. The older children or an adult lit the skyrockets, although every child knew that he or she was perfectly capable of doing it.

Even the young children were allowed to hold the Roman candles as they shot their eight or ten flaming balls into the air. But they were constantly reminded to be careful where they pointed them. We also had sparklers, and we would run around the lawn waving them and writing our names with sparkling flames in the air. The final activity of the Fourth was collecting any burned sparkler wires that might have been dropped on the lawn. Otherwise they might get caught in our reel-type, push lawnmower and nick the blade.

Thanksgiving. The Thanksgiving Day celebration was a family holiday that simply meant getting together and feasting. We generally didn't work in the fields unless the weather had delayed harvesting the corn. If some corn was still in the fields and the weather was good, we would likely be working shucking corn. We generally had about 50 acres of corn, and a good worker could harvest about one acre per day of shucked ear corn. We always shucked our corn as opposed to snapping it with the dried shucks left on the ears. It was a bit slower, but less storage space was needed and Dad preferred shucked corn for hog feed. Since Thanksgiving was a celebration of the harvest, if the harvest was not complete, postponing that celebration made sense. If we worked on Thanksgiving Day, we would always get together with our Smerdon grandparents and Uncle Willie's family on the following Sunday.

In those days, the University of Missouri and University of Kansas closed out their football season with a Thanksgiving Day game. If we weren't working, we would listen to the game on the radio. That was the big game for both teams, and the team that won had a successful season, regardless of its overall season record. My father liked football and enjoyed listening to the games on the radio in those pre-television days.

The Thanksgiving feast was large and consisted mostly of the food we had grown. Since we didn't raise turkeys, we never had a turkey on Thanksgiving Day. Mother usually cooked a hen, and we also had home-cured ham. The hen was a nice, fat one that was no longer producing eggs and was converting the feed consumed to meat instead of eggs. The hen would be dressed that morning. Candied sweet potatoes, mashed potatoes, gravy and several home-canned garden vegetables, freshly baked buns made from scratch, butter, homemade blackberry jelly and home-harvested comb honey were also part of the normal fare. Dessert included pumpkin pie baked that morning and perhaps a cake.

Since Thanksgiving was a four-day break from school, I tended to associate it with an extra day of weekend work. If the corn harvesting was done, we probably wouldn't work on Thursday. But we could count on working with Dad on Friday and Saturday -- usually in cleaning manure from the barn. The portion of the barn used for milking and for the horse stalls and calf pens had a dirt floor covered with straw bedding. During the season, animal waste would build up in this bedding and it made excellent, high-nitrogen fertilizer for the fields. Dad liked to spread manure on the fields scheduled to have corn the following year. So on Friday and Saturday after Thanksgiving, we usually hauled ma-

Spreading manure in a field.

nure. As a matter of fact, we hauled manure many Saturdays during the winter when we were home from school. Dad never kept us out of school for work no matter how far behind he was because, to him, school was most important. But he sure expected us to work on Saturdays.

We had a very fine horse-drawn manure spreader. It had a creosote treated, wooden box with a conveyor chain along the bottom. Two reels studded with spikes would rotate and tear into the manure as it was slowly conveyed to the back of the spreader, flipping the manure chunks back into a rapidly rotating spreader. This spreader would throw the manure out in a fairly wide and uniformly spread band. Large drive wheels at the rear powered the contraption, which was pulled along by a team of strong horses or mules.

Loading manure with four-tined pitchforks was hard work. Although we all helped load the spreader, Dad and my older brother, John, were stronger and did most of the loading. When the spreader was loaded, I would often drive it to the field and spread the manure. It was fun when I was unloading and the manure was flying everywhere, with a chunk occasionally hitting me in the back. I certainly didn't want to look back with my mouth open when the spreader was operating.

I remember one incident that could have been a tragedy. A neighbor, Donny Ritter, had ridden out with me to unload the manure. Coming back he was standing in the empty spreader box on those wet and slippery creosoted boards in the bed of the spreader when he slipped and fell over the side. I heard a yell and turned from my seat at the front behind the team just in time to see the large rear wheel of the spreader roll over his chest. I don't recall whether this occurred on a Thanksgiving weekend or not, but we could all be thankful that the spreader was not loaded. If it had been, Donny's chest could have been crushed. As it was, he was only bruised and frightened after the broad rear wheel rolled over him. He was sore, but no ribs were broken.

Until we got a mechanical corn picker, I thought of Thanksgiving weekend as a time of plenty of food, football on the radio and work. When the corn could be harvested in less than two weeks with the mechanical picker, as opposed to about 50 man-days by hand harvesting, Thanksgiving became more of a true holiday. Dad could justify taking off and celebrating without feeling guilty.

Christmas. The Christmas season was a time of happiness and high spirits. But it didn't start until the middle of December, although shopping started before then with the orders of Christmas clothes from the Sears & Roebuck catalog. In fact, sometime in the middle of December, usually on a Saturday, the family would make a shopping trip to Joplin. This one special shopping trip to the city of more than 30,000 was a big event. We might see Santa at the big thee-story department store, and the dime stores were large and well stocked. With our limited amount of cash, we children found the dime store to be a good place to shop for gifts.

We went in the morning and shopped until mid-afternoon, so we were in town for dinner (lunch). We usually ate at a place on Seventh Street, just off Main, where you could get what they called a 'plate lunch' for 15 cents. Since we had a lot of milk at home, there was no need to pay a nickel extra for a glass of milk. The meal was served on a thick, heavy, white plate, usually with chips on the edges. The plate had ridges dividing it into three sections, one for each food item. The larger section would have some thinly sliced, well cooked roast beef with mashed potatoes beside it. Brown gravy covered the meat and potatoes. Another section had vegetables, usually canned green beans, and the third section had coleslaw or cottage cheese. You got one slice of bread and a small pat of butter. No substitutions were allowed except the choice of coleslaw or cottage cheese. It might not have been the best plate lunch in town, but it was the best for the price. With our young appetites we cleaned those plates.

I recall sitting on Santa's lap and telling him that I wanted a cowboy suit, with a Western shirt, a vest, a bandanna, cowboy hat and a toy pistol with a holster. There were usually a lot of children there and you didn't get much time with Santa. We couldn't wait too long because we had to get home and do the chores and milking. And the days were short that time of year.

We didn't put up our Christmas tree until a few days before Christmas. We didn't buy a tree. We children would go up on the hill pasture and look for a small cedar. Sometimes these were a bit scraggly, but that didn't dampen our spirit. The decorations weren't extensive, consisting of a single, inexpensive string of lights that were wired in series. That meant when any one of the bulbs burned out, the whole set was out. Sometimes it was the children's task to take a new bulb and one-by-one put it in each socket to see if that was the bulb that needed to be replaced. This was frustrating work, but we managed to keep the lights going and thoroughly enjoyed them.

We kept the Christmas-tree decorations in a box under one of the beds in the children's bedroom in our old house. That box included small, four-inch-long candles of several colors. We were reluctant to discard anything useful in those depression days and Mother kept them in case she might need some small candles. Those candles were from the days before homes had electricity and candleholders were clipped near the end of the Christmas tree branches. They would be tilted outward so the flame wouldn't start a fire, but the fire hazard was still very great. I suspect those who used candles only lit them for Christmas Eve and Christmas Day, and then only when adults were present. We never used those candles, but I still remember the one time when I saw a Christmas tree with candles for lights. That was at Aunt Cora's and Uncle Eb's. We were there on Christmas Day but the candles weren't lit. I could see how the tree was decorated in the days before electricity.

Our Christmas tree was decorated with both red and green paper garlands, icicles, and the lights. We sometimes had a little artificial snow, and that was it. Some people made decorations by stringing popcorn on a thread, but I don't recall doing that. In school, the early grades might make colorful chain-like garlands, by cutting strips of colored paper and pasting them in interconnected loops.

Christmas was the only time that we had candy available on a regular basis. Most of the candy was homemade and included fudge, divinity and sometimes taffy. Making taffy was tricky, and Mother generally didn't consider it, since pulling taffy by hand was a big chore. Sometimes, however, the teenagers would make taffy, since working together in the kitchen pulling taffy – and flirting – was fun for teenage boys and girls. Fudge was my favorite, and it was the most common candy we made. I never liked to work in the kitchen, but I would certainly help Mother or John or Helen make fudge. We might have one box of store-bought chocolate candy and that was nursed along, with only one piece per night during the short Christmas season. That store-bought candy might be chocolate-covered cherries, which was the least expensive around. Dad loved sweets and probably enjoyed the candy as much as the children.

Christmas at school was also a festive time. We would decorate the classroom and at some point get a Christmas tree. The older boys were usually given the opportunity to find a nice cedar tree, certainly larger than the one we had at home. I remember one time in the 7th or 8th grade that I volunteered with Johnny Hilton and Jackie Ingram to go up east of Ritchey and find a suitable tree for the classroom. Our teacher, Mr. Meyers, told us that we must get permission from the owners before we cut it down. We went up through our pasture, on through Roy Marion's pasture, and beyond the house where Mrs. Crayton, the 3rd and 4th grade teacher, lived. We had looked carefully but couldn't find that perfect tree. We were up on the Spangler place, which was owned by two widowed or spinster women, whom we felt sure would not give us permission to cut a tree. Moreover, Jackie was sure that the women would shoot at us if they saw us, and he was uneasy about even being there. About that time we saw this cedar tree, too big for the Christmas tree but it had a perfect top.

Johnny and I decided that we would just top that larger tree to have the perfect Christmas tree for our classroom. We had been gone a long time and we knew that Mr. Meyers would be concerned since we were missing class. I climbed up the tree with the handsaw, with Johnny and Jackie below, the latter nervously saying we were going to get shot. I quickly sawed about six feet out of the top of the tree and dropped the handsaw to the ground. Jackie apparently was looking at the Spangler house for signs of danger when the saw landed on the end of the blade. It made a crack like a rifle shot and Jackie took off at breakneck speed toward Ritchey. It was so funny that Johnny and I could hardly get the school Christmas tree down and start back to school because we were laughing so much. I never realized that a handsaw could make a cracking sound like that, but I shouldn't have been surprised since some hillbilly musicians can coax music from them. Our class had a beautiful tree that year, 'obtained with proper permission and all of that,' of course.

At school we drew names for Christmas, and gifts were to cost no more than a quarter. I hoped that one of the poorer children wouldn't get my name because I feared the gift wouldn't amount to much and might even be something that wasn't new. As I reflect on it I'm more than a little ashamed at my lack of genuine Christmas spirit. It's possible that the only gift some of these children from the hills around Ritchey received at Christmas was the gift they got at school.

One night, during the last week of class before the one-week long Christmas break, there would be a Christmas pageant with angels, shepherds, kings and of course, Jesus, Mary and Joseph. I was usually a shepherd, and we would cut our own crooked staff, which we would have to bend and wire into the U shape on the end. That, plus a robe and a towel around your head, would complete the costume. I was probably not sufficiently disciplined to get a speaking part. On the last day of school before Christmas, which was often the 23rd, Santa would come in his old, ill-fitting Santa suit and stringy white beard. There was one Santa costume in Ritchey that Arthur Largen kept, and it was used by the churches, school and anybody else who needed a Santa. Santa would hand out all of the gifts. As we left for the holiday, Santa and the teacher would give us each a small, brown paper bag of candy. That bag would usually have two chocolate drops, several pieces of hard candy of various shapes including some ribbon candy, a pecan or two and an English walnut. We also were given a fresh orange. I suppose the teachers paid for these goodies. It wasn't a lot, but it may have been the only treat that some of the kids would get.

The churches also had a Christmas program. Usually the Sunday school classes would put on a pageant, usually not too different from the one at school. Each child would get some small gift and another small, brown bag of candy, nuts and an orange.

Christmas was a family affair. Mother's family lived in Oklahoma, more than 300 miles away, and wasn't involved in our Christmas. Usually, Grandma and Grandpa Smerdon, Uncle Willie and his family, and our family would be together on Christmas Eve, after the chores were done. We would alternate locations, one year in Ritchey and the next year at their place. Since the only way that Grandma and Grandpa could see their grandchildren open gifts was to do it on Christmas Eve, which was our family tradition. I don't know how we resolved the issue of Santa coming during the night, since none of the houses had fireplaces and Santa's gifts were handed out on Christmas Eve. But, it didn't seem to be an issue with the children.

However, one year we did have a Santa Claus, and he came to our house on Christmas Eve. Mother borrowed the Ritchey Santa suit and dressed up as Santa with a large burlap bag for gifts. Our grandparents and Uncle Willie's family had arrived, including Bob and Jack, who were about 4 and 6 at the time. Glenn was also young and in the Santa spirit. Mother in her Santa outfit came around the house to the front door and knocked. Grandpa went to the door, and to his surprise, there was Santa with a bag of gifts. His startled look caused mother to break stride and her best, husky "ho, ho, ho" was mixed with chuckles. Santa passed out the gifts, checking to be sure that all the small children had been good, and left by the front door only to appear from the kitchen later in her dress as if nothing had happened. I don't believe any of the young ones suspected anything. It was the only time that Santa appeared in person at our house when I was growing up. However, Mother gave the same performance for her own grandchildren, more than 20 years later in the early 1960s.

Christmas day was usually at Grandma and Grandpa's, and included our family, Uncle Willie's family, and other relatives. The women all brought covered dishes and there was more food than you could imagine, usually most of it grown on the farm. The several meats didn't include turkey because none in the family raised them. The meal was buffet style, if there were more than the Smerdon families there. But if it was only Grandma and Grandpa, and their two sons and families, it was a sit-down Christmas dinner (at noon) around the large dining table, with all of the leaves in.

The children played with their toys all day Christmas day. The women spent the morning in the kitchen preparing the food and the first half of the afternoon cleaning up. The men would often journey to the barn, to be out of the way, for philosophical discussions on politics, taxes, the travails of farming or whatever. When at Grandpa's place, they might enjoy a nip of bourbon from a bottle that he kept hidden in the recesses of a corncrib wall. There would be no nips of bourbon at the barn when they were at our house, since the only bourbon at our house was the half pint kept in the dresser drawer in my parent's bedroom – for medicinal purposes only.

Easter. Easter was another time when there was candy available for a short time. Again, it was usually a family holiday. The children will remember the Easter-egg hunt in the yard where the boiled and dyed eggs were hidden. The Easter-egg hunt was in the morning, usually after chores and before church, so Dad could watch. Later in the day, we would be with Grandma and Grandpa and they would give us each an Easter basket with candy eggs and maybe a chocolate-covered marshmallow rabbit. There were usually a handful of jellybeans of assorted colors in the basket. The candy would be gone before the end of Easter Sunday. However, the colored, boiled eggs that each of us collected plus the bowl of them on the dining room table would last for several days, even more than a week. You can only eat so many boiled eggs, even if they are colored.

Halloween. I remember Halloween not so much for the trick-or-treating, but because it was the one day each year when mischief was accepted – and even expected. I only remember going trick-or-treating one time. Helen was in high school and helped me dress as a girl. I didn't wear a mask, but had a sunbonnet to cover my short hair. Most people couldn't guess who I was, thinking that dressing as a girl would be the last thing a Smerdon boy would do. We didn't have special Halloween costumes and Mother didn't have time to make them. She was an excellent seamstress, but her sewing was for regular clothes that you could wear all the time. I don't recall how much candy I got trick-or-treating that time, but I'm sure that it didn't last long.

During Halloween, teenage boys would often get together to plan some sort of mischief. The girls would also get involved, but not in the serious stuff. They would make a paste of Bon Ami and water, and then paint the windows at school and at Ray's and Largen's stores, and maybe do scary things like tell ghost stories. That latter activity wasn't restricted to Halloween, and some pretty eerie ghost stories were told, maybe even causing a nightmare or two among those children who were naturally apprehensive and had fertile imaginations.

Older teenage boys liked to turn over outdoor privies on Halloween. As I reflect on that, I'm tempted to call to question the thought process in those young minds, including mine. I'm sure that we never considered the consequences of a misstep during that process. As I think about it, it is pretty gross. I don't know if anyone tried to turn over our privy on Halloween, but, if they did, they never succeeded. Ours was a very sturdy pit privy, bolted down to a solid foundation, and Dad felt it was safe. The vulnerable ones were those without a pit that just sat on top of the ground. They were easy to turn over and, fortunately, easy to set upright again.

Another favorite trick of the boys was to pull some piece of farm equipment downtown and park it in the middle of the street. I remember one time when some boys pulled our side-delivery rake nearly a quarter mile from the field and parked it in front of Largen's Store. I must confess that we talked more about the things we were going to do than actually doing them. I have heard stories of putting a farm wagon or some implement on top of a barn, but I doubt if it happened. Certainly, I never saw that.

I vividly remember one time when I was about 15 that some classmates and I were going to make an organized attack on the easy-to-manage privies in town. But a rumor got started that Alec Marion, the town constable, was looking for us and that he had a pistol. Caution prevailed to the extent that no privies were upended. Frank Meyer, a classmate agreeable to any trick, and who lived six miles from Ritchey, and was with us, tells of one incident that dark night. Somehow, he got separated from the group. Frank was in one of the back alleys and stopped to get his bearings in this strange village. As his eyes adjusted, he saw a vertical railroad tie that he thought was a corner post of a fence. Being a tall, athletic type, Frank decided to make a run and, using the top of the post as a vaulting platform for his hands, vault over the fence and not miss a stride in his getaway.

But when he did this, he felt the top of the corner post, shaped like a human head, sag some as he wildly jumped over the non-existent fence. Realizing that he had probably used Alec's head as a vaulting platform, only added to his speed as he sprinted away. Alec was very short man, about the height of a railroad tie corner fence post, and was probably having as much trouble seeing Frank as Frank had in seeing him. Subsequently, Alec, who lived across the street, asked me if I knew who was out prowling around on Halloween. He said he knew the boy wasn't from Ritchey since he wasn't familiar with the town's back alleys. I assured him that I didn't have any idea who it was.

Birthdays. Birthdays weren't big in our family and we didn't have birthday parties. We would receive gifts, usually clothes, from the family and from other close relatives. We would also have a cake, with plain icing and candles, but otherwise undecorated. Work went on as usual and, although the birthday was recognized as important, it didn't lead to days off or anything like that.

Birthday spankings for young boys, given with affection, were a part of the family celebration. These were friendly, though maybe slightly stinging, with one whack for each year as the years of one's age were counted aloud. We also got a 'year-to-grow-on' swat. We would usually get together with Grandma, Grandpa, and Uncle Willie's family on the Sunday before or after a birthday. That's when the gifts from relatives would be given and the spankings would occur. While birthdays were special in their own way in my family, they were not major causes for celebration as they were in my wife's family. As a girl in Neosho, she always had a birthday party with a lot of her friends. As a result of Joanne's birthday experiences as a child, our children could no more have a birthday without a birthday party with friends, than fly to the moon.

EXPERIENCE WITH GRANDPARENTS

Grandma and Grandpa Smerdon lived about ten miles east of Ritchey on the farm where my great grandfather had settled soon after he emigrated from England in 1872. Grandpa was born there in 1873 and lived on that same farm continuously until he died in 1946.

My maternal Grandma and Grandpa Davidson lived in Oklahoma southwest of Oklahoma City, more than 300 miles away, and we didn't see them very often, perhaps making a trip there once every four to five years. They did occasionally visit us in Missouri, but it was probably only every two or three years if that often. So I wasn't as close to my grandparents in Oklahoma as I was with those who lived only ten miles east. We would be together with the latter at least twice a month, usually on Sunday, and we were together virtually every holiday.

Grandpa Smerdon was a country gentleman who owned two farms. His father bought one of them in 1874. Grandpa obtained full ownership by buying out the other heirs when his father died. He purchased the second farm that we lived on in the early 1920's. Grandpa was a white-haired man, about 5-feet, 7-inches tall and had a bushy, white, coffee-stained mustache. His ever-present smile was engaging, and he always seemed relaxed and in good spirits. When I knew him, he always wore belted trousers and a light-colored shirt, not the bib overalls and blue-denim work shirt Dad and his brother, Willie, usually wore. He enjoyed working around cattle and usually carried a heavy, oak cane that he used as a cattle prod. Dad was a sharecropper and provided Grandpa a third of all the crops he raised as rent on the farm. Dad owned his own dairy cows, hogs and chickens, and I believe he and Mother kept all the income from the milk, eggs and hogs when he took them to market.

We had one pasture on our farm that was in the hills north of the creek bottom. It was used for grandpa's cattle during the spring and sum-

Grandpa and Grandma Smerdon.

mer months. Grandpa would drive down almost every week during the summer to check on those cattle, usually driving his Chevrolet car up the hills to his cattle's pasture. He would always ask us children if we wanted to go with him, and I always did. I would open pasture gates for him and, when he was driving slowly in the fields, he would let me ride on the front fender. What a thrill! There was a hood ornament on cars in those days that I could hold onto. Still, Mother wouldn't have approved if she'd known about it.

It was often hot and humid and the cars didn't have air conditioning, so, after he had checked the cattle, Grandpa would ask if I would like a bottle of pop. This was a rare treat, and I never refused. So we would stop by a tavern in town, locally called a 'beer joint,' where I would get a Nehi soda, usually orange or grape, and Grandpa would get a Falstaff beer. These drinks were both kept in a refrigerated cooler with cold water that opened from the top. The Nehi cost a nickel, and I think the beer was a dime.

Grandpa Davidson.

When we returned home, Mother no doubt knew that Grandpa had been drinking a beer because she had a very sensitive nose. I suspect that it would be impossible for anyone who had a beer or other alcoholic drink to conceal it from Mother. But she never said anything to him. She respected him and loved him, and knew that any beer or drink he might have was not in excess and, more importantly, was not depriving his family of food or any other needed support.

Although the bottomland was a fertile loam, the hills in the Ozarks were very rocky. That was the case in our hill pastures, and it was too rocky to mow the weeds in the pastures. There was one particularly objectionable prickly weed called 'thistle' that would grow in the pasture where Grandpa kept his cattle in the summer. Grandpa despised thistles because the cattle wouldn't eat the grass close to the weeds. He would pay us grandchildren a penny for each thistle plant we grubbed out in that pasture. Although Glenn was too young to participate, Johnny, Helen and I, each with a garden hoe in hand, would walk perhaps 30 feet apart back and fourth across that 40-acre pasture scanning for thistles. We kept a meticulous tally of each thistle that we hoed out. When Grandpa next came to Ritchey, he would check on what we had accomplished and pay us in cash. I think my older brother and sister were better at spotting the thistles, but even I as a ten year old could get more than 100 thistles, and earn more than a dollar for maybe four hours of walking back and forth across that pasture.

Grandma Smerdon was of German descent. Her family descended from the Liste family, originally from Hildesheim, Germany, dating back to the 1600's. Her maiden name was Rohn, and they had settled in Wisconsin. Grandma had black hair and every strand was always in place. She didn't drive so, no doubt, Grandpa took her to the beauty parlor in Pierce City. Although it never occurred to me that she might have her hair dyed, as I reflect on the fact that the day she died at age 68 she didn't have one gray hair. It would seem highly probable that she colored her hair.

Grandma was a proud woman, and she definitely thought her family was superior and could do no wrong. She had dressed my father in clothes much finer than were common for boys in the area when he was in elementary school. He was no doubt teased for dressing differently from others and this may have been the reason that he spent much of his time reading books rather than playing with his schoolmates. Dad once told me that his mother expected him to be above the others. She dressed him in white shirts with ruffles and in knickers. He resolved never to do that with his own children, and he didn't. Dad dreamed of being a civil engineer, but Grandma wanted him to be close by and insisted that he study agriculture, and that meant being on a farm and always near her.

Grandma always pampered her grandchildren. She invariably had candy for us in a bowl in the dining room, always lemon drops and sometimes chocolates as well. When we visited, I would suck on so many lemon drops that my tongue would get sore. Sometimes she would ask us to stay with her for a week. We always looked forward to it. My cousin, Billy, lived across the road from her, and it was a time that we could play cowboys-and-Indians, or cops-and-robbers and relive the scenes we had seen at the picture show. Grandma would get a cowboy outfit for us and we had toy pistols. It was great fun.

Each morning, Grandma would bake fresh coffeecake with cinnamon and sugar on top, which we enjoyed with our milk. She would bake cakes and pies, so we had more sweets than were probably good for us. Grandpa would take Billy and me to Pierce City in the afternoon to get a bottle of Nehi pop – and he would have a beer. So it was a lot of fun being with Grandma and Grandpa for a few days. Also, even as a small boy I had chores to do at home, such as bringing in wood for the cooking stove, and I never had to do that at Grandma's. I fondly remember staying overnight at Grandma's.

I don't recall that my Smerdon grandparents ever gave me any personal advice. But I was 14 when Grandma died. Grandpa died two years later. No doubt, if they had lived until I became older they would have given me advice.

I will always remember, however, one piece of advice that Grandpa Davidson gave me in 1945. It was near the end of World War II and I was 15 at the time. Grandma Davidson had died earlier, and he had come by train and was visiting us during the summer. He had asked me to go back to Oklahoma with him for a visit and Dad said I could go after we got a crop of hay harvested and in the barn. It kept raining, which delayed the haying operation and postponed the time I could leave. Grandpa Davidson, who chewed tobacco, was getting impatient. He had agreed to stay until I could return with him on the train, but he was anxious to get home.

One day I was sent to the neighboring town on an errand and Grandpa went with me. Although I was only 15, I drove the car regularly. Grandpa chewed tobacco, and carried an empty tin can with him on the floorboard of the car that he used as a spittoon. We were riding in silence when Grandpa suddenly spoke up and ask me if I used tobacco. I answered truthfully that I didn't. Suddenly, getting philosophical, he said that he didn't recommend the use of tobacco. He then added this advice, "If you ever decide to use tobacco, chew, don't smoke." Grandpa Davidson had never smoked, but during the times I knew him he always chewed tobacco. I did not smoke until I was about 20 and not much then. But, for several years I smoked a pipe and an occasional cigar. But I was never tempted to follow Grandpa Davidson's advice on chewing tobacco.

EPILOGUE – RITCHEY A HALF CENTURY LATER

Several years ago the city limit sign at the edge of town looked like this:

CITY LIMIT
RITCHEY
POP. 126

When I was a boy there were about 212 people living in Ritchey, including many children, and that was much less than it was at the turn of the century. One newspaper article in 1915 described Ritchey as a beautiful little town of 300 inhabitants. But the sign on the edge of town today says the population is 76.

The natural beauty of Ritchey and surrounding countryside is still there. But it isn't a place with job opportunities, so most that live there are retired or they drive some distance to work. Few of the small farms that once supported families are in operation now and much of the land is for pasturing cattle. The small businesses are all gone. Few houses have been built in the last fifty years, but most existing houses will have TV antennas on them, or perhaps satellite TV hookups.

Among the families living there in the 1930's were many children and the school was active. Originally there were one-room country schools throughout the countryside and students walked or rode a horse to school. These small schools were consolidated to form Consolidated Ritchey School District No. 10, with all twelve grades bused in to school from the country. Those in town walked to school.

Eventually, in 1940 the final two grades were discontinued and the junior and senior students were bused to Midway High School six miles to the south. Then in 1943 all four high school grades were moved to Midway. I was in that first class to go to Midway all four years of high school. Finally, the grade school in Ritchey was discontinued in 1955 and all students from Ritchey went to Midway in a further effort at consolidation. Now even Midway is gone and students in the area go to grade schools in the Triway School District, and then to a single East Newton High School. But there are no schools within about 10 miles of Ritchey.

The Ritchey Post Office closed in 1973. The railroad is still there, but the depot has been razed and the mail is no longer delivered by kicking the incoming mail bag from a fast train, and the hanging outgoing mail bag being snared by a pickup arm from the mail car of that same train. This train mail delivery occurred twice a day when I was growing up. Now all mail is delivered by a mail vehicle just like in the rural areas.

In the past, the lives of the people in the area were centered in that small town. It was not a bedroom community where work and play is generally in other places. Ritchey was our town. Hopefully, the small town traditions and the trust and neighborliness are still there. Loss of that would be sad.

Ritchey came into existence because Mathew H. Ritchey saw the beauty of the area and abundance of natural resources in 1832. He was the first settler in the area and built a log cabin, and cleared timber from the bottomland so he could farm it with his yoke of oxen. He became a very successful businessman and laid out the town, originally called Ritchville, but later changed to Ritchey. It boomed for over thirty years, helped by fertile Shoal Creek bottomland soil and the railroad bringing goods in and shipping products out. But transportation changed and Ritchey no more benefits from the railroad than a lonely barn adjacent to the track in the countryside, where the trains always pass at high speed. The economics of very small farms became iffy, and all of Ritchey started the inexorable downturn that continues today.

I don't think the town will die. It will always be a nice place to live. And many will take advantage of that. Opportunities for recreation, the natural beauty and history of the region may be attractive to some. But, sadly, it will not return to what I remember.

My hope is that the stories in these essays may bring fond memories to those of my generation who lived in small rural towns in America. More importantly, I hope they provide understanding of what life was like in rural America for young people from the 1920's to the 1940's.

The essays describe life on a farm on the edge of a small village in the Ozarks of Southwest Missouri in the period from before 1930 to 1950. At the beginning of that period, many did not have cars and few had running water in the kitchen or indoor plumbing. Almost no one had any education beyond high school and many did not have a high school diploma. In 1930, those who lived on the farms in the countryside surrounding Ritchey did not have electricity. Few had radios but as time went on these became more common for those without electricity through the government Rural Electrification Administration. Ritchey was not unique – it was similar to all small towns in rural America at the time.

Trust was a very important part of the culture. During my boyhood, we did not lock our house even on the very rare occasions when we would be gone for a few days. A business deal was affirmed and became a verbal contract with a handshake. Virtually no one had any business with a lawyer except in a real estate transaction or perhaps a will. In fact there were no lawyers in the county except in the county seat.

The schools taught the basic three Rs, reading, 'ritin' and 'rithmetic, and the grading in grade school was plus (+), average (Ave.), and minus (-). They meant better than average, average and poorer than average. In school most students were passed on to the next grade, but not all. Contrary to Lake Wobegon, all were not above average in the eyes of the teachers. In fact, most were average and as many were given below average grades as above average. The ethic was work and honesty. Crime, as we know it today, was virtually non-existent, although pranks were committed, particularly by teenage boys at Halloween. Some of these pranks were insensitive, but never intentionally malicious.

The guiding principle was that if you wanted to get ahead, you had to work hard. That is an underlying theme of this book. In Ritchey, no one thought of getting ahead through dishonesty or taking inappropriate advantage of one's neighbors. It was through hard work that one gained and improved, and that was not just physical labor but hard work of the mind.

Few, if they think about it, would want to bypass the advances that science and technology have brought us. I disliked stoop labor and my dreams were to not have a life of that. So we all worked hard to provide the opportunity for a better life. But looking back, it is hard to imagine a better setting in which to grow up than what we had.

The 1900's was a century of innovation. It saw the electrification of the rural areas, the advance of the automobile and the airplane during my boyhood, the coming of labor saving household appliances, the development of safe water supplies, the radio, agricultural mechanization, and many others. Since I left my home village, we have seen electronics, television, computers, unimaginable telephony, spacecraft, the internet, amazing imaging, advanced medical technologies, lasers and fiber optics, and high performance materials. We do not want to give up any of these. So if returning means going back to the physical conditions of the thirties, we cannot and should not return.

But there are values that have been lost and we can return to them – at least I hope so. We can return to honesty and trust. We can return to caring for our neighbors, even those in other countries who need our help. We can expect honesty in those who lead the major corporations and to have a less litigious society, where a person's word is his or her honor, and a handshake has more meaning than it seems to have today. We can return to the values that I so greatly cherish after over seventy-five years, the first twenty-one living in Ritchey and that great community of friendly, caring people.

Towns and communities like Ritchey are disappearing from the face of America. In the late 1800's, Ritchey was a thriving railroad town. But when U.S. Highway 60 was built and bypassed the village by two miles the fading of the town started. When I was a boy the population of the town was 212. It is now said to be 76, but it may be lower. We need to remember these places where our parents labored hard to make it possible for us to accomplish as much as our abilities permitted. That was one motivation in writing this book. Another person from Ritchey, a few years younger than I am, has established a web site on Ritchey. He is Howard Dale Ritter. Dale was from a typical family of modest means. But he, like his brothers and sisters, was very intelligent with a lot of potential and he became a successful government servant in several locations in the world. To get more information on Ritchey, visit http://www.vvm.com/~ritterh.

Can we ever return? I would like to think so. But I don't think that is realistic. However, we can return to the humanistic values that I learned as a boy. In this world of global conflict, that is the hope we must nourish. Ritcheyites cared about their neighbors. In my youth one's neighbors were those in the immediate area. But now our neighbors are all of our fellow world citizens, regardless of color, religion or culture. I fear we will experience endless world conflict if we do not find a way to return to the basic values that made Ritchey such a great place. One weakness of Ritchey is that it was a monocultural town. We did not think enough of the people of the world whose cultures are different, religions are different, races are different and hopes are different. We will have eternal conflict unless we learn to understand and accept these differences and gain their trust, just as trustworthiness was a basic quality of our Ritchey people.

Ritchey population.

A HISTORICAL FOOTNOTE: IT DID HAPPEN

There weren't any minorities in our small farming community of Ritchey. In fact, our school didn't have a single African American, Asian, or kid of the Jewish faith in the student body. Moreover, I didn't know of any Roman Catholics in our community. It was a homogeneous community, dominated by white Protestants of European origin.

We didn't think that we were prejudiced, but how could we know? There wasn't an opportunity for us to display concern for those who were different. While there were differences in the economic status and what people had, none felt in any way that they were 'above' the others. No one was rich, that's for sure. We had a fine farm and our parents were leaders in the community. All dressed alike at school. There were no designer jeans. The boys wore inexpensive overalls and the girls all wore similar cotton dresses, often homemade by their mother. So, to me, in those days, I didn't think about prejudices. But, on reflection, that was not the case, even if we didn't have occasion to demonstrate it in our community, where no one was different regarding race or ethnicity.

I think people in Ritchey were like the people in all the nearby small, rural towns. Most were directly or indirectly engaged in agriculture. I now realize there were prejudices among us. Many locals migrated from Tennessee, Kentucky and the Appalachian states, and their prejudices had come with them. How else could we make 'nigger flippers' (sometimes called beanie flippers or sling shots), or play a group game at school called 'blackman,' (see the essay entitled, Games) or have in our small bag of nuts and Christmas candy a nut we called 'niggertoes' (Brazil nuts)? No, the latent prejudice was there. We just didn't see the outward manifestation of it, as we might have if our community had been more diversified. We must not be naïve and let ourselves become too proud. We need to recognize weaknesses and learn from the past.

When I was about 12, Dad told me of an incident in Pierce City, only 12 miles east of us, and where he went to high school. It happened in 1901, when he was three years old. Except for that one time, when Dad told me of a tragic incident of racial hatred, I never heard anyone speak of it. Dad felt disgust and shame that it occurred in his hometown, even if he was too young to personally remember. It is sad that I never heard about it in school or read about it. It was as if it didn't happen. To this day, if Dad hadn't told me and my siblings of the incident, I probably would not have known of it.

As best I can recall, here's what happened. In rural areas, when you wanted to go to town, you often walked, if the distance was only a few miles. Usually the rural roads were used, but if the railroad track followed a more direct route, its right-of-way would be your walking path. We always viewed it as safe, and we didn't have fear of the hobos (we called them tramps), who would sneak a ride on a freight train. We knew of hobos because we occasionally saw them riding on the freight cars out of sight of the engine or the caboose. Sometimes, when a freight train was on the siding in Ritchey, a hobo would come the few hundred feet to our home asking for food. Mother knew they were down-and-out, and she would have them wait outside, and then provide a sandwich and other food to them. They usually offered to work, and she might have them chop wood while they waited.

Dad couldn't have personally remembered the details of the Pierce City story, since he was only three when it happened. So he must have heard of it from his father. I recall it this way.

A young farm girl was walking along the tracks between her parents' farm and Pierce City. Apparently, she was molested by someone traveling along the tracks. Dad did not give us details of the incident. But I don't recall that the girl was killed. It was a terrible thing and the person responsible should have been apprehended and tried for the crime. Apparently the molester was black. I do not know if he was identified, but the incident led to mob action in Pierce City.

The record I have recently seen on the web confirms what Dad told us. Some men in town amassed in racial hatred and, as a result, four African Americans were lynched and several houses were burned. There was no arrest or trial. It was a brutal action of a mob. Quite likely, none of those lynched or whose houses were torched was guilty. Equally tragic, all of the Blacks in Pierce City were run out of town. They left in mortal fear for their life. They gave up all of their property and didn't receive any compensation. This was one of many sad cases, particularly in the Deep South, where minority groups were denied their rights as American citizens. This happened over a century ago in a little town only 12 miles from Ritchey. I never thought of the area as the Deep South, but these actions in 1901 were as vicious as occurred anywhere. And it happened in our area.

More information is at: http://orig.clarionledger.com/news/0112/03/m04.html and http://www.mamiwata.com/murder.html.

On August 18, one week after my father's third birthday, the event reported in the two web sites listed above occurred. Both provided the same quote from the *Lawrence Chieftain* newspaper, published in the county seat of Lawrence County, where Pierce City is located:

> "In Pierce City, Mo., 1,000 armed whites burned down five black-owned houses and killed four blacks on Aug. 18, 1901. Within days, all of the town's 129 blacks had fled, never to return, according to a contemporary report in The Lawrence Chieftain newspaper. The AP documented the cases of nine Pierce City blacks who lost a total of 30 acres of farmland and 10 city lots. Whites bought it all at bargain prices."

APPENDIX I

THE REGION

The village of Ritchey, Missouri is located in Newton County in Southwest Missouri in the foothills of the Ozark Mountains. There is no county in Missouri west of Newton County and only one to the south. Specifically, Ritchey is 24 miles east of the Oklahoma border and 31miles north of the Arkansas border. A crow flying just slightly north of a line due west of Ritchey could reach the southeast corner of Kansas in about 25 miles. So Ritchey is tucked in the southwest corner of the state. You won't find Ritchey on a map of the State of Missouri in the 1952 Encyclopedia Britannica World Atlas section with individual state maps, but it is usually on state road maps, fortunately.

The Newton County area was known as the country of the 'Six Bulls' as a result of a trip to that area by Edmund Jennings. This North Carolinian left Jackson County, Tennessee to hunt in the West in the early 1800's and is said to have lived, hunted, trapped and fished with the Indians in the region. The hunter referred to his adventures and mentioned 'six boils' which were understood by listeners to be 'Six Bulls.' The 'six boils' were the six great springs that fed Indian Creek, Shoal Creek, Center Creek, Spring River and North Fork, according to historians. Ritchey is located at the edge of the Shoal Creek bottom, the flood plain of the valley.

Newton County was officially organized in 1839 and in 1840 had a population of 3,970. It had grown to 18,344 in 1880 and about 26,000 in 1888, according to History of Newton, Lawrence, Barry and McDonald Counties, Missouri published in 1888. If that last figure is correct, growth slowed considerably, because the county's 1950 population was 28,240, and had reached 40,555 by 1990.

Ritchey is located in the well weathered foothills of the Ozark Mountain range. It is at the edge of a beautiful valley with low rolling hills surrounding it. Adjacent to the hills are prairies such as the Sarcoxie Prairie to the northeast and the Oliver's Prairie (now generally called Newtonia Prairie) six miles south. Further north are relatively flat prairies. If one goes fifty miles south, the higher mountains of the Ozarks with very rough terrain dominate. The immediate region around Ritchey is characterized by beautiful blue or blue-green streams and many springs. These assets must have been a strong drawing card for the settlers from Tennessee, Kentucky, Virginia, the Carolinas and other Southern and Middle States. The 1888 history of the region said, "Shoal Creek is the leading stream in the county."

The hills were covered with many varieties of trees with oak, hickory, walnut, and ash among the hardwoods. The predominant softwoods were soft maple and elm. As expected, there were many saw mills in the early days and that continued on into the mid-twentieth century. Apple, peach and pear orchards did well in the rolling hills and there were a few grape vineyards. In fact an early viticulturist named Jaeger with vineyards west of Newtonia won an award from the French Government for his grape cultivars which were transferred to France and later were the rootstocks that helped overcome a blight problem in the French vineyards.

The prairies and bottoms were good for wheat, rye, barley and oats. Corn was well adapted to the creek bottoms where the soil was naturally more fertile and soil moisture more dependable in the heat of the summer. With good culture, average wheat yields of 25 bushels per acre and oats and corn yields of 40 were reported in the 1888 history of the region. If those figures were correct, the yields of those crops had not improved much by the 1930s and were probably less in many cases. Little chemical fertilizer was used in those days. The soil fertility, which was not naturally high in the region, contrary to some early reports, was probably being depleted.

The geology of the area was one of layered limestone hills with chert interspersed. Commercial minerals were mostly lead and zinc and a few producing mines existed in the county within a few miles of Ritchey. Granby, six miles southwest of Ritchey, was a mining town organized in 1848 and those commercial mines were still operating in the early 1940s. There also was a commercial mine in Wentworth, a similar distance to the northeast. But there were no commercial mines in Ritchey, although there were minerals at an unprofitable level in most of the surrounding hills. A small two-man mining operation operated during the 1940s a half mile east of town and I suspect similar operations had existed in the past at other nearby locations. I remember going down in that local mine on the lift which was fabricated by the miners and powered by a winch driven by an old automobile engine. The only light was the carbide light on the miner's hat, typical of underground mining in the old days.

The bountiful supplies of lead and zinc in the area is said to have been a potential cause of interest in the region by the Confederate Army in the Civil war. Several Civil War Battles were fought in the region in 1862 including one at Neosho on April 22, and two in Newtonia, one on September 30, and another on October 28.

The climate of the region is typical of the rest of Missouri. Arctic storms on rare occasion could venture that far south and cause very cold weather. The coldest winter of record was December-February 1929-30. By chance, the coldest temperature ever officially recorded in Neosho was 31F below zero on January 19, 1930 – the very night I was born in a farmhouse in Ritchey. Fortunately, that extreme belies the normal more mild winter temperatures where the coldest night in a winter might approach zero. Wind chill factors were not used then, so these were actual thermometer temperatures. Snow regularly occurs in the winter but usually only stays on the ground a few days. Severe ice storms are more feared because of the damage to trees and power or telephone lines caused by the heavy ice load and these storms happen every few years.

Missouri summers can be very hot and sultry. Southerly upper wind flow brings moist air from the Gulf of Mexico to the region and this can make the occasional 100F heat very stifling. While hot summer days in Ritchey see some nighttime cooling, it is never enough. Summer thundershowers are not uncommon and always provide a refreshing and cooling (but still humid) break.

Rainfall and snowfall at Neosho were measured by John C. Smith after 1880. During the eight years through 1887 the average annual rainfall was 53.7 inches with the range being from 31.7 to 70.7 inches. Smith reported snowfall of 43 inches in 1881 and only 3 inches during the following year. The eight year average was 19 inches, about 2 inches of water equivalent. As of 2008, records show the overall average annual total precipitation in Neosho to be 45.88 inches. Four severe droughts were reported between 1828 and 1888, with the period without a drop of rain or any dew ranging from twenty-four to forty-two days. To my knowledge, later severe droughts occurred, particularly in the 1930's and early 1950's.

Ritchey is a place where one experiences four distinctive seasons. While the spring is a beautiful time, it can be very wet and cause Shoal Creek to flood the bottom farmland. Although Shoal Creek has at one time been out of its banks (flooded) at Ritchey during every month in the year, the heavy floods which are devastating to crops in the bottomland usually occur in the spring. Fall often sees a kaleidoscope of colors on the timbered hills. While autumn rains can often play havoc with harvests, fall is a beautiful season with a wonderful smell in the air. Early fall sees the new apple and pear crops come in and apple cider abounds.

There is considerable evidence that Indians lived in the region around Ritchey. Excellent springs existed along the hills on both sides of the Shoal Creek Valley. These no doubt were ideal encampment sites. Many arrowheads were found in the Shoal Creek bottom. The farmers' tillage operations in the black soil in the river bottom fields would bring these arrowheads to the surface. After a rain had washed the soil from these carefully shaped light colored flint stones, farmers crossing the fields could easily spot them. My Father had found many, perhaps a cigar box full.

On one occasion in the late 1960, when I returned to Ritchey with my family, I learned that a grade school classmate who still lived near Ritchey had unearthed an Indian burial site about a mile east of town. We drove there and my wife and I were taken to a knoll on the edge of the creek bottom overlooking the valley and facing south. The area had large trees perhaps a hundred or more years old. I believe my former classmate clung to the thought that his discovery might be of some value. He showed me the hole about five feet deep that he had painstakingly excavated which uncovered two skeletons. In the digging he appeared not to have disturbed those remains in the slightest way. These Indian remains were in a fetal position and the roots of the large trees had grown through openings in the skeleton, including through the eye of one skull.

In response to my query if my friend had reported the finding to any official group, he said he had reported it to the University of Missouri Archeology Department. He seemed to be disappointed that the person he talked to had shown little interest in his finding, reportedly saying that such Indian burial mounds were very common in that region and apparently not worth a 250 mile expedition to see his discovery. We assumed the rounded knoll could have been an Indian burial ground.

Before Joanne and I left, we were also invited in my classmate's small unpainted shack of a house and shown a large glass covered wall mounting displaying a large artistically arranged collection of Indian arrowheads. My father had a small collection which he kept in a cigar box, but nothing like this. Those arrowheads had all come from a small area east of Ritchey and close to our farm.

An 1888 history of Newton County reports, "In 1832-33 the Osages were accustomed to visit the settlements and to seize corn, hogs and other property, believing that the country was theirs. On one occasion the Indians camped between the cabins of M. H. Ritchey and Gideon B. Henderson, and resorted to their ordinary methods. The two settlers, with ten men from the Mount Pleasant District, well armed, visited the Indian camp, and reasoned with the Indian interpreter in such measured terms and led them to leave the country. There were no fatal meetings in Newton or McDonald Counties, but just north of these counties there were a few murders of both whites and Indians."

The above account is of particular interest to me since M. H. Ritchey was the founder of the Village of Ritchey. Moreover, the farm I grew up on was originally settled by him. The many arrowheads found in the area clearly show that the Indians were there long before the settlers. It is comforting to know that there reportedly was no bloodshed between whites and Indians in Newton County, at least until 1888.

Neosho, the county seat of Newton County is about 12 miles as the crow flies from Ritchey. Neosho is an Indian name and other towns were named after Indian Tribes, such as Seneca on the west edge of the county on the Missouri-Oklahoma border. The following poem neatly describes the area.

cholera at St. Louis the day after his departure; of Union, the county seat of Franklin County, where the trail forked to the northwest and southwestern frontiers, and where the narrator's party set out via Mapes Iron Works, on the dim trail to Harrison's, on Little Piney Creek, ten miles south of what is now Rolla; thence to Kickapoo Prairie, the site of Springfield, known as the Three Forks of the White River, passing but one house until arriving at John Fullbright's, where Springfield now stands, west of which were the homes of John P. Campbell and Joseph Miller, settlers of 1830. John H. Miller, afterward of Ritchey, settled there with his parents when twelve or thirteen years of age.

The same 1888 history has an account of a journey by 'Old Sixty Four' to the Ritchey area. It is not clear who 'Old Sixty Four' was. This account, written in 1877, is of interest because it describes the area where my Great Grandfather settled in 1872. The farm which great Grandfather Smerdon settled was about two miles west of Pierce City on Clear Creek and was part of the original Looney farm. The account follows:

After leaving the house of John Williams, a day's travel took us to Prewett's Creek, now called Clear Creek. Prewett had settled one and one-half miles west of the site of Pierce City, and being the first occupant, the creek bore his name for awhile. Sampson Looney and John Ross came into this neighborhood in the spring of 1832. Here part of our company stopped, but Gideon B. Henderson, who married my only sister, and I concluded that we preferred to get near the junction of the Six Rivers, and so moved on west. At the mouth of Prewett's Creek we struck the beautiful valley of Shoal River. Delighted with the scene we drove on down the valley, though the trail was difficult of discovery, until we drove into a large timbered bottom; one mile west of where Ritchey now stands. Making our way through the forest we came upon a high cliff, out of which gushed a large spring of bright and clear water, rolling, tumbling, leaping, singing, down to the valley beneath. This looked attractive to a youngster from the prairies of Illinois. Near by was a log house just built, without chinked cracks, a floor or shuttered door. In front of it stood a man of whom we inquired how the road led out. By this time a woman moved the quilt which covered the aperture for a door, and, surrounded by a swarm of children, came out of the cabin to do the talking. She said: "There's no road further west; if you want to travel a road, you must turn round and travel back the way you came." I replied, "We wish to go west as far as we can without going out of the settlements, and make improvements." Here the old man broke in and said, "I'll sell my improvements." Gideon B. asked, "What will you take?" The old man responded, "I'll take less than the work is worth." Gideon B. Henderson asked, "Will you take that yearling colt?" at the same time pointing to a colt which was running with us. In plumped the old lady: "Take it, Jim, I want to get away from here." "Do you have the chills?" said I to her. "Something worse; no chills," she answered. At that moment I saw a curious grimace on Jim's face as he shot an appealing, warning glance at his wife, who evidently understood it and added simply, "We've lived here long enough." Gideon B. Henderson and Jim had now traded, the ladies of both parties being well pleased. This family was named May, and came there that year. My mother and sister were glad that their tiresome moving was ended, and the others were happy to move elsewhere. Next day we were left in full possession of our western house, but not without ascertaining Jim's wife's anxiety to get away. While Jim and his son-in-law were absent from home one day, some Osage Indians visited the cabin and stole a saw, an ax and other tools. Discovering the theft the men pursued to obtain restitution. The Indians, strong in number, abused the two whites, whipping them with Osage gun-sticks. A few weeks after our settlement I fell back east one mile and built a cabin. The house which I built in 1832, one-quarter mile west by south of Capt. Ritchey's residence, was only 12x14 feet, yet I had to go ten miles to obtain eight men (who lived where Pierce City is) to aid in raising it. One door, one window and an earthen floor characterized the building for three months; subsequently doors, shutters and lofts were made; ax-made clapboards, floors laid with hewed puncheons, bedsteads set against walls with one peg; axles were greased with honey and meantime farming was carried out on a small scale. A few who had raised corn were liberal in dividing it, hogs were scarce, pork hard to get, but wild game was so plenty that one hunter with his dog could supply all the pioneers for a week from one day's hunt. Honey was so plenty that it could be had for 25 cents per gallon, and in comb at 1 cent a pound. Meal for bread was beaten in mortars, the coarse remains being used for hominy. Until the fall of 1833, over a year, I had but one grist ground, and that at Cane Hill, Ark., sent there by a neighbor. In the fall of 1833 George McIntosh started a small mill and a blacksmith shop which won all the custom for fifty miles around. I worked on the construction of his mill-race for 50 cents per day. From the 1st to the 10th of June, 1833, the waters in creeks and rivers were higher than at any time prior to the floods of July, 1865, when they raised three feet higher than in 1833.

The first settlers in what is now the town of Ritchey were Judge M. H. Ritchey and his family in 1832. His son, Capt. J. M. Ritchey, was born there in 1836. I do not know the exact location of the original log cabin of M. H. Ritchey. However, later a large home on a knoll overlooking the Shoal Creek valley in the north edge of the town was built by J. M. Ritchey and was called the Ritchey Mansion. A small spring fed branch stream flowed just down the slope thirty to forty yards east of the mansion and continued due south to Shoal Creek. Locally, that stream through Ritchey was referred to as 'The Branch.' By all descriptions, The Ritchey Mansion was an elegant home. That mansion later burned and, according to one report, was the result of Bushwhacker doings after the Civil War.

Among the early physicians to serve the people of Ritchey, was Dr. G. L. Slavens who resided there in 1884. His father and mother, Dr. and Mrs. James H. Slavens had moved to the Newton County area in 1832. The elder doctor was also a Methodist preacher, reportedly the first in Southwestern Missouri.

Crawford County embraced all of Southwest Missouri until 1833 when it was divided to create Greene County. In 1835 Barry County joined these two. The original Barry County comprised all of what is now Newton, Lawrence, Jasper, Barry, McDonald, Barton, Dade and part of Cedar Counties. Prior to the organization of Barry County, Squire Vivion was the only justice of the peace in the whole region of the Six Bulls. One major duty of the justice of the peace was to join the young couples in holy matrimony. Although Newton County was organized in 1839, there is no record of marriages in that county prior to November 1863. Before then many of the marriages of Newton County couples were apparently performed in Barry County.

The first known blacks in Newton County were Neese and his mother who settled on the prairie eight miles northwest of Neosho in 1833-34. In about 1840, a freed slave named Lewis from Bedford, Tennessee moved to the county. According to the 1888 history of the area, the last slave transaction in Newton County was a sixteen year old slave girl named Frances who was sold to Thomas M. and Eleanor S. Johnston for $1000. The deed was drawn by Attorney David B. Bullard on April 6, 1860. The girl fled a few years later and reportedly was not heard from afterward. African Colony lands were established near Cedar in July 1881 and by November twenty-five black immigrants had arrived to take possession. Apparently a Rev. Mr. Harlow of the Colored Baptist Church was involved in this enterprise. In the fall of 1881, he was contracted to teach the Pleasant Hill School (perhaps a school for the blacks), three miles northwest of Neosho.

Although there were few blacks among the settlers of Newton County, the most famous of all of the natives of the county was George Washington Carver. Carver, who became internationally famous as an agricultural researcher, was born of slave parents in 1864 on a farm near Diamond Grove (now known as Diamond), Missouri. As a baby, Carver and his mother were stolen by a band of night raiders. Carver was said to have been bought back by his parents' master in exchange for a race horse, but his mother was never found. His birthplace in the north central part of the county is about 10 miles northwest of Ritchey.

George Washington Carver was very bright, always interested in nature and plants, and was given the opportunity to attend the black high school in Neosho. He worked his way through school, studying art at Indianola College in Iowa and later botany at Iowa State College where he received his Master of Science degree in 1894. He stayed at Iowa State as an assistant botanist for two years when he went to Tuskegee Institute in Alabama where he spent his lifetime in agricultural research. A broad range of products (about 200) were developed by Professor Carver, principally from the peanut, sweet potato and pecan. Before plastics were attempted, he had developed synthetic marble from wood shavings; dyes from clay; and starch, gum, and wallboard from cotton stalks. He was made a fellow of the Royal Society of Arts in London in 1916, an honor given to few Americans. In 1951, The George Washington Carver National Monument was established by the Congress of the United States on 210 acres of the Newton County farm where he was born.

IMMIGRATION OF SMERDON ANCESTORS

My Great Grandfather, William Smerdon departed Devonshire England with his family in early June, 1872, en route to Missouri. The party included my Great Grandmother Emily Pitts Smerdon, Great Uncle William, Great Uncle Thomas (who died fifteen years later at the age of eighteen), and Great Aunt Emily who was seventeen months old when they departed. My Grandfather, John Smerdon, was born fourteen months after his parents' departure from England. Two years later in 1875 another son, Henry, who died as an infant, was born. Two years after that the last child, a daughter named Thirza, was born. Great Grandmother Smerdon died a year later leaving her husband with five children to raise, feed, clothe and educate.

The following is an account entitled, "The Voyage from England to Missouri in 1872," a description of the original William Smerdon farm entitled, "Pierce City 1874-1875," a description of a flood on Clear Creek entitled, "The Flood - July 3, 1875," and a description of the year of farming after the flood entitled, "1875-1876." Since Great Uncle William Smerdon was born on December 21, 1867, he was less than ten years old when these events he writes about occurred. No doubt his remembrances come from the descriptions he heard as a child as well as his own recollections. The accounts as Great Uncle William Smerdon wrote them follow:

THE VOYAGE FROM ENGLAND TO MISSOURI - 1872

In the early days of June, 1872, we - Father, Mother, myself, my brother Tom and sister Emily who was a baby in arms - embarked for America. I can remember the sea was mostly calm during the trip, although the ship sometimes rocked and lurched. There used to be a saying by immigrants that they "had been rocked in the cradle of the deep." We made our crossing by the light of the moon. I remember Father taking me on deck to watch the waves roll in the moonlight. After a voyage of twelve days, we arrived at Ellis Island, New York.

And there my Father exchanged his gold coins for American paper money. He had brought 500 English gold sovereigns with him, each worth five dollars at par value. He told me in later years he got a large premium for his gold - as he remembered, about $675.00 for his 500 gold sovereigns. This was brought about by the Civil War of 1863. The Government had borrowed a large sum of money from England to carry on the War and it was inserted in the contract that both principal and interest must be paid in gold. So at this time, the United States was paying this premium for gold to pay the interest on the loan.

I remember we left New York City by train and stayed one night in Buffalo, evidently in a cheap hotel, as my Mother told a few years later that was where she got her first knowledge of bedbugs. In England they never have those bugs, mosquitoes, house flies, ticks, chiggers nor venomous snakes - only a few grass snakes and a few large blue flies that cause maggots.

We came through Chicago soon after the disastrous fire that was said to have been caused by upsetting of a coal oil lamp by Mrs. O'Leary's cow as she was being milked in the barn after dark. I recall it seemed to me acres of buildings had burned. The train went through the wholesale district. I saw from the car window high stacks of dishes that were ruined by the fire.

ATLANTA, MACON COUNTY, MISSOURI - 1872-1873

From there we travelled to Atlanta, Macon County, Missouri, a small country town near where an old school friend of Father's had located several years previously. We moved into a two-room box house that was vacant on his farm. Father bought a few things - a cook stove, table, chairs and bedstead. He unpacked a couple of large boxes 6 feet by 3 feet high and 3 1/2 feet wide, which were shipped by rail after being taken from the same ship we were on. Mother had brought three feather beds, some quilts, blankets and linens, and several tanned sheep skins with long wool that we used for foot rugs at the bedsides. Mother had two sets of dinner dishes - half at least were broken. Father had a shot gun and some tools. He had been told he was going to a new country and might have difficulty in getting such things. But this was unnecessary as everything one needed could be purchased at the stores.

It was now the first days of July. The days were long and hot. The oats harvest was at hand. Father was asked to help with the harvest. He did the shocking, as it is called by the farmers. Oats shocking in hot weather is one of the hardest jobs that I have ever tackled myself. Not being accustomed to such a hot climate, Father became overheated during the harvest - said he thought he had a sunstroke. To make things worse, a bowel trouble set up and he was a dangerously sick man. I have heard him say since that he told my Mother that he thought that he would surely die and Mother cried to think that fate had taken us so far from dear friends and relatives. But in time he recovered and some of the folks in the neighborhood tried to sell him a farm. But they could not get him interested. The soil was fertile, but the crops were corn, oats and hay, and there was no market except to cattle feeders and at a very low price.

Someone told Father that Southwest Missouri was the place of opportunity and that they were building a new railroad into this district and were giving cut fares to prospective settlers and homesteaders. In December of the same year he bought a 'homeseekers' ticket, as the railroads called their reduced fare, and went on a tour of investigation. He left Mother with us, we three children. We had a ton of coal and a supply of provisions. The nearest house was a quarter of a mile away and the snow was a foot deep.

It was in the early days of January, 1873, we were watching for Father's return. I well remember one sunny afternoon about 3 o'clock I saw Father coming down the Prairie road through the snow covered field. After he had greeted us all in the usual loving manner, he told Mother he had found the place we were going as soon as we could get away. He said that over in Southwest Missouri there was no snow, the wheat fields were green, the birds were singing and there were pebbles in the bottom of the streams.

Within two weeks we were living in one room of a two-room house. It was hard to get a place to stay as the town of Pierce City had just been incorporated the year previous. New homes and store buildings were under construction. They were completing the new brick public school building that stands there now on the hill with its additions.

The Frisco Railroad was then being built westward to Neosho, Missouri, a branch of which had been built to Carthage, Missouri. It was the only railroad into that part of this new country at that time. St. Louis was the only market for surplus products of wheat, cattle, hogs and sheep, hides, wool, furs, rabbits and quails, which were very plentiful in those days. A sportsman I knew told me he had bagged as high as eight dozen in one day and sold them for one dollar per dozen to the shippers.

A few years later, when the country became closely settled by people coming from the many Eastern states, the game became so scarce Missouri passed laws to protect and preserve the quail and wild turkey and deer and later wild ducks, also the fur animals.

We were in Pierce City only about two weeks until an Englishman who had come to America a few years previously and bought a large farm, heard about a newcomer, an English farmer. He came to see Father and persuaded him to farm his place in co-partnership - Father buying a half interest in all stock, implements, seed and growing wheat - and pay $1.00 per acre rental for all tillable land, which was on the basis of $2.00 for one-half of the acreage. He, not being a farmer, moved to the village town of Verona and furnished a man to do his part of the labor on the farm. This was a good farm - mostly fertile valley land - about 150 acres of plow land, a small orchard, plenty of timber free for the chopping, three log houses with fire hearths and chimneys - very comfortable.

Father's contract was for two years. He had good crops and good prices. Brother John was born on this farm August 29, 1873. He was the 4th child of the family. Sometime during this year Father's eldest brother died in England, age 48 years, a single man. He willed Father a reasonable sum in gold (the exact amount is not known) and Father got a premium on this for U. S. currency as before.

PIERCE CITY - 1874-1875

In the winter of 1874, Father began to look for a farm as his contract expired the coming March 1st. Father now decided to buy a farm for himself. So in looking the country over, he decided on a place one and one half miles west of Pierce City. Both the Frisco Railroad and Clear Creek run down the valley. There was a nice spring of crystal clear water always running.

This was a part of what was known as the Old Looney Farm. Mr. Looney was an early day settler - located there in 1835 when the county was named Barry County and about

100 miles square. The county seat was located on a hillside near a large spring adjoining the Looney farm, this being the center of the county, and Mr. Looney was the first County Clerk of this Barry County - at the magnificent salary of $25.00 per year.

Early in 1875, Father purchased 120 acres - one half being good bottom land with a one room log house on it. This part of the place was fenced and 20 acres cultivated and the balance mostly thick brush everywhere and heavy timber. There was also a good two-story, 4-room frame house south of the spring on the hill. This half south of the creek was mostly on the hills and limestone bluffs in its original wild state - anybody's cattle, hogs and sheep ran at large in those days. All of the cultivated land being rented and in growing wheat, Father only raised some potatoes and garden that year besides plowing and seeding the land to wheat. As the large house was occupied, we moved into the one-room log house. I clearly remember our moving in the early days of March, 1875 to our permanent home - this farm!

THE FLOOD - JULY 3, 1875

A never to be forgotten experience happened this summer. On the night of July 3, 1875, there came up one of those terrible summer deluges with thunder and much lightening, and the upper reaches of Clear Creek and its drainage were flooded. About 3 o'clock in the morning Father was awakened by the roar of the rushing water in the creek and got up to investigate. The muddy water was about to come into the house. The floor was only eighteen inches off the ground. They awakened us children and said we all must get, as this was within fifty yards of the main channel of the creek. We waded out to higher ground in the darkness as we had no lantern. We could only see where we were going by the flashes of lightening. We waded in water for about 250 yards. I remember it waist deep to me and sometimes came up to my armpits. We went to our nearest neighbor's home, a James Looney, who very kindly took us in for a few days until the water ran down and we could clean the house where the water had been four feet high in the house as shown by the mud on the walls.

At daylight next morning, the rail fence that we had followed in wading out was all gone. Everyone said that if we had been one hour later coming out we would most likely all have drowned as we were on the downstream side of the fence. The next day some folks were taken out in boats from their homes in the Bottoms. This is the first Fourth of July that I remember. In the year 1875! My mind is as clear on this as though it had happened quite recently. I waded in front of Mother. Mother carried brother John, who was the baby. Father carried sister Emily, and brother Tom, who was next eldest to me, held Father's hand as he waded along by his side. He sometimes lost his footing and just floated along. Rail fences were swept away and lodged in drifts in the timbered bottoms.

1875-1876

The following fall and winter, Father cleared out - grubbed out with mattock - eight acres of persimmon, sassafras and swamp willow, and wild rose and blackberry thickets. The next year this was included in the wheat acreage. The crop was fine, but this ground having poor drainage, the water would be several days going off. Just as this wheat was ripe and ready to harvest, there came one of those heavy summer thunderstorms and this field was under water like a pond. After a few days the surface water drained off, but the soil was so soft it would mire a horse to cross it. So father got three men who were experts at swinging a cradle to cut this wheat. A cradle is a scythe blade with fingers attached to it so that it laid out the grain in a flat swath convenient for tying. This tool went out of use entirely as the age of harvesting machinery had just arrived. The grain was threshed by a machine operated from a power plant known as a horse power. Four and sometimes five teams of horses were hitched to long levers and travelled around in a circle causing a large wheel with cogs to turn a small pinion to turn a long iron rod to revolve. This was attached to the threshing machine. The capacity was small. They threshed 200 to 300 bushels of grain in a day. The last year that Father farmed the Wallen farm he fed the men and horses for two weeks while threshing 1500 bushels of wheat and 1000 bushels of oats.

APPENDIX II – BIOGRAPHIES OF SETTLERS

The biographical sketches of some early settlers of Ritchey have been included to provide the reader with additional background information. The sketches of Judge Mathew H. Ritchey, Captain James M. Ritchey, Herman J. Rohn and Joseph H. Davidson are taken verbatim from, "History of Newton, Lawrence, Barry & McDonald Counties, Missouri." Published in 1888 by The Goodspeed Company, Chicago, the preface contains the following disclaimer by the publisher.

"In all cases the personal sketches have been submitted by mail, and in most instances have been corrected and approved by the subjects themselves. The publishers disclaim responsibility for the substance of the matter contained in the Biographical Appendix, as the material was wholly furnished by the subjects of the sketches."

JUDGE MATHEW H. RITCHEY

"Judge Mathew H. Ritchey is one of the very earliest settlers of Newton County, and the founder of the town which bears his name. He was born in Overton County, Tenn., February 7, 1813, and is of Scotch descent. His father, Abel Ritchey, was a farmer of Overton County, Tennessee, and died when Mathew H. was but four years of age. His mother's name was Mary Wasson. Judge Ritchey was reared among the scenes of frontier life, and lived in Tennessee until 1829, when he went with his mother to Morgan County, Illinois. After remaining here for two years, and at the age of nineteen, he started for Missouri (then a Territory), carrying his effects in a two-horse wagon drawn by a yoke of steers, and taking his mother with him. He crossed the Mississippi River at St. Louis, pushed on through the State, and finally, in 1832, located where Ritchey now stands, being attracted by the fine bottom lands on Shoal Creek. His nearest post-office was 100 miles away, and the nearest mill was eighty miles from Ritchey. He had an excellent rifle, which he valued very highly, and being a good marksman, had no trouble in procuring meat for the table, as the country abounded in wild game, and the streams were full of fine fish. He built his first log cabin on the site where the residence of R. E. Armstrong is now standing. In 1835 he married Miss Mary King, daughter of Sanford King, who was born in Kentucky, of Irish parentage, his father being a Tory from Ireland. Sanford was in the War of 1812, and his father was so angry at him on this account that he forbade him to return to his home, but was afterward glad to accept the hospitality of his son, who on account of difficulties in Kentucky, had sought refuge in Missouri. Judge and Mrs. Ritchey were the parents of ten children: Capt. James M., Nancy J., Mary M., Martha E., Christopher C., Amanda M., Amillia A., M. Sue, Margaret E., and Sanford H. These children were all born on the old homestead except Sanford H., who was born in Newtonia. The children all lived to maturity except Nancy J., who died in infancy. Judge Ritchey was elected constable in 1836, his jurisdiction extending over an area thirty miles square. He was elected county judge, which office he filled for several terms. He was also elected representative to the State Legislature and has been State Senator several terms. He was also captain in the State Militia. He was a delegate to the State convention, called to decide whether the State of Missouri should secede from the Union or not. Judge Ritchey voted for the Union amidst much opposition and excitement. He was a staunch Union man, and was always true to his principles. During the war he was paymaster, with the rank of major. The family lived at Newtonia during the war. Mrs. Ritchey died here in 1855, and Judge Ritchey married Mrs. Mary E. Clark, a widow lady, who is yet living by whom he had three children: John C., Julia, and Charles G., who died in infancy. Judge Ritchey ran his mill (being engaged in the milling business at that time) all through the war, and afterward still continued this business. He was also engaged in merchandising both at Neosho and Newtonia. In 1871 he laid out the town which bears his name, and in company with his son, Capt. J. M. Ritchey, constructed the mill and dam, the hotel and store, and other buildings, thus founding the town. Judge Ritchey was a member of the Masonic fraternity, joining that body in 1846, and was a charter member of Newton Lodge No. 175 of Newtonia. He continued a member of that lodge until 1884, when he changed his membership to assist as a charter member in organizing Ritchey Lodge No. 530, of which he is now a member. Judge Ritchey joined the Cumberland Presbyterian Church in 1840, and has taken a great interest in the same, having held the position of ruling elder over twenty years. He has been clerk of the session, also a delegate of the General Assembly of the United States several times. He was originally a Democrat in his political opinions, and was one throughout the war. He became a Greenbacker when that party was organized, and was a candidate for Congress on the "Greenback" ticket in 1876. Judge Ritchey laid out and built Newtonia in 1854, and took an active part in the establishment of Newton College. He is a man of iron constitution, and one of the best known citizens of Southwest Missouri. He is now the owner of 1,000 acres of land and a large amount of town property in Ritchey and Newtonia."

Matthew H. Ritchey.

CAPTAIN JAMES M. RITCHEY

"Capt. James M. Ritchey, who is engaged in milling and stock raising, is a native of Newton County, Missouri, born in the year 1836, on his father's farm, in the old log cabin which was built by his father in what is now Ritchey. He was the first white male child born in that county, which was then a wilderness, inhabited by wild animals and Indians. The Captain, as an infant, was rocked in a cradle hewn out of a solid log, and made by his father. In this wild and unsettled region he grew to manhood. He was the son of Mathew H. Ritchey, whose sketch will be found above. The Captain received a rather limited education, but by reading and observation he is accounted a well-informed man on all subjects. During his youth he assisted on the farm, and at the youthful age of nineteen married Miss Calodonia D. Logan, of Lincoln County, Tennessee, daughter of Benjamin and Elizabeth Logan. To the Captain and wife were born three children: Henry M., Milton H. and Mathew A., who died in 1886, at the age of twenty-four years. After marriage Capt. Ritchey began farming, and then engaged in the stock business with his father. At the breaking out of the late war he was in New Orleans with stock for that market, but lost, through the failure of the purchasers to pay their notes, which he had taken in payment. He returned home and entered the secret service of the United States, in July, 1862, and there remained until October, 1862, when he was appointed enrolling officer for McDonald, Newton, Barry and Jasper Counties, Missouri. He then organized Company I, Seventy-sixth Regiment Missouri Volunteers, October 10, 1862, and December 17, same year, he was appointed captain, having previously filled the office of lieutenant. In March, 1863, the regiment was disbanded and Capt. Ritchey's company was consolidated with Company C, of the Seventh Provisional Regiment Missouri Volunteers, and at same date he was appointed quartermaster. Capt. Ritchey then organized Company K, Fifteenth Regiment Missouri Volunteer Cavalry September 19, 1863, at Mount Vernon, Missouri, and was ordered to move to Newtonia and take charge of the post there. Here he was on active duty, being in almost one continuous skirmish. January 16, 1864, Capt. Ritchey received orders to proceed with his company to the vicinity of Keetsville, Missouri, and protect the telegraph communication from Springfield, Missouri, to Fayetteville, Arkansas. This was an arduous undertaking, and the company was in many skirmishes. The company was engaged in this campaign until February 19, when they returned to Newtonia. They had accomplished the object of their enterprise, and driven the band of rebels from that part of the country. The country was infested with bands of guerrillas and partisan bands, and Capt. Ritchey was in many engagements with them. His experiences at that time would fill a volume. In 1863 he captured some rebel mail, and among the letters was one from his present wife to a young gentleman in the rebel army. She was at that time a young lady of decided rebel proclivities. The last year of the Captain's service he was on detached duty, and was mustered out July 4, 1865. He then engaged in the saw-mill business near Granby, Missouri, where he remained until May, 1866, when he went to Newtonia, and, in company with his father, Judge Mathew H. Ritchey, engaged in the flouring-mill business enterprises. They were engaged in merchandising at Pineville, Rocky Comfort, Newtonia and Ritchey, and have been active in building up Newtonia as well as Ritchey. Capt. Ritchey has made most of his money in stock raising and dealing. He, in company with Mr. B. A. Duvall, at Newtonia, have control of about 1,000 acres of land for stock raising purposes, and have a fine herd of Durham Cattle. The captain joined the Masonic fraternity at Newtonia in 1869, and has held all the offices of the Blue Lodge. He was elected master in 1871, and continued in that office, with the exception of one term, until 1884, when he organized Ritchey Lodge, No. 530, he being honored with the name by the Grand Lodge as master, and at present fills that office. In 1875 he was appointed deputy grand master of the district, and held this high office until 1886; also held the office of Masonic district lecturer for the same term of years. He was grand sword bearer of the Grand Lodge of the State of Missouri for two years, and is also a member of the Royal Arch Chapter. He was a charter member of Newtonia Lodge, No. 230, I. O. O. F., which was organized May 19, 1870, and is still a member, having filled all the offices of the lodge, including noble grand. In political opinions the captain is independent. His first wife died May 15, 1865, and November 15, 1866, he married Miss Martha L. Wills, daughter of Dr. Lewis Wills, a prominent physician of Neosho. Captain and Mrs. Ritchey have two children: Mary L. and Jess M. The Captain is still in active business, and stands deservedly high in the opinion of the people."

The following biographical sketch from the 1888 History, is on Herman J. Rohn, the great-grandfather of the author. He was the father of Irma Helene Rohn, who married John Smerdon. Their oldest son, John Erle, is the father of the author. Herman J. Rohn married Mary Von Listen, also listed in family records as Marie Liste. They had four children, Charles William (1869), Cora Marie (1873), Irma Helene (1875) and Curt Herman (1877).

HERMAN J. ROHN

"Herman J. Rohn is one of eight surviving members of a family of ten children born to the marriage of William and Theresa (Thonn) Rohn, who were born in Germany. The father was born about 1803, and was a lumber merchant and coal dealer, shipping to Saxony and Prussia. He came to the United States in 1843, and located on a farm in Washington County, Wisconsin, where he has since made his home. He owns 280 acres of land, and has always been held in high respect by all who know him. He has held the offices of justice of the peace, chairman of the county supervisors, judge, and has represented his county in the State Legislature. He was also colonel of the old State Militia, First Regiment, and in his political views is a Democrat. He has always been an honorable and upright citizen, a man of great force of character, and will long be remembered by his descendants as the founder of his race in the United States. Herman J. Rohn was born in Germany in 1829, and in 1840 came to the United States when only eleven years of age. He received a fair German education, and attended school at Milwaukee, graduating from the high school of that city. He can speak German, Bohemian and English languages, and has some knowledge of the Latin language. In 1863 he enlisted in Company G, Forty-fifth Regiment, Wisconsin Volunteer Infantry, and served as a private until the close of the war. He was at the siege of Nashville, the battle of Franklin and in many skirmishes, and while in the service rose to the rank of first lieutenant. In 1867 he was married to Mary Von Listen, daughter of Baron Carl Von Listen and Maria (Klepsch) Von Listen. Baron Von Listen came to the United States in 1866, and bought 200 acres of land in Washington County, Wisconsin. He was very highly educated, being a graduate of four universities: Jena, Heidelberg, Goettingen and Zurich, and could speak fluently Latin, Greek, German, French and English. His patent of nobility dated back to the fifth or sixth century, some of his ancestors having been present at the Crusades for the recovery of the Holy Sepulchre. He lived in Wisconsin until 1871, when he died at the age of sixty-four years. Mr. Listen and wife are the parents of the following named children: Mary, Helen, Herman, Charles, Josephine, Otto, Hermina, Antonio and Paula. Mr. Rohn was in the insurance business in Milwaukee for some time, when he purchased and lived on a farm in the county until 1876 and thence came to Newton County, Missouri, and located on his nicely situated farm of 140 acres. He has held the office of justice of the peace, and in his political views is a Democrat. Mrs. Rohn was highly educated in Germany before coming to America, and can speak and write German, English, French and Bohemian. They are one of the first families in the county, and are highly cultured and intelligent."

Joseph H. Davidson, described in the 1888 sketch following, was the great-grandfather of the author on his mother's side. His son, Thomas Lewis, married Elizabeth Ann Motley, January 29, 1889. To their union were born ten children, Stella Jane, December 1889; Harold Adron, August, 1891; Velma Leota, June 1894; Asa Eugene, March 1896 (who died three years later); a daughter, January 1898, who died at birth; Eula Luella, June 1900; Ada Pearl, June 1902; Vera Lorene, January 1905; George W., April 1907;

Thomas Welzie, May 1909. Ada Pearl married John Erle Smerdon, parents of the author.

JOSEPH H. DAVIDSON

"Joseph H. Davidson, farmer, is the son of Thomas Davidson and the grandson of William Davidson, who was born in South Carolina, of Irish descent, was married in Illinois, in 1813, and was one of the pioneers of Sangamon County, that State; he died in Macon, Illinois. Thomas Davidson was born in South Carolina, and came with his father to Illinois when a lad of seven. He here learned farming, and here married Miss Celia Hawey, the daughter of Joseph Hawey, of Illinois, but formerly from Kentucky. To Mr. and Mrs. Davidson were born twelve children: America A., Joseph H., William H., Elizabeth M., Daniel T., Lucy F., George W., Lutitia C., Melinda L., Elis L., Thomas K. (killed in the late Civil War) and Colwin J. (who died young). Mr. Davidson lived on his farm in Macon, Illinois, for many years, and is still living, at Decatur, Illinois, at the age of eighty-one. He is a Democrat in politics, was a prosperous farmer, and he and wife are members of the Cumberland Presbyterian Church. His son, Joseph H., was born in Macon County, Illinois, in 1836, and was reared on his father's farm. In 1861 he married Miss Lydia A. Kimberlin, daughter of Lewis and Nancy (Lamb) Kimberlin, and to this union were born seven children: Anna L., Thomas L., Elizabeth, Nelson, Nancy, Charlie and Oscar. Anna L. married C. T. Humbard, of this county. Mr. Davidson resided on a farm in Macon County, Illinois, until 1871, when he moved to Missouri, and located on a farm in Jasper County for about ten years. In 1881 he came to Van Buren Township, Newton County, and purchased his present property of eight acres, where he is now living. Mr. Davidson, like his father, is a Democrat in politics. He is a member of the Farmer' Alliance, and he and wife are members of the Methodist Episcopal Church."

APPENDIX III – A 1931-32 RITCHEY SCHOOL SURVEY

A school Survey of the Ritchey School was dated December 2, 1932. It is a nice history of the school from its very beginning in 1860. The survey was written in longhand and is 17 pages long. Below is a condensation of this survey. It starts, "A study of the educational system of the Ritchey community has brought fourth many interesting fact." Here is the first part of this survey and is quoted directly:

"The first public school opened in the Ritchey community in the year 1860. It was began in a brush arbor, and later moved to a log house. The place was located about one mile north of the present site of Ritchey. It had formerly been a place where camp meeting was held. The second term (1861) of school was held in the same place but with a different teacher. This term of school closed before its regular time because the teacher entered the army. The schools were financed by the parents paying tuition to the teacher for instructing their children. The first three years were all that were attempted in the state course of study. Some readers, arithmetic and Webster' spellers were on the list of text books. The school was held only two or three months each year. In 1868 a log house was built north and west of the present school building. It was a typical building for that time. It was a subscription school, and was well constructed. It was held from two to three months each year. In 1872 a one room frame building was built. It was built north east of the present building. Eight grades were taught. One teacher was employed. In 1887 the community changed from one to six directors, and a new two room building was erected (Note, these were two rooms of the six-room school I attended and my fifth, sixth, seventh and eighth grade classes were held in these rooms). It is the present rooms with the folding doors. Two teachers were employed. Eight grades were taught along with two or three high school subjects. It was known as a common or grade school until 1900 when one year of high school was added. In May 1901 the first class ever graduated received their diplomas at a public graduation exercise. There were nine in the class. A Job School was later erected and held two or three terms. In 1911 a third room was built north of the original structure. Three teachers were employed. In 1917 another class was graduated. It consisted of about ten pupils. Two or three years of high school work was offered but was not considered creditable in better and larger schools. This was the last class to graduate before consolidation. Only the common subjects were taught between 1923 and 1926. Two teachers were employed during that time."

"The income is formed in two ways. Taxes which are paid by everyone who has or has not any children going to school. The tax levy is 65 cents. The amount of state aid that the Ritchey Consolidated School received in the year 1931-32 was $3,000. The difference in expenses and state aid is $993.53. It has been said that not near as much state aid was received as there should have been."

"In the last 72 years or since school began in this community the teachers have increased from one to six. Several years ago teachers had to only have an eighth grade. A few years later they had to graduate from the twelfth. Now they require a certain amount of college work. A higher qualification of teachers has now improved the schools. The men were the first teachers, it was thought that women's place was to keep house. The following table will show the qualification, salary and grades taught by each teacher; year of 1932-33.

NAME	GRADE TAUGHT	QUALIFICATION	MONTHLY SALARY	
Joslin	first, second, third	state	$65	(taught my 1st & 2nd grades)
Ross	fourth, fifth	state	$50	
Williams	sixth, seventh, eighth	state	$70	
McClary	first to eighth	state	$60	
Craton	first to eighth	state	$65	(taught my 3rd & 4th grades)
Danner	High School grades	B.S. Degree	$75	
Frazier	High School grades	B.S. Degree	$80	
Henry	High School grades	B.S. Degree	$120	(was School Superintendent)

"The total monthly salary paid to eight teachers for instructing 222 pupils is $585. The average amount paid to each teacher is $73.13."

"The school resembles the nations of the world in some ways. It consists of president, directors, treasurer and secretary. In 1887 the community changed from one to six directors. The following table shows the occupations and ones holding the positions:

Year of 1932-33.

Mr. Erle Smerdon	President
Mr. J. J. Jack	Treasurer
Mr. G. T. Laurance	Secretary
Mr. G. E. Henry	Superintendent
Mr. H. C. Douthitt	Director
Mr. J. H. Ferguston	Director
Mr. A. H. Wolgamont	Director
Mr. V. L. Shore	Director"

In 1860 only three subjects were taught in the elementary grades. By 1931, ten subjects were taught. At the time high school subjects taught had advanced from the three in grade school to 14 in high school. The high school library now is worth $425.32 and contains 309 volumes. Of the 222 pupils in the consolidated district, 152 are in the 12 grades in Ritchey and 37 and 33, respectively, are in the eight grades in Green Valley and Mountain Grove.